Contents

Part 1: Employment

Part 2: Moving Out

Part 3: Getting a Ride

Part 4: Money Matters

Part 5: When "It" Happens

Part 6: Life Skills and Social Necessities

On Your Own for the First Time

A Guide to Starting Off in the Real World

Jeff Bowers

On Your Own
for the First Time

Library of Congress Card Number: 00-111969

ISBN: 0-9706667-0-5

5   4   3   2   1

Pyramid Publishing
P.O. Box 1128
Cincinnati, Ohio 45071
www.pyramidpublishing.com
888-997-3257

Dedication

The difference between being alive and really living is sometimes as simple as who we spend our time with. The happiest people I know are those who have found special people to support them and help them want to succeed. For many of us, finding people that can motivate and inspire us is difficult; probably because in most cases we are too busy simply surviving to recognize the need for such encouragement.

Motivation without inspiration is like love without passion. In both cases the absence of the other complementary force keeps an otherwise perfect situation from truly reaching its potential. On rare occasion life presents us with people who possess and exemplify the very essence of those complementary forces. I have found such a person without even looking. My life and all I have to give has been greatly influenced by their unselfish gifts of shear energy and encouragement. I am grateful and fortunate to have been given the opportunity to meet this person and I cannot imagine moving from this point on without them.

Bethany, For all you have done for me I dedicate this book to you.

Acknowledgements

To my parents Marie and Raymond Bowers and to my children Anastassia, Israel, Alexander and Jeff, thank you for your support and inspiration

Credits

Editor
Hope Stephan

Proofreader
Tammy Norton

Cover Designer
John Windhorst

Book Design & Art Production
DOV Graphics
Michelle Frey
Tammy Norton
Cathie Tibbetts

Printer
C.J. Krehbiel Co.

Introduction

Within these few short chapters you will learn how to better prepare yourself for life after leaving the nest.

Being on your own for the first time marks the beginning of a new level of maturity filled with uncertainty, anticipation and excitement. When you first find yourself away from home, you suddenly realize that you are totally responsible for establishing your own place in the world. This book will help you avoid mistakes that millions experience every day simply because they do not have the basic knowledge that you will have if you take the time to read this text. Each chapter gets right to the point and starts teaching you what to watch for and how to avoid easily made mistakes. This book should help you in many areas of your life and serve as a reference tool as the individual subject matter becomes relevant.

The difference between success and failure is directly proportionate to how prepared you are. There is more to surviving on your own than simply bringing home a paycheck every week. What you do with your money is far more important than how you earn it. Learning the fundamentals of living and surviving on your own is going to be hard enough without stumbling through new experiences unprepared. So, do yourself a favor and read this book.

Life is a series of memories, try to collect as many pleasant ones as you can.

Part 1
Employment

1

Resumes & Cover Letters

Searching For a Job

How many people do you know who have graduated or left home, secured a good job the next day, received a salary advance, and started living a self-sustaining lifestyle? Before you decide to get out on your own, consider the task of looking for a job well in advance. If you're still in school, take advantage of employment bulletin boards, your student counselor, job placement services, and any other reference sources that might be accessible to you. If you're not in school, but are planning to leave the "nest" soon, get really serious about a source of income while someone else is still paying the bills. Regardless of what situation you're in, getting an early jump on your job search is critical.

Take full advantage of workshops that deal with career searching, resume writing, interviewing, and negotiating. Local newspapers will most likely have a section devoted to employment and employment-related opportunities and services. The yellow pages will also prove to be useful, and let's not forget the library and the vast resources of the Internet. Leave no stone unturned while keeping your eyes and ears open at all times.

If you do not have any job prospects or contacts through parents, guardians, or friends, get the local paper and start narrowing down your choices. You will quickly discover that the longer you look, the shorter your list of potential jobs will become. Some jobs will be eliminated because of location, pay, and hours, while others will simply be out of reach due to prerequisites and required experience. Some job classified ads will give instructions on how to apply, while others will just have a number to call. Once you have made your list of prospects, start calling to find out what is required for the job. They could want you to just stop by for an interview, or they could require that you send them a resume first. If they want a resume, you'll be better prepared to write one after reading this chapter.

Decide in advance what is more important, the pay or the job. When moving into the world of employment, you will rarely find great jobs that pay well right off the bat. For example, digging ditches or operating a jackhammer is hard work and will probably pay much higher than waiting tables or being a lifeguard. At first, be prepared to work wherever it takes to pay the bills. However, if the job itself is more important than the money, be prepared to whistle while you work and cry on payday.

Employment Agencies

If you have exhausted all available job search resources, perhaps it's time to consider an employment agency. State employment agencies, aside from usually being free, are an excellent source for jobs. However, the majority of their listings are for non-skilled positions and are on the lower end of the pay scale. Despite this, state agencies can match you up with a number of potential employers from which to choose. Private employment agencies historically offer a better selection of jobs; however, unlike the state, they charge a fee, which varies from state to state and from agency to agency. An example of such a fee would be a finder's fee payable in advance, while other agencies might get a percentage of your first check. Regardless of the terms, utilizing the services of a private employment agency will probably result in a better job.

If you plan to use the services of a private employment agency, remember that the agency works for the person paying the fee. In most cases, all fees are paid by the employer who is paying the agency to find it candidates. Therefore, the agency will be working in the best interest of its client, (the employer) and not you. You may be offered or convinced to take a job that is right for the client, but not necessarily right for you. On the other hand, if *you* are paying the fee, the agent will be looking for what *you* want, making every effort to answer to your needs. For maximum benefit, screen prospective agencies to find one that specializes in the particular field in which you are interested. An agent that has clients in your field of study or interest will have knowledge of available jobs and, at a minimum, a client base that you can send unsolicited resumes to.

If you are going to solicit the services of a headhunter or employment agency, carefully read any agreement before you sign it. Make sure you understand the terms of your agreement with the agency. For example, if you pay the fee, find out what the fee includes. You might be paying a fee at the end of a certain date whether they have found you a job or not. Use agencies to help in your search, but don't rely on them completely. When looking for an agency, check them out by calling the Better Business Bureau. Take note of any information it may have on the prospective agency. If you know of someone else who has used a particular agency, consider that referral as well.

If you have a really impressive resume and skill mix, you might consider contacting a headhunter. Headhunters are usually looking for a specific educational background and work experience mix. They are usually working for a corporate client who wants to interview only the best candidates. Headhunters' fees are usually much higher than those of a private employment agency; therefore, they are constantly looking for that special handful of candidates to send out for an interview. If you are approached by a headhunter or if you contact one, read the agreement carefully. As with any document, take the time to read it over and understand what it says. Do not let your desire to find a job overshadow your common sense. If you are unsure about a particular point, get clarification. You might be able to negotiate the fees, due dates, and so on. Remember, though—headhunters are usually interested in either well-seasoned candidates or those with particularly unique skills.

Reality Check

There will always be a smarter, more attractive, and better-qualified person than you. Get over it! Instead of being consumed with that thought, consider that some of your peers just might think that *you're* that person. It's all relative, wouldn't you agree? Be realistic and humble about your first job or two. With that in mind, start thinking about what you are qualified to do in addition to what you want to do. Accepting the fact that you'll probably be struggling at first will make your first working experiences easier to deal with. Go to work each day realizing that you're not going to be working there for the rest of your life. The important thing is that you are working and making money, no matter how little the amount. Also realize that you need to be dependable and productive while you're at work. Working hard and being a good employee will help you to get a better job reference when you're ready to leave.

Resumes

Before you can begin writing an effective resume, you must first take a good hard look at your experience, regardless of how limited you may think it is. Also, be realistic about the types of jobs that you are qualified for right out of school.

A good way to start drafting your resume is to outline your strengths and weaknesses. Write down any accomplishments or achievements from prior jobs, if you've had any. Include enough information about your background to interest the reader, but don't ramble on about your life story. Pick a good format for your resume. If in doubt, the chronological format is very popular and easy to read, because it takes the reader from the beginning of your employment history to the day you write the resume. The best resumes will incorporate many of the suggestions found in this chapter.

What to Include

Resumes include key elements which are expected by employers in some form or another. These basic elements give a brief and, hopefully, accurate picture of the applicant in one or two pages. How you lay out the elements and the method in which you prioritize them will depend on how much experience you have and what the specific employer is looking for. The following elements are listed with a brief explanation:

> **Heading**: As a rule, the heading is placed at the top in either the center or at the left margin. Include your full name, address, and phone number(s).

> **Employment objective**: This optional statement helps an employer know where you want to go and how you want to get there. If you include this element, keep it short, from a single sentence to no more than a short paragraph. For example: "To secure a position in the food service industry and eventually train for restaurant management."

➤ **Education**: Depending on your level of experience, this could be your most important asset, so address it accordingly. If you have graduated, list the dates of graduation and degree(s). If you are still in school, list the anticipated graduation date.

➤ **Special Academic Honors/Awards**: This is where you list inclusion in an honor society or special academic award.

➤ **Special Skills**: This section can be really important, especially if the position requires specific computer-related courses and skills. Also include special talents and experience that could be beneficial to a prospective employer.

➤ **Employment History**: This should be the focus of the resume, listing, in reverse order, your employment history and including, at a minimum, employment dates, employer names, and duties/responsibilities.

➤ **Licenses & Certificates**: If, for example, you have a teaching certificate, then include that information. If you have applied for, but not received, a certificate or license, list it as "pending."

➤ **Professional Memberships**: Use this section to list affiliations with a union or organization such as the United Auto Workers.

➤ **References**: Unless you are specifically instructed to include references, include the statement "References are available upon request."

What to Leave Out

➤ Complex sentences, excessive use of fonts, bolding, italicizing, and long sentences.

➤ Wordy phrases and too much description.

➤ Potentially discriminatory information such as religion, race, and sex.

➤ Personal information like hobbies (unless specifically requested by employer).

➤ Salary information. This is best included on an application or during an interview

Action Verbs & Adjectives

By using action verbs and adjectives throughout your resume, you can better emphasize past accomplishments. Action words help highlight initiative, a key value-added aspect of any applicant's resume. Take full advantage of the following words, realizing that this is only a partial list:

Action Verbs

Adapted	Demonstrated	Implemented	Invented	Produced
Analyzed	Developed	Improved	Modified	Researched
Centralized	Enhanced	Increased	Motivated	Restructured
Coordinated	Formulated	Initiated	Negotiated	Supervised
Decreased	Generated	Innovated	Organized	Upgraded

Adjectives

Accomplished	Competent	Determined	Excellent	Resourceful
Adaptable	Conscientious	Diverse	Flexible	Responsible
Aggressive	Cost-conscious	Dynamic	Honest	Results-oriented
Ambitious	Creative	Efficient	Patient	Skilled
Committed	Dependable	Energetic	Reliable	Versatile

While You are Writing Your Resume, Consider the Following Questions:

➤ How dependable is my transportation?

➤ Is there any reason why I can't travel, say, 50 miles one way to work?

➤ Are there circumstances that would prevent me from working any shift that is offered?

➤ Do I need to receive a paycheck every week, or will every two weeks be acceptable?

➤ What do I definitely *not* want to do?

➤ Will I be willing to work overtime?

➤ Will I be willing to work nights, weekends, and holidays?

Don't Forget

When writing your resume, remember three things: clarity, brevity, and impact! Keep your resume short and to the point, generally no longer than one page. You are probably thinking, how can I possibly tell my potential employer how great I am in just one short page? Believe me, in one page you can condense a tremendous amount of information. Concentrate on your strengths and provide references only upon request. If possible, never include reasons for leaving your last job—that type of information is best left for the one-on-one interview.

Preparing a professional-looking resume is your key to getting an interview. Remember, most employers scanning through a stack of resumes will look to find those that are well prepared and professional in appearance. So, take your time and do it right, paying special attention to grammar and spelling.

Sample Resume

TED WILEY
1321 Tumbleweed Drive
Florence, AL 12121

OBJECTIVE	To expand upon my current computer-related skills and to enhance my ability to develop office-related spreadsheets and database programs.
EDUCATION	Florence High School Florence, AL 12345
	University of Alabama: Related courses: Two years of computer-related courses, including: Microsoft Word, spreadsheets, and database. I am scheduled to complete my B.S. in Computer Science in two years.
EXPERIENCE	Overnight Mailing Company, Muscle Shoals, AL, From 10/2/99 to present. *Job Title*: Inventory Management Assistant. *Duties*: Maintained the database of packages both incoming and outgoing. Assisted in the development of the spreadsheet to track all inventory.
SKILLS	30 semester hours of computer-related classes
NOTE	References are available upon request

Cover Letters

A good cover letter is brief, as a rule one page, and should be written to specifically address the experience and skill mix that the prospective employer is looking for. If the job advertisement is for a marketing assistant, don't ramble on about your experience as a night shift gravedigger. Instead, summarize your resume, emphasizing experience or skills that best suit the job for which you are applying. Tell the reader where you saw the advertisement and why you are sending the resume. Let the employer know what you have to offer, while remembering to incorporate clarity, brevity, and impact.

Sample Cover Letter

Ranger Shipping Company
Mr. Wally Hodges
1212 Queensbury Lane
Florence, Al 12345

November, 12 2000

Dear Mr. Hodges:

I am very interested in the position of Inventory Manager which was advertised in the *Florence Times* on Sunday, November 8, 2000. I have relevant experience in inventory management and I am currently working toward my B.S. in Computer Science. I have enclosed my resume, which lists my experience in inventory systems from both the academic and employment standpoint.

I look forward to your response.

Sincerely,

Ted Wiley

Resumes & Cover Letters: The Rest of the Story

Pulling It All Together

As with any first impression, consider the writing of your resume carefully, because it will be the first impression you make with an employer. When recruiters, interviewers, or company representatives start to read an applicant's resume, they see only an 8½ X 11 sheet of black and white paper. The fact that you have excellent verbal and communication skills is irrelevant at this point. There's no way the reader can see how dynamic and articulate you are. If the position is customer service-related, they can't tell how well you relate to people or how diplomatic you are by reading a resume. If you're thinking, "just wait until they meet me," think again. Without a good resume and cover letter, you might never see that day. What a shame, don't you think?

If you plan to rely solely on your personal ability to sell yourself, you could be making a serious mistake. Seldom do applicants get in to see a prospective employer without having their resume evaluated beforehand. Never discount the power of a well-written, well-planned resume.

Like it or not, one of the purposes of a resume is to screen out candidates. If a company interviewed every person who filled out a job application, they would be swamped all the time. Conducting an interview is time consuming and expensive. For this reason, only the top applicants are invited to interview. Resumes help employers filter out candidates who don't have the educational credentials, experience, or skills to meet the job requirement.

Before you start to compile all the information that you think a resume should have, stop and try to consider what information an employer would find useful in making a hiring decision. For example, you might think working for a fast food restaurant is useful because you dealt with customers every day. You would be right if applying for another restaurant job or a position that requires those skills. On the other hand, if the position for which you are applying requires you to sit at a computer terminal and input data all day, leave out all the particulars of a former restaurant job. Instead, just list the job, employer, and the dates of employment. Of course, if your responsibilities in the restaurant industry included inventory control or computer usage, then by all means include that information. Knowing what to include and what to leave out is critical. You can have plenty of experience, but if you don't know how to relay it, you might as well have no experience at all.

Before you start outlining a resume, carefully consider the position. Tailor the resume to fit the needs of your prospective new employer. Consider what skills and accomplishments are most applicable to the position. Are there any job-related or private projects that would be important to include? A good job-related project would be any team effort in which you played or contributed and made a difference in the outcome. Merely being on a project team, although somewhat valuable, is not enough. Showing or indicating how your input made a difference is the key. An example of a private project or program would be the local 4-H club or Habitat for Humanity. If you were the chairman of a project that required you to put a team together and then manage a project like Toys For Tots, that could also be useful.

Always look beyond your work history for valuable experience. Whether you were paid to accomplish something is not the issue here; it's how well you performed. Working on civic projects teaches teamwork and organizational skills. Do not disregard what you have learned and how you may have contributed to a successful team project. If nothing else, being involved in extracurricular activities shows that you care about the community and that you're probably not just sitting around the house playing *Crash Bandicoot* on your Sony Playstation.

If, while in school, you worked in the bookstore, include this information if handling money or customer service skills are relevant to your next employer. If including this type of experience makes up the bulk of your resume, spend whatever time is necessary to effectively relay that experience to a prospective employer. Remember: Try to show how the experience learned would be beneficial to their organization.

Internships

If you were lucky enough to have worked under the auspices of an internship program, make sure you list it. Employers know that, for the most part, internships are awarded to only the best candidates. If you were involved in an internship that is directly related to the position for which you are applying, then your chances of getting hired have just increased.

If you know someone who has completed an internship, ask them about the hours, pay, and how potential employers viewed their experience on their resume. If you want to work as an intern but can't seem to find an internship, approach a company and offer your services. If they are interested, they will develop the program. If you are offered a position, seek out someone you can get along with and try to recruit them as your mentor or supervisor. Of course, some companies will have defined duties and responsibilities for interns and there will be little room to deviate. If for some reason, you are not given much to do, use your time learning the various software packages. If you are considering working for the company permanently or for a similar industry, learn as much as you can about the business in general. If you really want to work for the company, at some point ask what your chances are after your internship is over. Having experience in an internship can be vital information, so examine the applicability and go from there.

Do I Really Need More Than One Resume?

If you are going to send resumes only to companies within the same industry, one resume is enough. Companies that perform the same service or produce similar products will require the same basic skills. For example, if you are applying for a position with any company that manufactures snowboards, then one resume format is sufficient. However, if you plan to expand your search to include companies that make apparel for snowboarding, advertise and market snow-boarding events, and or raise capital for snowboard merchandising outlets, then you will definitely need more than one resume.

Tailoring your resume to match the needs of a diverse industry instead of a general resume will improve your chances of getting an interview. For example, if you want to work with a company that produces marketing and advertising for snowboards, emphasize your marketing and advertising background. Leave out information that would not be relevant to a marketing and advertising position. On the other hand, if you are interested in the actual manufacturing of snowboards, then emphasize any manufacturing, design, or engineering skills you possess. The key is to include only what would be important to the specific position.

When writing your tailor-made resume, include any common element that would highlight or enhance your interest and personal connection with the product or service. Let's say you are the reigning Northeastern snowboarding champion; by all means mention that in all of your snowboarding-related resumes. Having professional recognition in any industry is an excellent selling point and benefit to a company that is associated with that product or service. However, be careful not to make your extracurricular accomplishments the brunt of your resume. Having the ability to race down a hill at sixty miles per hour does not automatically make you a valuable employee.

When you go to the extra effort of writing a resume that targets a specific position, your time will be well spent. Compared to the resumes of other applicants applying for the same job, a resume tailored to a specific position will stand out from the rest.

Layout

Now that you've got everything together, let's walk through proper layout techniques. The order in which you organize your resume will determine how effective it is. You need to list the elements in an order that stresses your most desirable attributes and achievements. You have limited time and space to grab a prospective employer's attention, so use only the information that will get them interested and make them want to know more. As mentioned earlier, carefully tailor your resume to fit the position. The reverse chronological resume format is your best bet. By listing your most recent experience first, the reader can quickly ascertain what you have been doing or working on most recently.

Because you rely on your resume to do most of the work for you, pay special attention to how it reads and how it looks. The quality of your resume confirms a commitment to making sure that what you do and how you do it is as professional as possible. If your resume is average, it will be treated as such; however, if it is well written and visually flawless, your chances on having it read are good. The following suggestions relative to layout and content should be considered when preparing your resume:

➤ Use a margin of 1 to 1¹/₂ inches on all sides.

➤ Be consistent in using similar type headings. If you underline and bold headings, be sure to do the same throughout the rest of the resume.

➤ In your work experience section, list more than your duties. Employers know that there is sometimes a big difference in what your stated duties are and what you actually did.

➤ Avoid using acronyms, especially if you are applying for a job in another field. For example, don't highlight your accomplishments as an ALARA technician if the company doesn't know what ALARA stands for or if you are not going to be doing that kind of work anyway.

➤ Be consistent in your use of line spacing.

➤ If you have letters of recommendation, refer to them, if applicable.

➤ Unless you have been working for many years, try to keep your resume to one page.

- Keep the variation of font types to a minimum. Professionalism is important, so keep the font relatively basic. Besides, anyone can change a font.
- Use boldface to make different job experiences more evident.
- If you are going to make a sublist, use bullets or asterisks.
- To be really professional, remember to use the same writing style in both your resume and your cover letter.

Proofreading & Printing

Once you have finished your resume and have read it over for mistakes, read it again. Spellcheck and other computer options can help you proof your resume, but don't put a stamp on it until you're absolutely sure the spelling and grammar are correct. Even the most sophisticated of spellcheck tools will sometimes miss a mistake. If you don't want an old English teacher to look over your resume, at least give it to friends and relatives; that is, those who can spell. Don't spend days organizing and writing a resume if you are not going to spend whatever time is necessary to make sure it's right.

Aside from spelling and grammar, make sure your resume is uniform in its appearance. If you use bullets under one job description to highlight key points, don't use numbers or asterisks under another. Check the margins, font, and overall appearance. Also, make sure the resume has clarity, brevity, and impact. Remember, your resume will be the first indication of how well you convey ideas, communicate in writing, and check for accuracy. Don't blow it. Even if you are faced with a deadline, never send out a resume until it's ready.

Once you are absolutely sure your resume is correct and ready to mail, you can start thinking about paper and printing. If you have a good computer and ink jet or laser printer, you will only need to select a good paper. Resumes should almost always be printed on good quality 8½ X 11-inch bond paper. As a rule, stick with conservatively colored white or bone-colored paper. If you don't have a computer or access to one, take your typed or handwritten resume to a resume service and have it converted to allow top quality printing. If this is the case, make sure you proofread the resume again once it has been reconfigured on a computer. Never assume that a professional resume service will not make mistakes.

If you are smart and tailor each resume to fit a specific company, the resume preparation process will be a time consuming but valuable effort. Do not simply write one resume, proof it, and then hit print for fifty copies. If you do, don't expect the phone to ring off the wall.

Punctuation and Mechanics

The spellcheck tool on your word processing program can only help you to an extent. The rest of your grammar, punctuation, and mechanics will have to come from what you retained from those exhilarating English classes or a good writer's guide. However, if you consult this next section during your writing, I think most of your questions will be answered. When writing a resume and cover letter, keep the following rules in mind:

Capitalization

➢ Capital letters are most frequently used to indicate the beginning of a sentence or to show that a word is a proper noun.

➢ Capitalize the first word of a sentence and the first word of a direct quotation that is a complete sentence.

➢ Capitalize the names of days, months, holidays, and special events. Do not capitalize the name of a season unless it is part of a proper noun.

➢ Capitalize the names of awards and documents

➢ Capitalize the names of academic subjects that are languages or that are followed by a course number. Also, capitalize proper adjectives in the names of academic subjects.

➢ Capitalize the names of structures and the names of organizations such as businesses, religions, governmental bodies, clubs, and schools. However, capitalize a word such as *school* or *club* only when it is part of a proper noun.

➢ Capitalize trade names. Do not capitalize a common noun that follows a trade name.

➢ Capitalize most proper adjectives. Use a lower-case letter for a proper adjective that is in common usage.

➢ Capitalize both letters in the two-letter Postal Service abbreviations of state names.

Punctuation

➢ Use a period at the end of a declarative sentence, a mild command, or a polite suggestion.

➢ Use a period after most standard abbreviations, including initials that are used as part of a person's name or title.

➢ When a period in an abbreviation precedes a question mark or an exclamation point in a sentence, use both marks of punctuation.

Commas

➢ Use commas to separate three or more words, phrases, or clauses in a series. Use a comma after each item except the last.

➢ Use a comma to show a pause after an introductory word or phrase.

➢ Use a comma to separate sentence parts that might otherwise be related together in a confusing manner.

➢ Use commas before and after the year when the year is used with the month and the day. Do not use commas when only the month and the year are given.

➢ Use commas before and after the name of a state, province, or country when it is used with the name of a city. Do not use commas between a state and its ZIP code.

➢ Use a comma after the greeting or salutation of a social letter and after the complimentary close of any letter.

Semicolons

➢ Semicolons are used to connect independent clauses and to clarify meaning in sentences that contain a number of commas.

Colons

➢ Use a colon to introduce an explanatory phrase or statement or a list of items that completes a sentence.

➢ Use a colon after the salutation of a business letter. For example, Dear Mr. Bowen:

General Mechanics

➤ Use quotation marks to call attention to the special nature of such words as technical terms.

➤ Use quotation marks to set off a word that defines another word.

➤ Place a comma or a period inside closing quotation marks.

➤ Place a semicolon or a colon outside closing quotation marks.

➤ Use an apostrophe to show possession.

➤ Use an apostrophe to replace letters or numbers that have been left out in a contraction.

➤ Use a hyphen to divide a word at the end of a line.

➤ Use a hyphen to separate compound numbers from twenty-one to ninety-nine.

➤ Use a dash to show an interruption in a thought or a sentence. Use a second dash to end the interruption if the sentence continues.

➤ Use parentheses to enclose material that is not basic to the meaning of the sentence.

➤ Use brackets to enclose explanations or comments that are inserted in a quotation but that are not part of the quotation.

➤ Italicize letters, numbers, symbols, and words when you are referring to them as words or symbols.

➤ Spell out numbers of one hundred or less. Spell out numbers that are rounded to hundreds that can be written in two words or less.

➤ Spell out any number that begins a sentence, or rewrite the sentence.

➤ Use numerals to express dates, street numbers, room numbers, apartment numbers, telephone numbers, page numbers, and percentages. Spell out the word percent.

Resume Samples

The following resumes are provided to use as a reference. Their layout format, depth, and impact vary by experience and level of education. So, before you write your resume, review these examples for style and continuity. Each resume reflects differently the individual characteristics of the person writing it. Create your own style after reviewing the following examples:

Resume Samples

Jeffery K. Sithen
2334 East Baker Avenue
Five Oaks, KY 76543
(654) 876-9876

Objective:	Employment in food service, preferably in a salaried position.
Education:	Deep Creek High School, 1995-1999 General education/college prep courses
Experience:	*Harold's Mexican Adventure*, 1998-1999 Assistant night manager responsible for inventory, ordering, and scheduling personnel. Dealing with customers and employees has enabled me to better appreciate the operation of a restaurant. *Happy Days Children's Emporium*, 1996-1998 Waiter and food preparation duties.
Capabilities:	Good organizational skills; proficient with operation of cash register; familiar with Microsoft Word.
Activities:	Deep Creek High Football Team Deep Creek High Track Team Deep Creek High Golf Team Deep Creek High Senior Class Treasurer
Awards:	National Honor Society, 1997 and 1998
References:	Available upon request

PETE BECK
478 First Street
Tennis Green, KY 23234
550-988-9876

JOB SOUGHT:	Computer-Aided Graphic Designer
EDUCATION:	University of Alabama Bachelor of Arts, 1998
WORK EXPERIENCE:	*University of Alabama Graphics Department*, 1997-1998 As the Assistant Designer, I developed layout and design ideas for the University Brochure *Art's Photography Studio*, 1996-1997 Layout Technician, responsible for scanning and converting industrial photographs to overheads for sales presentations.
MEMBERSHIPS:	Art Designers of Alabama since 1996 American Design Council since 1997
REFERENCES:	Available upon request

SUSAN WILSON
129 Pleasant Street
Arkansas Valley, AR 03851
876-987-9898

CAREER GOAL: Attorney-at-Law

BAR MEMBERSHIP: Mississippi State Bar, January 1999

EMPLOYMENT EXPERIENCE:

Jackson Public Defender's Office, Jackson, MS
Law Clerk, 1998-1999
Researched for civil cases and processed subpoenas; interviewed witnesses and wrote reports. Prepared trial briefs.

Raymond, Lee & Towers, Jackson, MS
Law Clerk, 1997-1998
Researched legal issues and prepared investigation reports.

Bowen & Bowen, Jackson, MS
Law Clerk, 1995-1997
Researched legal documents and prepared investigation reports. General administrative work.

EDUCATION:

Mississippi State University
Juris Doctor, December 1999

Class rank: Top ten percent
The Ohio State University
MBA Finance, 1994
B.S. Finance, 1992

HONORS: National Honor Society

REFERENCES: Submitted at your request

JIM STANFORD
101 Profit Street • Toom Lake, NY • 987-909-8349

GOAL: Paralegal

SKILLS:
- Prepared legal documents
- Compiled case citations
- Interviewed witnesses
- Attended hearings

WORK EXPERIENCE:
Sawyers & Milkin, Toom Lake, NY
Legal Assistant, 1997 to present

Niles, Rivers & Chandler, Peakskill, NY
Legal Assistant, 1996-1997

EDUCATION:
Columbia University
Paralegal Program, Certificate, 1996

Columbia University
B.A., Political Science, 1995

REFERENCES:
Available upon request

Joan Beckman
876 Shy View Court
Brattleboro, VT 76666
787-903-5421

Goal:	Social Worker
Education:	Master's Degree in Psychology, 1995
	B.S., Psychology, 1992
Coursework:	Social Welfare
	Case Analysis
	Abnormal Psychology
	Sociology
	Comparative Religions
	Criminal Justice
Field Study:	Counselor, Brattleboro Battered Home Institute, 1993-1995
	Counselor, Southern Vermont Drug Rehabilitation Center, 1992-1993
References:	Available upon request

DAVID MCCRAWLEY
2345 Western Branch Court • Spring City, OH 65432 • 515-726-8655

OBJECTIVE
Management position with an environmental restoration firm.

EDUCATION
MBA, University of Finley, Finley, Ohio 1998
B.S., Environmental Science, University of Finley 1995

EXPERIENCE

Fluor Daniel Fernald Construction   Engineer 1990 to present
Fernald, OH

Mid-Western Environmental Inc.   Environmental Sampling Coordinator
1989-1990
West Chester, OH

ACHIEVEMENTS
Created a statewide database for environmental samples.
Supervised a twelve-man survey/sampling team
Managed two environmental soil clean-up projects, value: $750,000
Managed four facility decontamination projects, value: $2.9 million
Eliminated need for post-sampling plan (cost-saving value: $75,000)

MEMBERSHIPS
Society of Environmental Professionals
American Management Association
Utilities & Manufactures Robotics Users Group

REFERENCES
Available upon request

"Caution"

The resume you are about to write is a legal document that is used in screening and hiring decisions. Therefore, information counter to the truth, whether it be salary or position-related, is grounds for immediate termination if found to be intentionally false. When a prospective employer is reading a resume, it is generally assumed that the information is as accurate as possible. Listing information that is questionable or vague is sometimes associated with an individual who has been in the workforce for, say, twenty-five years. After 25 years, not being able to remember how much a first or second position paid is somewhat understandable. However, when you are just getting started in the career world, information like that should be fresh and accurate. If you are hired based on false resume information, don't be surprised if one day, when you least expect it, you get a call from your manager, who wants to meet you in the human resources office. At this point, you will have serious questions to answer.

If you are terminated for the falsification of a resume, you will most likely have no recourse. In addition, your chances of receiving unemployment compensation are slim at best. If this situation is not bad enough, imagine explaining the situation to your next prospective employer.

Cover Letters

Why Have a Cover Letter?

The cover letter is a business letter used to introduce an applicant to a prospective company. Cover letters are almost always sent with a resume and are intended to be read before the resume. In a sense, the cover letter is a business transmittal letter for an applicant's resume. A well-written cover letter will introduce an applicant's credentials while creating enough interest to make the employer want to know more. The ultimate objective in crafting a well-written letter is to get a potential employer to read your resume and to then grant you an interview.

The best cover letters are written with the employer in mind. Therefore, the more research and knowledge you have obtained about the company and position, the better. Make no mistake about it; you will not be the only person with a good resume and cover letter. With that in mind, you can see just how important the wording, format, content, and overall tone of resumes and cover letters can be. Competition is stiff, with only the best of the best being asked to interview. If you really want an excellent cover letter, do your homework on the company and find out as much as you can about the position. Even if you are not applying for a particular position, having knowledge of the company is highly recommended.

Getting Started

Once you have written, proofread, and printed your resume, you will now need to draft the perfect complementary cover letter. If you had the opportunity to hand deliver your resume and were interviewed on the spot, the cover letter would not be necessary. However, this is usually not the case. All too often, companies want to see a resume long before they even want to think about seeing you.

Like your resume, the cover letter should be well organized and error-free. Remember, always write with these three ideas in mind: clarity, brevity, and impact. The best resume and cover letter combinations will be coordinated. They will use basically the same font size, spacing, and layout and they will be printed on the same quality paper. Cover letters should have the following basic information:

> ➤ Your name and complete address, including phone numbers.
> ➤ The date you are sending the letter out.
> ➤ The company name and the name of the person to whom your resume package is addressed.
> ➤ A greeting/salutation like Dear Ms. Williams or Mr. Smith.
> ➤ A brief opening paragraph explaining why you are sending them the letter and resume. For example, the brief opening paragraph could refer to a previous meeting or phone conversation, or it could refer to a trade publication or newspaper advertisement.
> ➤ Several short, concise paragraphs detailing why you want to work for the company and what credentials you can bring to the organization.
> ➤ A closing paragraph that requests an interview or, at a minimum a telephone call.
> ➤ A closing phrase, such as Yours Truly or Sincerely.

Regardless of how talented you are, work to keep the cover letter to one page. Mention just enough to get the reader interested in the attached resume. Stay focused and professional throughout the letter. Do not try to fit your entire resume and cover letter content on one page. As I just mentioned, your resume will be the next sheet of paper the reader will see. If the cover letter is good, the reader will move to your resume with optimism and anticipation. A really good letter will have the reader wanting to thoroughly go over your resume, which is exactly what you want.

Cover Letter Tips

To assist you in creating the perfect cover letter, read the following tips and highlight those topics you have not considered. This quick list should act as a check list, if nothing else, and serve to improve any aspect of business letter writing skills you may possess:

- ➤ If you do not have a computer or access to one, spend the money to have your handwritten or typed cover letter reformatted on a computer and printed out with an ink jet or laser printer. If you do not have paper left over from the printing of your resume, purchase the exact same type for your cover letter. The two documents should be printed on the same paper.

- ➤ Remember that the resume and cover letter are working together on your behalf, so prepare them in a complementary fashion.

- ➤ Mention some of the resume's key selling points in your cover letter.

- ➤ Never use a form letter. Tailor each cover letter to its intended reader. Be sure to address the letter to a certain person and included his or her name in your salutation.

- ➤ If you have made prior contact with the company, refer to that in the cover letter.

- ➤ Have others proofread your cover letter.

- ➤ When writing your cover letter, limit the use of *I* and *my*.

- ➤ In your cover letter, state why you are the ideal applicant for the position.

- ➤ Avoid trying to sound like someone else when you write. Make an effort to write the same way to talk. If you do not normally say *therefore* or *perhaps*, then don't write that way.

Characteristics of a Poor Cover Letter

As with any first impression, the overall appearance of your cover letter is critical, so draft your letter including only power-packed statements. If you try to include too much, the page will run to the bottom, leaving little room for an easy transition to your closing line and signature. A trained, experienced reader can glance at a resume and form an almost immediate opinion as to its overall value based solely on its appearance. If the layout is poor, or if any errors are detected, the candidate's chances start to quickly diminish. Poorly written cover letters suggest that you do not thoroughly check your work and are most likely not very conscientious, neither of which is very flattering. Applicants who submit cover letters with poor grammar and spelling risk having the reader think that they are either poorly educated or, even worse, that they don't care.

Cover letters written without clarity and focus will also be an instant turnoff. If an applicant does not know how to break down a simple thought and relay it without rambling on, then most likely they will also be an unorganized employee.

Good cover letters are written with a mild dosage of self-confidence. However, if the applicant goes overboard, then all is lost. There is nothing worse than a letter filled entirely with "I did," "I accomplished," "I solved," "I improved," and so on. If you are *that* good, why are you unemployed or looking for a job? The same goes for being pushy. Don't insist on an interview with the employer by giving them the dates and times that *you* will be available. Instead, suggest an interview or request a follow-up phone call. If you insinuate that the employer would be foolish for not hiring you on the spot, then you might find out that the only thing your cover letter is good for is a coffee coaster.

Cover Letters Suited for a General Audience

Like a resume, cover letters should be tailored to fit the reader—unless you are going to write a generic resume to send out to many different companies. If this is the case, then an all-purpose resume is what you need. If you have recently graduated and you are not sure you know what you want, then write a resume to highlight your education, your experience, if any, and any other characteristics that would be attractive to a wide range of employers. However, if there are a handful of employers for whom you would particularly like to work, don't send this type of resume to them. Instead, tailor each resume to the specific company. Even though a cover letter to a general audience is somewhat generic in its content, you must still pay strict attention to detail and grammar.

Letters to Headhunters and Employment Search Firms

The biggest difference between preparing a cover letter for a generic resume and one for a headhunter or employment agency is what you should add in terms of individual preferences and requirements. All cover letters will have the basic information: a return address, date, salutation, an opening introductory paragraph, several short position-related paragraphs, a closing statement, and the closing phrase. When you send a cover letter and resume to a headhunter or search firm, you know that the information will be used to find a position from an existing database of clients. To save you and the agency time, include your minimum salary and required benefits package. Some could argue that this might be a way of limiting yourself, but if you are definitely not willing to work for less, state that in your cover letter. The agency will not bother to call or recommend you for any position that does not meet the minimum compensation package. If you are adamant about travel and relocating, include that as well. This is a difficult requirement to include because so many professional positions require occasional relocation and travel. In this respect, you really could be limiting yourself. Not wanting to travel is a personal decision, one that should be carefully made before you write your cover letter. By all means, include your travel and relocation requirements if you are absolutely not willing to consider a position that requires them.

Aside from your individual requirements, include any value-added information that would be applicable to specific positions or industries. For example, if you have a track record of saving money through innovation, include that and give examples. If you have been successful in redesigning or remodeling a system, program, or process, include that as well, giving examples of your accomplishments. Remember, your objective is to get an interview based on your cover letter, resume, and the recommendation of the headhunter or agency.

Cover Letters Used in Responding to Newspaper Ads

This type of cover letter is highly focused, because it is written in direct response to an advertisement. The requirements are usually listed in the advertisement, which makes writing the letter much easier. By knowing what skills are required, you can leave out unrelated experience and focus on what the employer is looking for.

Most likely you and several hundred of your closest friends will also be responding to the same ad. This kind of response is typical for a position listed in the local paper. With that in mind, you must grab the reader's attention quickly by being clear and concise.

Sample Cover Letters

Allen Noteworthy
235 East West Park
Eastern Field, OH, 34343
513-987-0987

February 12, 1999
Mr. Bill Later
Corporate Credit Director
Crocker Foods Inc.
39 Industrial Park Suite 45
White Plains, AL 85310

Dear Mr. Later:

It was a pleasure meeting with you last Tuesday to discuss the position of credit supervisor with Crocker Foods, Inc. I thank you once again for your time and valuable information. The meeting was most informative, and I left with a much better idea of what the position requires.

After reviewing my notes from the meeting, I feel confident that my educational background and experience would make an instant impact within the credit department. The plans for overseas expansion are particularly interesting to me. My undergraduate degree in Finance combined with my MBA concentration in International Business will match well with the company's plans to diversify overseas.

I hope my response to your questions about my previous position with Max General Foods was sufficient and that a mutually beneficial working relationship will result. I look forward to hearing from you.

Thank you again for your time and consideration!

Sincerely,

Allen Noteworthy

Donna Marino
6 South Beach View Miami, FL 02223
704-988-94334 Work
704-988-0900

March 1, 2000

Mr. Dobbie John
Corporate Headhunters Inc.
7 Park Avenue
Playground, NY 22220

Dear Mr. John

I am writing to you to see if you would consider representing me to your clients. I wish to work for a company that offers travel and relocation opportunities. My experience in Computer-Aided Drafting (CAD) and my B.S. in civil engineering have allowed me to work for Power Engineering and Global Construction. These two employment opportunities have allowed me to travel to several countries and learn a variety of new engineering techniques and building code variations.

If you have any clients in the construction engineering industry who are looking for someone with my credentials and who also need employees to travel, please let me know. My verbal and communication skills are very good, so interviewing will not be a problem, but rather an advantage for me.

Very Truly Yours,

Donna Marino

Rick Brennan
4113 Crownpoint Avenue
Apartment 89
Richmond, VA 32322

December 7, 2000
Ms. Debra Cochran
Wakefield School District
87 Court Place
Richmond, VA 23233

Dear Ms. Cochran:

I am writing to inquire whether the Wakefield School District has an opening for a math teacher. Having a master's degree in education and a B.S. in mathematics was beneficial in my last assistant teaching job at Marymount Elementary School.

Having three children of my own and experience in a day care center has helped me learn how to better mentor children in large numbers. In addition, I have committed my time to the annual fund-raiser for a new elementary school after-hours program held each summer.

I would appreciate the opportunity to discuss my qualifications and abilities with you at your convenience.

Sincerely,

Rick Brennan

Final Note

As you get older, your chosen profession will be increasingly more important. However, for now you need to concentrate on earning a livable wage. As the adage goes, it's easier to find a job if you have one. You should start considering your career goals as soon as possible, but you will most likely change your mind every few months. Some individuals in their fifties don't know what they want to be when they grow up, so don't spend time trying to find the perfect job today. Concentrate on finding a source of income that will pay the bills.

2

Job Interview Tips

Once your prospective employer has reviewed your resume and contacted you, start preparing for the interview right away. Try to find out as much as you can about the company and prepare some questions for the interviewer. However, be sure that you ask your questions only after the interviewer has finished. Waiting until the interviewer is finished is not only using good business etiquette; it will also show that you are a good listener. Keep your list of questions out during the interview and cross off those that are answered during the course of the interviewing process. You might just be surprised by how many of them are eliminated, thus leaving less for you to inquire about after the interviewer has finished.

The interview gives the applicant and the interviewer an opportunity to talk about information that's relevant to the position at hand. Try to find out what type of interview is being scheduled, because your method of preparation will differ accordingly. For example, a one-on-one interview is quite different from a group interview. On occasion, the type of interview will not be revealed. Instead, you will simply be instructed to meet at a predetermined place and time. In either event, bring a copy of your resume, a writing pad and pen/pencil, and prepared questions to ask. Once you arrive, it will be up to you to "feel out" the situation and respond accordingly.

If you are concerned about the interview itself, remember that questions are only difficult if you have not fully prepared for them. Before you answer a question, make sure you understand it first. If you stick to the facts, you can't say anything wrong.

Interviewing Types

Interviews come in many different forms and are used for different reasons. The following breakdown of the individual types of interviews will help you better understand the reasons for the different formats. Understanding the anatomy of a specific interviewing type will be a critical part of your preparation.

Screening

A *screening* interview is used to screen out inappropriate applicants, thus eliminating them from the pool of potential candidates. Many applicants who attend screening interviews are not called back, which is precisely why they are conducted. This type of interview is used for several reasons, one of which is to respond to an expected crowd of stampeding applicants. Another reason is that screening interviews are short and sweet. The screening takes about ten minutes, and you're usually left with the standard "don't call us, we'll call you" type of response. If the interviewer is trying to move you along, take the hint. At this point, it's too late to change the interviewer's mind, so avoid being persistent and just be pleasant and leave.

Series

Series or *serial* interviews are designed to guide the applicant through many different one-on-one sessions with various departments, managers, or even potential coworkers. They usually start off with a recruiter or human resources person and progress from there. As a rule, a series interview is long and tedious. If you are scheduled for a series interview, make several copies of your resume and be prepared to stay as long as necessary, giving each interviewer your undivided attention and enthusiasm. Each person involved in the interviewing process will be asking you questions, so it is essential to remain fresh and focused as the day wears on. This is easier said than done, given the circumstances. It will, however, be more tolerable if each one-on-one session goes well.

At the end of the series interview, each member of the interviewing team will form their own opinion; and in some cases they will compare notes and make a collective decision. With this in mind, treat each one of these mini-interviews seriously. Bring the same fresh assertive attitude to each one.

Stress

Increasingly rare, another interviewing format is sometimes called a *stress* or *interrogation* interview. The name comes from the manner in which the questions are administered. A series of questions are fired at you in rapid succession with little time to think in between. This type of interviewing technique is used to find out how prospective employees handle themselves under pressure.

Behavioral

The *behavioral* or *situational* interview requires the applicant to be able to think fast and put together a response in a logical manner addressing all aspects of the question. The interviewer will ask you to describe how you may have handled a specific situation. These types of interviews are difficult to prepare for; however, you can do well if you quickly think the question through and answer it honestly with a positive twist.

Panel

The *panel* interview is held in a room with you and several interviewers. Many find this format the most intimidating, because you are alone, answering questions from several strangers. With one interviewer, you can concentrate on making eye contact, and focusing on one personality type. When three or four total strangers are drilling you, the situation gets incrementally worse. While one person is asking you a question, you have to concentrate, knowing the others are listening and watching.

Panel interviews also provide a setting in which interviewers can see how potential employees handle themselves under pressure. A lot of information can be obtained about social skills and verbal communication skills during this type of interview. In most cases, members of the interview team are managers and supervisors who will be responsible for the candidate once hired. With this in mind, it is particularly important to approach a panel interview prepared and confident.

At the beginning of a panel interview, try to remember the names of the panel members as you are introduced. This could be difficult, but responding to individual questions by using their names will be impressive.

On occasion, panel interviews are held at lunchtime. This is sometimes because, during lunch, many of the key members are available all at once. However, don't let this relaxed environment lull you into a situation where you let your guard down. Always be professional and, regardless of the circumstances, avoid inappropriate conversation. Try to stay focused on the reason you're there. Remember that you are being evaluated all the time despite the setting.

At the end of a one-on-one interview, you leave with a certain feeling based on the chemistry between you and your interviewer. This is not the case with a panel interview. For example, one panel member might like you right off the bat, while another might have instantly taken a dislike to you. During the interview, you may get signs of encouragement from one person and arctic blast from another. To make the panel interviewing process easier, practice by having several of your friends ask you employment-related questions.

Group

The group format is usually held when many applicants are expected to be applying for the same position or various positions all at once. A typical group interview is held when a new business like a department store relocates to your city and places an ad like: "Ajax Inc. has a number of positions available for 1st, 2nd, and 3rd shifts. Apply in person at the Crown Convention Center on March 15, 2000." In this setting, you and many others applying for the same job are interviewed. The employer uses this format to observe the applicant's interpersonal skills, among other things. After the initial group interview, increasingly smaller groups are interviewed. If you are lucky enough to make the initial cut, applications are filled out and onc-on-one sessions are scheduled.

Selection

This is considered the critical interview because your work history, school history, social activities and general interest are discussed at length. If you have made it this far, you are all but drawing your first paycheck. However, make no mistake about it, if the interviewer has uncovered any inconsistencies in your resume or application, the interviewer will be questioning you about it. If the selection interview goes well, you are likely to get an offer the same day. If not the same day, you should at least know when.

Any one of a number of individuals, ranging from a recruiter to an immediate supervisor or department manager, can conduct the selection interview. Regardless of who the interviewer is, expect this type of interview to be detailed and extensive. Take this opportunity to impress the interviewer with strong communication skills and enthusiasm. This will be your opportunity to ask specific questions about the company's goals and how you fit in to those goals. Prior to being notified about this interview, be prepared to discuss your salary and benefits package. Know what you want and, more importantly, know what the company is offering. For example, don't ramble on about your desire to have a 401K plan if the employer doesn't offer one. Be specific and direct.

Make sure you don't leave the interview if major questions are unanswered. If salary and benefits are not discussed, find out when they will be. Finally, be prepared to give a decision relative to your acceptance of the position, including the agreed-upon terms and conditions of employment.

Telephone

For the most part, *telephone* interviews are held when applicants have applied for positions in other states. In this case, telephone interviews serve as a screening process prior to setting up an interview that requires a long drive or plane trip. Whether you've applied for an out-of-state or overseas job, have your resume, questions, and writing supplies handy in case you get the call.

A telephone interview gives the interviewer an opportunity to judge you solely on your accomplishments. Unlike an interview in person, the caller will not be observing your posture, appearance, and overall demeanor. However, don't slouch over on a couch while you talk. Regardless of where the interview takes place, you need to be professional and alert. This is hard to do dressed in your sweats and sitting on the floor.

Exploratory

An *exploratory* interview is one that an applicant would initiate to inquire about other companies. Typically, someone wanting an exploratory interview would contact the company in question and set up a meeting with specific members of a department or a human resource specialist.

Let's say you are currently working for a computer company and, for whatever reason, your manager—or team coach, as they are sometimes called—is making life on the job difficult at best. Before you decide to resign and possibly find yourself working in an even worse environment, you might call another computer company and request an exploratory interview through their human resource department. If you are lucky enough to get one of these interviews, do your homework and prepare questions specific to your concerns. On occasion, these types of interviews can result in an offer from the other company. Even if you don't expect that to happen, have an answer ready. After all, if you were happy with your current employer, you wouldn't be looking for a new job, would you?

When you arrive at your interview, regardless of what type it is, bring a current copy of your resume and note-taking supplies. During the interview, avoid negative comments about the previous company and any particular employee. As a rule, badmouthing another company or person is viewed as petty and immature. Instead, direct your questions and inquiries toward what the other company has to offer and how it perceives its future in the market.

Dress for Success

Before you enter the interview room, take a deep breath and try to relax. The first impression you create will be visual, and the importance of body language and composure should not be underestimated. As a rule, it's better to be overdressed than underdressed. So, if you don't know how to dress for the interview, be conservative and dress up.

For men, a suit will create the most impact, sticking to the dark-colored fabrics and a conservative tie. For women, a suit is also preferred; however, a base skirt and blouse of one color with a jacket of another coordinating color is acceptable. Both men and women should concentrate on looking alert and being energetic. Remember to make frequent eye contact and occasionally smile. Use your normal speaking style and don't try to be someone else. When you speak, be articulate and use good diction. Project your voice loudly enough for the interviewer to hear. Finally, don't get in a rush—pace yourself and emphasize key words when appropriate.

Six Basic Parts of an Interview

1. **The greeting:** Say good morning/afternoon, look them in the eyes, and if they offer you their hand, shake it somewhat firmly.
2. **Small Talk:** Break the ice with a general comment. For example, make a statement about the weather or say something positive about the office complex. Never break the ice with a negative comment like, "Finding this place was a pain in the butt."

3. **The Purpose:** This is the bulk of the interview. All parties exchange questions and answers, comments are made, and key points are clarified.

4. **Summary:** There should be absolute understanding between the parties.

5. **Path Forward:** One party will contact the other. You should leave knowing what is suppose to happen next and approximately when it will happen.

6. **The Close:** Offer an exit handshake, if applicable, and strong eye contact followed by a statement reflecting your thanks for their time and consideration.

Be Prepared to Answer These Types of Questions

Don't try to prepare for every conceivable question. Instead, master the content of your resume and try to figure out what the interviewer is looking for. The questions listed below will give you an idea of what to expect during an interview. However, don't memorize the answers to these qucstions, because the interviewer might change the content or meaning to fit a particular situation. Whatever you do, don't tell the interviewer, "I'll do anything" or "I'm a real people person." Instead be realistic, genuine, and sincere. Try to put yourself in the interviewer's chair. What kinds of questions are relevant to the position? What kinds of questions would you ask an applicant applying for the job?

Try These Questions on for Size

➤ What are your strengths? Make them relevant to the job.

➤ If you went to college, why did you select your major?

➤ What kinds of situations do you find most challenging?

➤ What frustrates you the most?

➤ What are your weaknesses? Offer one weakness and then explain how you are trying to improve it.

➤ What problems do you encounter in your current job?

➤ What are your primary responsibilities in your current job?

➤ Describe a typical day at work. In your current job.

➤ Why are you considering leaving your current employer?

- If asked to talk about yourself, just give general information about your family and hobbies.
- Explain how you go about prioritizing your workload.
- What do you enjoy most/least about your job?
- What do you hope to find in a job and company?
- Describe one of the best ideas you ever had for a current or prior job.
- How have you maneuvered around obstacles that prevented you from completing projects or responsibilities on time?
- In your current job, how is performance measured?
- Why have you chosen this particular field of employment?
- Would you be willing to travel or relocate?
- How long would you plan to stay if given the position?
- Where do you see yourself in five years?
- What contributions can you make to this position?
- How do you handle criticism?
- How does this position fit into your career plan?
- If you were laid off, why were you laid off?
- What prompted you to leave your last job?
- Have you ever worked on a team project?
- What has been your greatest accomplishment, and disappointment?

Consider These Questions to Ask During the Interview

Remember this one rule: Never ask a question if you are not sincerely interested in the answer. Save yourself and the interviewer a little time and concentrate on relative matters. Tailor your questions to the type of interview. For example, in a group interview with many other applicants, don't ask a personal question like, "How does my background meet your needs?" Instead be more general in nature, asking questions like, "What shift is this position for?" or "Is this a part-time position?"

Start with simple, non-threatening questions and move toward those that address specific issues. Remember, while you are asking questions, the interviewer is still evaluating you as a potential employee, so craft your questions well and keep them specific and relevant.

Consider Some of the Following Questions to Ask

> ➤ Describe a typical day for me if hired. This question is appropriate if someone is interviewing you in the department with whom you could be working. If someone is conducting the interview from human resources, don't expect him or her to be able to answer a question about the daily activities of another department.

> ➤ What would you expect me to accomplish first in this position?

> ➤ Who will I report to?

> ➤ Why is this position available?

> ➤ Is this position being offered to employees inside the company as well as outside?

> ➤ How is performance measured?

> ➤ What kind of career growth and promotional opportunity is there?

> ➤ How does the decision process work within the company?

> ➤ How does my educational history and work history meet your requirement?

> ➤ Will I receive training on the job?

> ➤ How is success measured in this company?

> ➤ Where do you see this organization in five years?

> ➤ When will I know if I am considered for the position?

> ➤ Is there a probationary period? If so, tell me about it.

> ➤ What are the normal work hours? How is overtime handled?

Prepare & Review

Prior to going to the interview, review all of your notes and questions. Practice answering questions from the above list and focus on the interview, not on the outcome. Make sure you have good directions and you know where to park. Also, make sure you know who you are suppose to see when you get there. Take several pens or pencils, a note pad, a copy of your resume, and organize them in a file or folder.

During the interview, save the issues of salary or hourly wages for last and try to get them to make the first offer. The reason is simple—you don't want to guess too high or too low. Once you and the interviewer have finished asking questions, there will be time to discuss other important topics, such as commissions, bonuses, medical and dental insurance, 401K plans, tuition reimbursement, vacation time, and life insurance. While conversing with the interviewer, be specific and give details. When asked a particular question, give the interviewer a particular situation relating to that question, and not just some general answer. Always listen carefully to the question, ask for clarification if necessary, and make sure you answer the question completely.

Closing

Each interview will be different in format, length, and personal chemistry. However, when the interview starts to draw to an end, you should be able to tell where you stand. When you sense the end is near, ask for some feedback. Try to frame your closing questions to fit the tone of the interview while inquiring whether or not the interviewer thinks there is a match. Some interviewers will be polite and noncommittal when, in fact, the second you leave, they record their true impression. Others might be direct and blunt, which could be good or bad, depending on the comments. In any event, at least you'll know where you stand. If the criticism is harsh, accept it as gracefully and professionally as possible. Avoid arguments, even if you know the criticism is unjustified. Arguing will only make a poor interview worse. At this point, it's best to accept the comments and move on. The quality of the outcome is directly proportionate to the experience and professionalism of the interviewer.

If you find yourself getting the same or similar negative comments from interviews, take a hint and start rethinking either your desired field of employment or your short-term goals. One interviewer could be wrong, but several less than stellar interviews should be painting you a picture.

If you can't tell how your final questions are being received, at least close the interview on a positive note. A sincere thank you while making strong eye contact with the interviewer will leave a good impression. It could just be the few extra brownie points you needed to get the job.

Ask any salesman what's the most important part of the presentation and they will tell you it's the close. If you don't try to close, then why make the call? All too often, applicants leave an interview without clear direction on what's next. Not every interviewer will tell you, so don't wait. Instead, ask where you stand or what the next step is. Is there going to be a follow-up interview or phone call? If so, when will it be?

After all you've gone through, don't leave without at least knowing what's going to happen next. If the interviewer tells you that, for example, you simply don't have enough experience, ask if they know of another firm that is looking for your level of experience.

Immediately following the interview, think carefully about what was said. If the criticism was directed toward personal characteristics or mannerisms that the interviewer found negative, and if they were justified, then by all means use the criticism to improve your next interview. However, if the cold hard facts revealed a lack of experience, then don't take it so hard. Only time can correct that. Use the critique to alter your job search approach by shoring up your good points and downplaying your bad ones. If you cannot take negative criticism and turn it into positive improvement, then you will spend many a night trying to figure out why you're not advancing in your chosen field of employment.

Follow Up

After the interview, it is acceptable to send a follow-up thank-you letter. This can be hand-written, but it should be brief. If you have a specific question, it's acceptable to contact the interviewer by phone. If you've been promised an answer by a certain date and you don't get it, once again, it's okay to call.

If an unusually long amount of time passes, remember that the interviewing and screening process for a given position can be time consuming. Don't expect a call or a Federal Express letter the next day. If you're becoming impatient, call and tactfully request an answer, explaining that another offer has come in and you need an answer by a certain time. This might be the interviewer's chance to tell you that you were not considered for the job and to accept another offer. This could also be just the nudge they needed to expedite the decision and make an offer to you. Either way, this tactic should be used only if you are truly under some time constraint. No one likes to be rushed into a decision, so try to relax and wait it out.

When the call or letter does arrive, be prepared to accept the results. If you did not get the job, ask why. This shows you are sincerely interested in improving yourself. If you lacked sufficient education or experience, consider that input and move on to a position for which you are more qualified. If, on the other hand, you were not considered because of a poorly written resume and less than impressive interview, take that criticism and use it to your advantage. Spend time rewriting or reorganizing your resume, and refine your interviewing skills.

If the interview went well and you get an offer letter, check it over for accuracy and content. If the letter doesn't include some of the agreed-upon issues, mention that in your response letter. Do not sign an offer letter with obvious mistakes, even if you are promised they will be corrected once you are hired. If they are sincere about hiring you at the agreed-upon salary and benefits package, they will correct any deficiency before they ask you to sign. Good Luck!

Reasons Why Some People Don't Get Hired

> They arrive late for the interview.

> They are much too aggressive.

> They are very nervous, which indicates a lack of confidence.

> They are not willing to start at the bottom.

> They make excuses.

> They have a poor personal appearance.

> They fail to look interviewer in the eye.

> They give vague responses to questions.

> They lack maturity.

> They lack interest and enthusiasm.

> They speak badly about past employers or co-workers.

More on Interviewing

Research

Before you can start your researching efforts, you must first decide where you want to work. Are you going to stay at home, where everything is familiar, or are you going to travel across the state or country? This, I'm afraid, is going to be a much bigger question to answer than selecting a company. The ramifications of this decision can and usually will affect the rest of your life. Are you going to stay at home and build a strong resume before you travel, or are you going to hit the road and start off in an entry-level position in the area you really want to live? Big questions require big answers! Take your time and think out at least the next five years of your working life.

Most job applicants fail to realize how important a little investigation can be prior to the interview. Researching the prospective company can separate you from other candidates in an interview. Having the prior knowledge of key aspects of the company and discussing them throughout the interview is impressive. If nothing else, it shows initiative.

Depending on the size of the company, your investigative techniques will vary. If you are going to interview with a multi-national corporation, obtaining an annual report from the corporate office is a good start. Larger corporations will also have information available through their public relations office, which can usually be located by calling the corporate information number. In addition, you can research the Internet and local libraries for articles on the company. Smaller companies require a little more work. However, a good way to find out about a small business is to use your contacts, if you have any. Knowing someone who works there or has worked there is a good start. Remember, when you're talking to an employee, his or her view of the company might be slighted, so be careful. If, for example, you know the person really well and he or she thinks you would be competing for his or her job if hired, he or she might try to give you negative or derogatory information. If you don't know any current or former employees, check the library for newspaper articles.

If you come up short on information, perhaps you can find out about other businesses that make the same products or offer the same services. A word of caution: If you use this method, be very careful how you approach the interview. You definitely don't want to ask foolish questions like, "The Ajax company had a really good year selling widgets last year. How did this company fare?" If the company you're interviewing with had a poor year, that could be a very sensitive question.

There is at least one more source of information that should not be overlooked. Take a trip to your former school and research using its career development center or job placement office. Many good schools have dedicated considerable financial resources in trying to place graduates in jobs. If you come up empty-handed, at least you can cross them off the list.

Your goal is to impress the interviewer with your questions and with the quality of your research. Armed with information about the company, prepare questions of both a general and a specific nature just in case the mood of the interview allows it. Some really good applicants use an interview to find out if the company is right for them instead of using the interview to learn if they are the right match for the company.

When conducting your research, use some of these questions as a guide to building a good base of information:

➤ What product or service does the company offer?

➤ If the product or service provided is seasonal, is employment also seasonal?

➤ How many offices does the company have in the area, in the United States, and overseas?

➤ What kinds of external circumstances affect the product or service?

➤ Does the company have a union or nonunion workforce?

➤ Does the company have plans to expand?

➤ Has the company laid off employees recently? If so, for what reason?

➤ Is the company part of a conglomerate?

> ➤ Does the company have an employee-supervisor relationship or has it implemented the team member/team coach approach. The latter work environment usually means the company is trying to stay on top of current management techniques.

Research plays an important role in your overall job search endeavor. The information you collect and transform into useful tools like interviewing questions could make the difference between you and another applicant. As with anything, doing it right takes initiative, diligence, and commitment. So you owe it to yourself to put together a research plan that includes places to look for information and a timeline for completing the research. Remember, it is highly unlikely that you will ever interview for the same company again. So, with that in mind, take your time and do it right

Recruiters

The word "recruit" means to enlist personnel for a party or organization, to hire or engage the services of, or to replenish, revive, and restore. If this sounds like a vital function, then you are correct. Ask any NFL sports franchise how important recruiting the right personnel for a team can be and they'll tell you that it is the difference between having an average season or making it to the Super Bowl. Like a sports organization, corporate America wants the best of the best, and to get them, they are committing tremendous financial and personnel resources. Make no mistake about it—recruiting services are big business. A good recruiter is judge, jury, and salesman all rolled in one. Some companies have their own recruiters, while others contract with private firms. In either case, recruiters for the most part are not only recruiting, they are conducting an interview to see if there's a fit.

Recruiters, at least professional recruiters, are articulate, analytical professionals who have excellent communication and organizational skills. Most companies who can afford to have their own recruiters hire them to work in the human resources department. Being a good recruiter is usually tied to the performance of employees they recommend for hire. Likewise, if the last five employees recommended for employment by a given recruiter turn out sour, then it's time to find them something else to do. If they're lucky, it will be with the same company. With this in mind, it could be inferred that the recruiters need you just as much as you need them.

In order for recruiters to be effective, they must truly understand what the company or manager is looking for. They must understand the position requirements relative to education and experience, and they must know what kind of personality traits would best fit the existing department in which the newly hired applicant would be working. To help recruiters make better decisions; they attend seminars and take related courses. Some have advanced degrees in disciplines that focus on employees like human resources, while others may hold general degrees in business.

Recruiters screen out applicants for interviews that follow at a later date. However, if you make it past the recruiter, don't think you've got it made. A recruiter could screen fifty applicants and schedule twenty interviews for a single position. On occasion, recruiters have the authority to hire without an interview, but this is usually the exception, not the rule. Making it past the recruiter means that you will now have the opportunity to interview, so get ready.

Private recruiters are constantly searching for candidates who will suit their clients' requirements for current positions and opportunities in the future. Many job seekers send resumes to private recruiters to expand their marketability. Recruiters usually scan or enter the resumes into data base programs and send them out as their credentials fit an open position. If you are planning to send a resume to a recruiter, make a note to update it as your experience and education warrant.

References

Good references combined with a strong resume and successful interview are all but tickets for your next paycheck. That is, of course, if your references are good. If you manage to have an interview scheduled as a result of a strong resume, you have only your references standing between you and your future job. On occasion, you can write an excellent resume and pull off a flawless interview only to be crushed by poor references.

References, especially for candidates from outside the company, are critical in the decision process for many companies. You can be very impressive and convincing in an interview, only to have your last two managers blast you when contacted about your prior performance. No matter how well you write and how impressive your communication skills are, the real measure of any employee is how they perform once they're hired.

References can also work in your favor. For example, let's say your mediocre resume got you an interview that went reasonably well, but your references were excellent. If call after call to former employers reveals an intelligent, dedicated, highly motivated employee who was as trustworthy as he was dependable, your chances of being offered a job have just increased. This kind of consistent complimentary reference from former managers will not go unnoticed. As a matter of fact, many companies view good references as a key aspect of an applicant's trio of offerings: resume, interview, and references. Even if your experience and educational credentials don't match up, many employers won't let such an obviously good employee get away.

Of the two main types of references, professional and personal, professional are considered the most reliable. This is due to the inability of the applicant to sway or influence the results. Personal references are those that an employee might get from a manager or supervisor who has favorable comments to offer and is willing to write them down. Few employees seek written personal references from managers that found their performance to be less than desirable. For that matter, professional references are viewed as better indicators of prior performance.

Because of slander lawsuits, many companies now have strict policies about providing references, usually insisting that calls about a former employer be routed to a human resource manager for comment. This can be bad or good, depending on how well you performed. If you were an excellent employee, your prospective employer may never know. Conversely, if you were the type of employee every company wants to avoid, your next employer might never find out. Calls that are forwarded to human resources personnel may only result in the verification of employment dates, the position held, and possible salary information. Knowing what policy your current employer has in relationship to references will help you better plan for your next job interview. However, trying to find that out could be difficult.

The following questions are a representative sample of those that could be asked by someone checking a candidate's reference:

- If the employee tries to come back to work for your company, would they be rehired?
- When did the employee start working? How long did he stay?
- What was their job title?
- What is your overall impression, say on a scale of 1-10, with 10 being excellent?
- How reliable and punctual were they?
- Was the employee a good team player?
- Did the employee display supervisory or managerial characteristics?
- What, if any, positive attributes did the employee have?
- What, if any, negative attributes did the employee exhibit?
- Can you verify their salary or at least give an approximate amount?
- How did they respond to management and supervision in general?
- What were their duties and responsibilities?
- Did the employee receive regular raises and/or promotions?
- How did the employee interact with their co-workers?

Some companies might be able to give out only information relative to employment dates. Again, before you leave your current employer, know what information they will and will not give out. This just might help you draft your next resume and cover letter.

Nepotism & Contacts

The million-dollar question is, "Does who you know or who you are related to make a difference?" Well, that depends on the individual policy of the company to which you are sending a resume. Nepotism is defined as favoritism to relatives. Even if a company has a strict policy against nepotism, it can always find a way around it if it wants to. So who fits the nepotism mold anyway? Here's the list: father, mother, son, daughter, brother, sister, uncle, aunt, first cousin, nephew, niece, husband, wife, father-in-law, mother-in-law, son-in-law, daughter-in-law, brother-in-law, sister-in-law, stepfather, stepmother, stepson, stepdaughter, stepbrother, stepsister, half-brother, and half-sister.

Organizations generally do not want a manager to appoint, employ, or promote a relative to a position within the organization where the manager has jurisdiction or control over that person. Many companies have policies that forbid the hiring of immediate family members and relatives if they will be working in the same department or if one will supervise the other.

Ladies and gentleman, competition is stiff, and you would be foolish to think that a good resume will keep the employer's niece from getting "your" job. The fact is, this type of favoritism is just another obstacle to overcome in your pursuit of a job. Sure, there are companies that discourage it, and in some branches of the government it is even forbidden. Yet the preferential treatment of family members and relatives is played out every day, so get use to it. Who knows? Your next job could be the result of nepotism.

Contacts—everybody needs them, yet nobody seems to have any. Why is it that, if you have any contacts, they always seem to work for the sanitation department or county jail? Why can't you have contacts—I mean really good contacts—with companies like Proctor & Gamble, Disney, CNN, Microsoft, and General Motors? But wait, if you had really good connections, you'd probably get hired on the fast track to senior management, and by age thirty, you'd be knocking down a $400,000 salary and getting $100,000 in annual stock options. But did you earn it? Who cares, where do you sign? The fact is, this is the exception and not the rule. Sure, everyone would like at least the opportunity to show their stuff, and if using contacts can make it happen, so be it. Reality check: Write a good resume with a complementary cover letter, practice for the interview, and hope for the best.

Just the Right Stuff

No matter how good your resume and cover letter are and how much you research and prepare for the interview, the chemistry exchanged between you and the interviewer during that first few minutes is critical. People like to talk to people with whom they "connect." Not all interviewers are professional enough to look past the lack of personal chemistry to see a promising candidate sitting across from them. So there you have it. The one thing you cannot prepare for or even remotely anticipate is the amount of chemistry, or lack of it, that you will experience when you open the door.

It is very frustrating to walk out of an interview with a company representative or recruiter and feel that the information exchange was good yet something was missing. You can usually feel or sense it as soon as the other person does. The lack of personal chemistry fills the room like a suffocating odor that only the end of the conversation can cure. Without the proper chemistry, a would-be recommendation or job offer could be lost. Of course, this could be a blessing in disguise if the interviewer was going to be your future boss. If you did not get along during the interview, chances are you would have been uncomfortable as a new employee. This is speculation at best, but would you want to drag yourself out of bed and drive to a job where you feel uncomfortable all day?

Most interviewers and recruiters are cordial, professional, and receptive to applicants, so don't be worried. Although you may sense that something is missing, your interviewer may keep the interview on schedule without the slightest indication that the chemistry was simply not there. When you left the interview, you knew something was wrong, but you did not seem to get that impression from the interviewer. "Perhaps it was just me," you think, and then boom! You get the bad news over the phone or in the mail. Now you're even more confused. Conversely, you might get an interviewer that is professional enough to recommend you anyway, despite poor chemistry.

There is another consideration for you to file away concerning the right chemistry. If you don't meet the personality type called for by the available position, then you're likely not going to be hired. For example, you could be interviewing for an engineering position for which you are overqualified, but not get the job because you have a monotone voice and melancholy personality. So why would that matter if you were qualified? Well, let's say the engineering position requires daily contact with high-profile clients and weekly interviews with public information officers. In this case, the company would probably prefer a good public speaker with excellent communication skills and an average engineering background to the opposite combination.

The bottom line is, don't assume that if the chemistry was good and you got along well in the interview, you'll get the job. The same goes for bad chemistry. Don't assume all is lost just because the chemistry was not there, because you can never tell. All you can do is greet them, close with strong eye contact and a firm handshake, and then wait for them to contact you.

Companies Want Problem Solvers

Applicants that have strongly proven problem-solving skills have an edge in today's highly competitive job market. It is easier to find a well-educated, talented employee who performs well above average than it is for companies to find true problem solvers. Few universities have curricula that include problem-solving courses, despite the increasing need for such sought-after abilities. Applicants that leave one company to work for a competitor or similar company, and know how to solve that industry's problems, are all but hired. Statements like "here is what I can do to solve your specific problem" are music to a recruiter's ears. Few employers will turn down those gifted individuals who have acquired these skills. To give your prospective employer a sampling of your skills, include one or two on your resume and cover letter.

In some cases, an interview will be structured to test your ability to solve problems. If an interviewer gives you a hypothctical situation to solve, first make sure you understand the scenario by asking them to be more specific or to give an example. The problem will most likely require that you work on it alone. If this happens, use the following steps when formulating your response.

Problem-Solving Tips

1. Define the problem, paying special attention to the nature and cause of the problem. Understanding the real problem is key to the rest of the process, so make sure you nail it. What is really going on and what internal and external factors are included?

2. Briefly brainstorm some possible options. If you are allowed to have a pen and paper, jot down some ideas by defining the elements of the problem.

3. As you start the planning phase, a few of the options will begin to appear more feasible than the others. Consider the resources of the company and the severity of the problem, and then select the best option. Remember, this is just a hypothetical situation, so you can make some assumptions as long as you justify them in your solution.

4. Again, given the company's resources and the severity of the problem, develop an action plan. While you are delivering your action plan, make sure you include a statement such as: "Of course, the first step would be to put together a team to solve the problem. Having the ability to include several others and drawing on their collective input would make the process more successful." A team player statement like this, along with a good action plan, is very impressive.

If you don't feel that problem solving is one of your strong points, then by all means don't put yourself in a situation where you will be challenged. Only you know whether or not you are a good problem solver. If you're not, and you want to be, start by using the four previously mentioned problem-solving steps in other areas of your life. Over time they will become easier to master, and if you move that thought process to your next job, you will slowly build your problem-solving skills.

When the Interview Starts to Go Bad

If the interviewer starts leading you through unfamiliar waters, accept the challenge and attack it as you would any problem. For example, if you are questioned about something on your resume, say a lack of formal education, you should first clearly understand the question and then proceed with the following approach:

> Acknowledge that the interviewer perceives a problem with your lack of education.

> Explain how another employer might have felt about the same problem before they hired you.

> Move into a short conversation about how, instead of finishing school, you were working and gaining valuable experience.

> Assure them that you have every intention of finishing school as soon as you are settled in a new job.

> Finally, assure them that what you might lack in academic achievement you more than make up for in experience.

The fact that you don't quite meet the education prerequisite might be tempered by suggesting that you plan to complete your degree at night and that, after you get settled in on your new job, you will be enrolling. You have not only acknowledged the interviewer's concern, you have given him justification and assurance that you will be working on obtaining a degree very soon. However, if you commit to completing a degree program, you had better do just that. If you have no intention of going back to school, then be honest and accept the outcome.

When questions start to get out of hand or become increasingly more difficult to answer, respond with a positive statement, then address the question and follow with a positive statement. I caution you about coming off as being evasive by trying to dance around the real issue. There is an art to answering questions thoroughly, honestly, tactfully, and with just the right amount of political correctness, while still addressing the issue. Having the ability to effectively respond to a challenging question is an art that needs to be honed like any fine skill.

As mentioned earlier, make sure you understand the question. If necessary, ask for clarification. Don't think you have to immediately respond the second the interviewer has finished asking the question. It's perfectly okay to pause for a few seconds while you collect your thoughts. It's best to make sure you know what to say before you start babbling incoherently about nothing as you desperately grasp for just the right response.

One way to avoid dealing with negative questions that might send the interview into a tailspin is by acknowledging some of the issues up front. If you know that an MBA is preferred for the position and you only possess a B.S in business, then bring it up first. Tell the interviewer that you understand that an MBA is preferred for the position and then explain how your experience will make up for the lack of having one. If the tone of the interview starts to decline because the interviewer is insistent on the academic credentials, then commit to enrolling in an evening degree program and completing an MBA in a reasonable amount of time. If this is agreeable, stick to the commitment; if not, take one final crack at trying to downplay the MBA by reemphasizing your experience.

If the interviewer stops asking questions temporarily, revert back to a topic that involved a positive dialogue. If this technique proves futile, don't push any further. Accept defeat and then ask if there is anything else that the interviewer would like to know about you or your resume. The response to that question will set the tone for the remaining interview. Despite the outcome, remain pleasant and professional. Why, you ask? Because, despite the lack of an MBA, your resume and application might still be forwarded for consideration. Never burn any bridges, especially in the working world.

If the interview has a defined time and agenda, let's say thirty minutes, and twenty minutes into the process the interviewer has not asked you about your credentials or even referenced your resume, politely ask if you could spend some time discussing them. On occasion, you might just have to take control of the interviewing process, especially if the subject matter starts to stray. For the most part, this situation is rare. Most interviewers are seasoned professionals, especially those interviewing for large corporations. However, you should be prepared and confident enough to interject whenever appropriate.

Sometimes the tone of an interview will change because your last response was construed as inappropriate or rude. If you think that's the case, ask if you can clarify the response or further explain the answer. In some cases, that's all it takes. The interviewer may simply have misunderstood. The best way to avoid this situation is to stay focused and concentrate on every syllable coming out of the interviewer's mouth. You will have plenty of time to think about other things later, but for now, your utmost concentration is required. If you can't do that, you could find yourself with an extra forty hours a week to sit at home while you ponder thoughts of the universe between soap operas and *Jerry Springer*.

Regardless of how the interview turns out, use the process to improve your communication skills. If all goes well, that's great. If not, take what you have learned from the last interview and look forward to your next opportunity to dazzle them.

So, Mr. Applicant, Tell Me Why You Were Terminated

Few of us can blow right through a question about termination, regardless of what the circumstance were. However, if you are smart, you'll make responding to this question a vital part of your interviewing preparation. What can you say? Well, the first thing to know is what not to say. Don't start off with "Hey, that guy is a jerk, nobody likes him, and I just got fed up one day and told him off."

True or not, this is a bad response. The interviewer will think your answer was immature and that you possibly have a hidden problem with authority. Neither of these is flattering, to say the least. A more professional approach would be to acknowledge the termination and then defend it without derogatory comments about the other party. A calm, clear response to a direct question, ending with a positive statement, is your best bet. Avoid getting angry all over again; even if you were in the wrong, take control of yourself and just answer the question. This is where prior preparation comes in handy. You should practice answering questions about termination to the point where your response will be flawless, leaving the interviewer with sympathy for you instead of agreement with the other employer.

Take this opportunity to assure the interviewer that, whatever the circumstances were that led to your termination, they have since been corrected. You have learned from the misfortune and have used the criticism to better yourself and your worthiness as a valuable employee. This kind of answer might sound corny, but if presented in the right manner, and with absolute sincerity, the results will be well worth it.

If you quit your last job and the interviewer wants to know why, again, be positive while avoiding negative comments about your former employer and fellow employees. Your response to this question, like the one referring to termination, should be well thought out in advance. Just give your side of the story and follow with a positive statement. Good interviewers will dissect your response to this question because they are looking for similar situations that you might be in if given the position.

Some applicants think that leaving an employer on their own terms is okay, when, in fact, it's not. Depending on the situation, prospective employers will not want to hire, train, and invest countless hours in a new employee only to have them quit when times or situations get tough.

Start the Interview Off Right

Few people are born with the innate ability to sweep people off their feet with a few well-spoken words. Because of that inability, they concentrate on making a good visual impression. This is because a well-dressed man or woman usually makes a reasonably good first impression. However, it's not until they open their mouths that the true first impression is formed. Perhaps it's simply easier to look good than sound good.

Making a good impression starts with arriving just a little early. The interviewer would rather have you sitting quietly in the waiting room than be waiting on you to arrive. By the way, if you're one of those people who is so important that you have to wear a pager and cellular phone all the time, at least have the courtesy to either set them to vibrate or turn them off. The best suggestion is to just leave them in the car. If either rings or vibrates and you look down to see the number, it will be distracting to the interviewer. Would you like for the interviewer to take calls or be jotting down messages during the interview? Be considerate of the interviewer's time and leave the pager in the car.

When you first introduce yourself, start off with thanking the interviewer for their time or make a casual positive remark about the weather. Needless to say, the first words are critical. Take a minute to establish some common ground through connection with a photograph of Little-League baseball players hanging on the wall or poster of a famous golf course. If you can both talk about something non-interview-related for just a minute, the tone and remaining session will be more relaxed. This short conversation will help you feel like you have in some small way made a connection. The power of this brief verbal encounter should not be taken lightly, nor should it be avoided in an attempt to jump right to the heart of the interview.

When the interview is set up, try to find out something about the person conducting the interview. This prior knowledge, no matter how minute, will give you an edge on preparing an opening remark or initial conversation topic. Sometimes a department secretary will schedule the interview; if that's the case, take the opportunity to ask a quick question or two about the interviewer. Relatively generic questions like "Does he or she play golf?" are harmless enough. Another opening sentence or two could refer to an earlier telephone call, e-mail, or letter. Take advantage of any common topic. If you do, the conversation can build on that brief exchange and make a somewhat uncomfortable situation less stressful.

If no agenda has been established, at least find out how long the interview is scheduled to last. This will help you keep track of the time. Knowing how long the interview is going to last is especially important if time starts to run out and you still have several key points to make.

As you move through the first few minutes, again, refer to any correspondence. For example, "I understand your department is researching a new product." This simple statement should prove to be another move toward creating a common bond. Referring to a previous conversation makes you seem less like a total stranger. Regardless of how you prepared for the interview, set aside some time for those first few critical words together.

Show Me The Money

 If you are concerned only about working with a dynamic organization that fosters and encourages your true creative ability, then skip this section. If working on something about which you are so passionate that just having the opportunity to work with others who share your enthusiasm is enough, then, once again, skip this section. However, just in case having enough money to buy food is important, you might want to at least skim through the next few paragraphs.

Talking with an interviewer about salary and benefits can be difficult and uncomfortable to say the least; however, it remains a major concern for most people. If the interviewer makes you an offer, they will probably be offering on the low end of a salary range. Despite the obvious advantage some interviewers have during salary negotiation, they find this part of the interviewing process equally stressful. It could be because money and benefits are very personal items and only the applicant knows how much they need to survive.

You seldom hear an employee talking about how much money he or she makes. Paychecks are given out in a ritualistic ceremony that rivals the Changing of the Guard at Buckingham Palace. Although the check amount has been memorized from prior weeks, the act of actually holding the check in your hand conjures an image of absolute ecstasy. Many larger companies send out checks to be distributed in tightly sealed white envelopes so only the individual receiving it can see the true mystery amount. As check time arrives each week, the anticipation builds to a kind of frenzy that can only be cooled when you open the check and confirm that the already known figure is visible in print. This short-lived thrill is beyond description, yet once you have mentally distributed the entire sum to bill collectors, it's back to the grind with only the thoughts of next week's check to keep you company. In a sense, the amount of money you make is perceived by others as a form of success or failure, depending on what end of the spectrum you're on. Some employees would go ballistic if they found out that a co-worker was making 5 or 10 percent more. For these reasons, the subject of salary negotiations is a very touchy and delicate subject.

Unless this is your first job, you will have some frame of reference for an hourly rate or salary. If you are applying for a job that you read about on a job placement board or newspaper advertisement, the likelihood of knowing what the pay will be is good. If the ad doesn't mention compensation, then you had best establish a minimum amount before you enter negotiations.

Salary negotiations should be discussed after the interviewer or company representative has made the decision to make you an offer. Talking about money too soon, especially by the applicant, is viewed as premature and overly aggressive. First, concentrate on selling yourself to the company, and then discuss the dollars and cents. If the interviewer raises the subject of money too early, the figure will be hanging out there like laundry to dry. If the offer is really good, the applicant will be so excited they could blow the rest of the interview by not concentrating. If the figure is really low, the interview, for all practical purposes, is over. The applicant is so discouraged by the low-ball number, the rest of the interviewing time is wasted.

One of the best ways to prepare yourself for salary negotiations is by researching the position. If you know what others are making with the same skill level and experience, use that information during your negotiation. If you can't find that out, contact a career counselor at a school, university, or vocational center. Leave no stone unturned. Researching the going rate or salary should take only a short time on the phone. Of course, if the salary is set, you know the benchmark from which to start negotiations.

If getting the job and experience are more important than the money, then adjust your negotiating tactics accordingly. Remember, sometimes the only way to get valuable experience is to start off at the bottom. Regardless, making the decision to work for less than you need or desire is a personal decision, one that should be carefully considered in advance. However, without gaining vital experience, trying to get considerably more money from the next employer might be harder than you thought.

On occasion, working for low wages can be detrimental. The reasoning is simple: if you were willing to work for less with your previous employer, then why should your new employer need to pay you more? Again, think long and hard about working for low wages.

When you start negotiating with an interviewer about salary, make sure the information you've given them is right. Deceiving an employer about prior salary or hourly wages is not only dishonest, it is grounds for termination.

The art of negotiating a salary can best be performed when a predetermined hourly wage or salary has not been established. For example, if you ride by a local McDonald's and see a Help Wanted sign offering $6.50 per hour, good luck trying to get $8. Many applicants have to accept the prevailing wage or set amount for a given position with little to no room for discussion. On occasion, an applicant's experience can warrant a slightly higher wage, but this is the exception and not the rule. An example of such an exception would be prior experience in the food service industry. In this case, McDonald's might just pay a little extra to hire an experienced worker. If the job market in your local community is good, you might have additional leverage for negotiating. Good employees are hard to find and even harder to keep, so many smart businesses offer a higher wage at the onset of employment to keep their employees from coming to work every day with the newspaper employment want ads in their back pockets.

Fresh out of school, many young, relatively inexperienced applicants are destined to "get what they can," so to speak. There are some fortunate graduates, however, who have no experience but possess sought-after educational credentials, such as computer engineering. These lucky individuals can not only negotiate their salaries, they have to contend with corporate headhunters and recruiters who seek them out.

How About Those Benefits?

Negotiating a good salary is a major part of an applicant's compensation package, but don't forget those benefits. When you're young and first starting out, the salary or hourly wage seems to be the most important part of the job. Salary is important, but if you consider the added financial benefits of paid medical, vacation leave, and a 401K retirement program, your compensation offer might be larger than you think. As a matter of fact, a job paying $35,000 per year with selected benefits might be a better offer than a position paying $45,000 with no benefits. Some applicants will say, "Give me the extra cash and I will get my own benefits." If you're one of those thinkers, consider having free company medical benefits vs. no medical benefit and having to pay $275 per month or getting sick and missing 10 days a year with no paid off days. In this example, the medical benefit alone is worth an extra $3,300, bringing that $35,000 to $38,300. Add in sick time, vacation leave, and a company-matched 401K program, and you are making the same as, if not more than, the $45,000-a-year job. To help you evaluate your options, review the following list of benefits that could be offered by companies as part of their total compensation package:

Most Popular Employee Benefits

401K Plan	Profit Sharing	Child Care	Life Insurance
Vacation Pay	Car/Van Pooling	Training	Tuition Plan
Sick Pay	Flex Days	Medical Plan	Pension Plan
Paid Holidays	Paid Parking	Dental Plan	Exercise Facility
Vision Plan	Personal Time	Prescription Plan	Company Car

Some of the above benefits are more meaningful to you than others. However, if you are enrolled in a degree program, or plan to be, the tuition reimbursement program could be a big benefit. If you have a child who needs day care, take advantage of the company's childcare program. Failing to consider the true net worth of a company's benefits package could cause you to accept a lesser offer with another company just because their salary offer alone is slightly higher.

After negotiating a salary, the benefits with some companies are just a standard part of their overall compensation package to new employees. There is no negotiation required—you have them and that's it. Well, at least that's partially true. For example, if a company offers a 401K plan, you will have to enroll in it before you can take advantage of the benefit. There are many different elements within 401K plans that should be understood before signing up. You should consider the amount or percentage you can put in, and whether or not the company matches any portion of that amount. Also, don't forget to ask about vesting. Knowing when you are 100 percent vested is also very important.

All of these questions can be answered by the human resources department, so use it for your point of contact. If discussion of the 401K plan sounds intimidating or slightly confusing, don't worry, it will be covered in detail in Chapter 12. In general, you will find few who have negative comments about a 401K plan. As a matter of fact, many financial consultants advise employees to put every extra dime in their company's plan.

Benefits, if they are offered, should be considered with any offer and taken seriously, regardless of the salary or hourly wage being offered. Smart employees will work hard to balance both salary and benefits before making an employment decision. (Note: During the interview, make sure you have a pad and pencil to write down key points and critical responses relative to salary and benefit negotiations. These notes will be helpful when you get an offer days later. Having the ability to refer to direct statements or key notes will make evaluating the offer that much easier).

You Can't Ask Me That Question, Can You?

Most job applications have the following statement or something close to it printed on their applications: *We do not discriminate on the basis of sex, religion, color, race, age, national origin, martial status, or physical handicap.* Discrimination on the basis of any of those is illegal. Regardless of how much information a company wants to know about you, some things are simply not relevant and are illegal to inquire about.

Despite the illegality, sometimes interviewers will slip up and ask questions they shouldn't. If you are in an interview and you are being asked questions that just don't sound right, it's probably because such questions are of a discriminatory nature. For example, if you are a woman applying for a job and the question is, "Do you have children or are you planning to have children?" consider the ramifications of your answer. If you say yes, the employer might view that as a negative response. Some companies are concerned that women with children, married or not, will be missing time to attend to a child's needs. Right or wrong, this is a real concern for some companies. Asking a question like that and then denying employment on the answer in today's workforce environment would be legal suicide. The lawyers would be six deep on your front porch the next morning wanting to represent you.

Can you imagine being asked on the phone by an interviewer if you were handicapped, or if you were over fifty years old, or what your race is? If a company wants to discriminate against you, they can find ingeniously illegal ways of doing so. Be careful how you respond to discriminatory questions. At the same time, don't blow up in the interview and storm out. Although you have every right to do so, you don't want to be known as difficult or overly sensitive. The choice is yours, of course, but instead of reacting emotionally, handle it this way; immediately after the interview, write down exactly how the questions were presented and keep your notes on file pending the outcome. If you are notified that you did not get the job, ask why. At this point, depending on their response, you could consider legal action if their response was based on an illegal or prejudiced question. However, make no mistake about it; taking a company to court could be a very difficult endeavor to pursue. Something like that could haunt you for the rest of your working life. On the other hand, if you were denied employment on the basis of illegal questions and you can prove it, call an attorney and set up an appointment. Even if you have the company "dead to rights," the waiting time will most likely be long and the impending lawsuit well publicized. Trying to find a job with this hanging over your head will not be easy.

To Accept or Not to Accept—
That is the Question

By the time the interview is over, you will have a pretty good feeling about your chances. If you covered everything on the agenda and the tone was upbeat and positive, chances are you will be getting an offer letter. If the interview was mediocre at best, you'll just have to wait and see. Sometimes what you perceive to be a poor interview turns out to be better than you thought. Of course, if you leave the interview with that sick feeling in the pit of your stomach, then it's probably justified and you might as well write that job off.

Getting an Offer

Well, you've got the job, or at least an offer, so now what? After the initial excitement and sigh of relief, get out your interview notes and look over the discussion relative to salary and benefits. Focus first on salary and benefits, because other issues like job title or position start date are of less importance at this time. There is usually little to discuss with regard to these. They are what they are.

If all the terms and conditions in the offer are the same as discussed in the interview, start working through the thought process involved in making your final decision. If the offer is different from what you discussed in the interview, keep reading—that subject will be discussed later.

The decision to accept an offer should include, among other things, the question of whether or not this position and offer are right for you. At this point, give careful consideration to your answers. Being offered a good salary usually means the company has high expectations. Are you sure you're willing to work long hours, overtime, and weekends if necessary? Arc you prepared to cancel your vacation at the drop of a hat if necessary? Can you deal with the anticipated daily pressure? If you are uneasy about any of these important considerations and you have other offers pending, stop and reconsider. However, if this is your only offer, remember that failing on a new job is not worth it. If you are offered a position for which you are just not ready, you had better consider the consequences of accepting it. But enough discussion about the negatives. If the company thinks you are worth taking a chance on, and the numbers are right, get out your pen.

Now let's discuss an offer containing inconsistencies. If there is a discrepancy about anything, you have two choices: You can call for an explanation or you can write for one. Either way, make sure you get a satisfactory answer, and if the correction is made, make sure you get it in writing before you sign. For example, if during the interview a starting salary of $35,000 was agreed upon, and the offer is for $31,000, then by all means call or write for an explanation. If, on the other hand, $35,000 was casually mentioned, and no firm preliminary offer was made, you might still call for an explanation, but don't count on a correction being made. If you have a real concern, and the company wants you badly enough, on occasion you can get a slightly better offer. This, however, is the exception and not the rule. Compa-

nies don't routinely use the bait-and-switch tactic to trick employees. If they are genuinely interested in you as a new employee, they are going to try to entice you, not deceive you. If the offer is not as discussed, give them the benefit of the doubt and seek an explanation. Be professional in your correspondence with them and remove emotion from your tone, whether you're writing or calling. Remember, before you sign on the dotted line, give the new position adequate thought.

3

Changing Jobs

Changing jobs can be stressful, regardless of whether you're resigning, being laid off, or being terminated. However, the attitude you take with you to a new job depends on why you are leaving. Resigning is voluntary and should be done only when you have another job lined up. Being laid off usually is the hardest to cope with, even more so than being terminated, because, for the most part, you have no control over it. Usually, when you're terminated, you know why, or at least you should know why, and thus it shouldn't come as a complete surprise. Regardless of your reason for changing jobs, don't dwell on the circumstances surrounding your departure; instead, concentrate on constantly trying to improve yourself.

Things To Consider

If your decision to change jobs is based on wanting more flexible hours, an easier commute, better chance for advancement, or higher pay, you should start considering a new job. If, on the other hand, you are considering a change because you're not vice president after working six months, or you think you are entitled to a 25 percent raise every year, then you should stop and rethink that decision. Moving up the corporate ladder at supersonic speeds and getting large salary increases every year is not only unrealistic, it is foolish.

Some people look at the success, fame, and fortune of movie stars, athletes, and rock stars, and they want that same level of success for themselves, NOW. When you're watching those superstar performers on television, it's easy to get caught up in the hype. Realistically, that level of success happens only to a tiny percentage of people. Although these types of professions are very impressive, their levels of success came only after years of hard work and little financial reward along the way. For example, consider that a professional football player has most likely played football for twelve years for free before getting paid a dime. He played midget league, junior high, senior high, and college for essentially nothing before making it big.

Think about the thousands of other players who put the same time and effort in the sport, graduate from college, and never make it to the pros. Just putting the time in doesn't always guarantee success. This example was used only to illustrate that you have to pay your dues while doing your best to succeed each and every day. If you do this on a consistent basis, the likelihood of achieving eventual success and financial reward is much higher.

Being a Model Employee

Before you decide to change jobs, remember that other companies are always trying to lure good employees away from their existing employers. Dedicated top-performing employees are sought after by many companies. Employees who take a lot of time off to travel or "find themselves" will more than likely not be wooed away for bigger and better opportunities.

No matter how good you are, if you're sitting at home, a prospective new employer will view that as an undesirable characteristic. Stay at work and become a model employee, putting your best effort and skills to work every day. Your reputation as a talented, hard-working employee is the best asset you can have, so don't just bide your time until something better comes along. Instead, work to improve yourself on a daily basis. Remember, your next employer is most likely going to call your former boss for a reference. What is your boss going to tell them? If you don't like the answer you just came up with, then work to improve it and be dedicated while you're still there.

What's Right for You

Before you change jobs, think about what you're really looking for relative to title, pay, benefits, location, and so on. If you don't have some kind of goal, then working toward one is impossible.

Know when to stop looking for a better job by establishing some sort of realistic criteria. You might become disillusioned if you've convinced yourself that you need a $10 million salary as president of a multi-national corporation to be satisfied. It's not that you shouldn't "shoot for the moon"; it's just that, realistically, you should consider being content with much less. The main objective should be to find some occupation that makes you feel good, is rewarding financially, and allows you to have an enjoyable life outside of work. Have you ever heard someone on his or her deathbed say, "If only I could have made vice-president," or, "If only I could have made more money?" Instead, you'd probably hear, "If only I had spent more time with the ones I love." Think about it. Your job should be a part of your life, not your whole life.

Resigning

If you have made the decision to resign, don't leave until you have a firm offer in writing from another company with every detail spelled out to your satisfaction. The offer letter should include at a minimum: the start date, starting salary, bonus and or commission information, benefits, and some form of a written job description.

Resigning, no matter what the circumstances are, can be an uncomfortable time for you and your boss, so choosing the best time to discuss the matter is highly recommended. The best time for a conversation like this is when you and your boss can get away from the rest of the workforce for a short time and give each other your undivided attention. A meeting at the beginning or end of the shift is usually conducive to both parties and should be scheduled ahead of time. Be considerate of your boss's time, realizing that he or she will probably be the one who gives your next employer a reference. During the meeting, stay focused on the positive aspects of your tenure even if your decision to leave was based on unsatisfactory working conditions or other negative reasons. Convey to your boss that the decision to leave was a carefully considered and difficult one to make. Also, give the standard two-week notice if possible. If your boss requests a longer time, say one month, honor the request if possible, remembering once again who will be giving you a reference.

Moving on is a sign of maturity and should be viewed as a positive growth opportunity. If leaving your past employer is based on a desire to take on new challenges, and, in parallel, make more money, then changing jobs can be exhilarating. The most accurate predictor of future performance is past performance in a similar situation. So, to be considered a valuable employee, be diligent, proactive, and innovative throughout your working career. Remember, it was your choice to leave, so take that positive attitude and inspiration with you to your new job every day.

A Manager's Response to Resignation

Try as best you can to be prepared for your boss's response to your leaving by putting yourself in his or her position. Consider that by leaving you could be putting your boss, manager, or your fellow employees in a bind. If your current employer has invested a lot of time and money in training you to run or operate a specific system or machine, then don't be surprised if he or she is not particularly happy about your leaving. If your boss offers you more money, a promotion, or better benefits to stay, be ready to respond to the offer.

As your last day draws near, you may be asked to give upper-level management an exit interview. Don't get uptight about it; many good companies want to know why employees are leaving, especially good ones. Be positive and truthful, focusing on as many positive aspects of the job as possible.

If you are leaving a small company, talk to your boss about your final check, any vacation time that is owed to you, how long your benefits will last, and which benefits, especially health insurance, will be available to you after you are gone. If you are leaving a larger company that has a human resource department, ask the HR representative the same questions before leaving. Finally, don't forget the adage *Never burn any bridges*. Who knows? You just may need to come back to work there someday.

Things to Avoid When You Decide to Go

➤ Avoid job-hunting on company time if at all possible.

➤ Don't give prospective new employers permission to call you at work. Instead, have them call you at home or make arrangements to talk during your lunchtime.

➤ Don't leave copies of your resume addressed to some other firm out in clear view.

➤ Avoid using your employer's office supplies to hunt for a job. This is disrespectful.

➤ If you get a job offer, resist the urge to brag to your boss or other employees.

Being Terminated

If you were terminated and you know why, take that criticism and turn it into a skill or characteristic that will lessen your chances of being terminated again. The first week after being fired is usually the worst. Get hold of your emotions as soon as possible, direct your energy toward understanding what happened, and convince yourself that it won't happen again. Being terminated is a humbling and sometimes devastating experience. Pull yourself together and make your new job a better one by understanding what your employer expects of you.

Once you move on to your new job, never badmouth your former employer. Your new boss and co-workers are not interested and will most likely view your complaining as petty. Instead, be positive and focus on your new job.

More Information on Changing Jobs

Take a Deep Breath

Even though changing jobs can be frightening, you should take this opportunity to consider what you really want to do with your life. It doesn't make any difference whether you have resigned, been terminated, laid off, or just want to make a move, changing jobs is stressful. Worrying about how the bills are going to get paid and about unemployment insurance benefits will drive the average person crazy. However, do not let your bank account drive you to a new position too soon. If you do, you might just find yourself doing the same thing, just for a different company. If that's what you really want, then go for it, but chances are you will once again be looking for another job really soon.

Before you can truly start to search for another job, you owe it to yourself to first identify what you didn't like about your previous job and what situations you want to avoid in the future. If you really enjoyed your last job but just couldn't get along with management or co-workers, stop and try to figure out why. Are you sure it wasn't at least partially your fault? Did you really try to get along? Take a hard look at these questions before you go any further. If you don't confront reality, you might be miserable no matter where you go.

Once you have identified the root cause for leaving, you've fought half the battle. If you have identified some personality changes that have to be made, by all means start working on how you plan to make those changes. Accepting responsibility for your own shortcomings is hard to do, but it's necessary before moving on.

Take this time between jobs to identify your needs both from a financial and intellectual point of view. If you have found through other jobs that you need continuous mental stimulation, then make the need for that your primary focus. If, in order to feel good about yourself, you need a challenge, then pursue those kinds of positions.

There are many jobs that require employees to work fast on their feet and to work under pressure on a daily basis. Whether or not the money is as stimulating as the job is quite another thing. In any event, you have to decide what's right for you. The starving artist loves his job and is perfectly willing to do without the financial rewards for now. However, if the almighty dollar is what you live for, then search for careers that pay the big bucks. For example, salespersons who work on commission and have the liberty to work as many hours and days as they want to will get a reward every paycheck. Which type are you? Are you one extreme or the other, or are you somewhere in between? Whether it is mental stimulation or money, the decision is yours and should not be taken lightly.

Understanding the Market and Yourself

Years ago, when workers entered the job market, they could count on doing a good job, being faithful to their employer, and being rewarded with lifetime employment if they so desired. Markets were relatively stable and company loyalty toward employees was good. Those days are all but gone. As soon as a product can be mass produced in Mexico, the company announces plant closures in the United States and starts laying off employees faster than you can say NAFTA. Most companies want you to be as loyal as possible; however, this is usually not a reciprocated feeling. When the market shifts, or the product line is changed, the hammer falls on the lowest common element— you, the employee. That's business, my friend. The survival of the fittest is no truer than in corporate America.

When you consider how many jobs are lost to out-sourcing or plant relocations, it's no wonder most people can't figure out where the safe jobs are. The fact is, no job is truly safe. With the ever-increasing introduction of technology and the Internet, who knows what's going to happen next? Good news for one industry or company is usually bad news for another. Your ability to adjust and diversify your skill mix is crucial to survival in today's working market. The more you can learn about different jobs and the more diversely educated you become, the better chance you'll have in maintaining steady employment. Realizing that the job market is volatile is also another good reason to start stashing a few bucks away for those times between jobs. Those who don't save, at least a little, will be much worse off than those who do.

If you're lucky enough to figure out what jobs will have the longest life, you then need to decide if you want to work in those professions. For example, you find out that making batteries for the new wave of battery-operated automobiles is the hot job of the future. Do you want to work in a battery plant all day? How about selling batteries, or stocking them on the shelves, or installing them in new cars? Do you want to do that? You need to look inside yourself and figure out what you want to do. Sure, you need money and, sure, the bills need to get paid, but many people are working jobs they can't stand out of sheer necessity. What are *you* going to do? You have to eat. It's a tough choice—one that only you can make. But you should at least think about what you want to do just in case another job or opportunity comes along.

Perception of Young Workers

Older workers see younger workers come and go on a regular basis. With that in mind, some older employees don't want to spend time training someone who is here today and gone tomorrow. They probably have forgotten that they were the same when they were young. Baby Boomers in particular are skeptical about younger workers. Of course, some of their skepticism is fear. A 45-year-old salesperson making $75,000 realizes that the newly hired 20-year-old will probably be matching his quota in just a few years. Management has a hard time paying $75,000 for the same results that $35,000 can buy. There's no wonder animosity is created between the ages.

The best way to avoid initial criticism is by producing on the job. Get to work just a little early and stay a few minutes late every day for the first few months. This will make your employer feel better about the decision to hire you and remove any discussion from other employees about your dedication or ability to show up on time. Also, before you get the job, make sure you can show up every day without needing to take off for first one thing and then another.

Don't bring your financial, emotional, or relationship problems to work. Get all your affairs in order—your apartment, banking account, utilities, and so on. Schedule doctor and dentist appointments after work hours, and if your car is not running properly, find alternative transportation. If you need to get a ride to work, try and get a relative or friend to bring you to work and pick you up. Don't ask a co-worker to pick you up. Don't give them any reason to think you are not dependable or that such a request could become a habit every time your car needs repair. Remember, you don't want your employer or older co-workers to know what is going on in your personal life. You are focused on the job and nothing else for at least the first few months. After some time has passed and you have proven yourself as a valuable employee, you can start to loosen up.

It's sad that young employees have to endure this type of scrutiny. Be proud of your age, and let your youth and vitality work for you by bringing new, fresh, and exciting ideas to work. Unlike the older, more experienced workers, you will not have any paradigms to overcome. You have the unique ability to see problems and offer solutions unlike other employees who can't recognize the problems because they have been working too close to them to see anything wrong. This look from the outside, so to speak, is unique to newly hired employees and is valued by their employers.

Education vs. Experience

Let's say you are the employer and you have to choose between two applicants. One has a bachelor's degree in business and three years' experience as an assistant sales manager for a department store; and the other candidate has two undergraduate degrees and an MBA but has no experience at all. Who would you hire to replace a management assistant who has just left for another position? You need this person to pick up quickly and run with the new job. In this particular situation, the experienced candidate is a better choice because, not only do they have experience, they might also be bringing a better way of doing business to the new employer. The fact that the candidate has firsthand experience will also mean they won't have to start from scratch learning the basics of what is not taught in school. For example, knowing how to deal with co-workers, subordinates, and management is something that cannot be taught in school; it has to be learned through experience.

In another employment situation, the MBA could be preferred because a more advanced understanding of finance, accounting, management, and human resources can be a valuable asset to a company. This is especially true if the company isn't planning on hiring someone to make an immediate impact on the department. If a company wants an employee with graduate-level knowledge, and is prepared to allow him or her to grow with the organization, then the applicant with the MBA will probably be offered the job.

So which is it, experience or education? The obvious choice would be a well-balanced mix. If you are determined to get an MBA, at least occupy some of your time working and gaining experience, preferably in a field related to your education. However, if you can't find that perfect position, having experience working in the local music store is better than no experience at all. At least the music store will provide some working knowledge of the employer/employee relationship and how to deal with customers. If you are convinced that experience is more valuable than getting an advanced degree, by all means work in that direction. But don't be surprised if, after ten years of dedicated service, the guy with five years and an MBA gets the promotion.

How To Stay Current

You have to stay current whether you're looking for a job or considering a change. At the beginning of a new millennium, no skill can benefit you more than computer skills. Knowing your way around a computer is not only advantageous, it's an essential skill in many positions. Learn the company's software and take every advantage to practice when you are not at work by going to the library and getting on the Internet (or if you're fortunate enough to have a computer at home, log on and start learning).

If you are going to be changing jobs soon, try to find out what kind of computer programs your new employer is using and start brushing up. Listing relevant computer skills on your resume will definitely help you get the job. While you're online, look up information about your profession and read something every day. If there are professional memberships, inquire about joining. This is the best way to stay on top of your job. Professional memberships will have all the current trends, studies, and new products. Another good way to stay connected or to learn something new is by attending trade shows that come to your area. These trade shows have on-site products and services to look at and read about. They are also a good place to make contacts, because many have employment information as well.

Be diligent in trying to stay current, but also realize that making a switch from one company to another is easy if you will be doing the same type of job. However, if you are a bartender, don't expect to jump right into a position with an investment-banking firm. Moving to a totally different career is difficult enough; being successful at it is really hard. So unless you are a wizard expect a transition period.

If you are considering making a career change, don't underestimate what you are going to be up against. The best way to make the change as smoothly as possible is by learning as much about the new position as possible. In order to stay current, learn the company or industry lingo and terminology and find out what computer software they use. Talk to others in the same line of work and make a trip to the library to log on to the Internet. Making the change is going to be difficult at best, so prepare yourself with as much knowledge about the business as you can.

Using the Internet in Your Job Search

If you don't have access to a computer with Internet access, make a trip to the local library. Most libraries are online and will be glad to give you the short course on how to log on and maneuver around the Internet. As with any tool, know how and when to use it. Once you have learned how to *surf* around from company to company, you'll find a wealth of information. The Internet places a vast amount of information at your fingertips in seconds. You can find out what's available, what the pay and benefits are, and what experience is required, all from the comfort of your chair.

Once you start to feel comfortable with the Internet, you'll ask yourself why you should try to find a job anywhere else. That's when your problem starts. So many people are so fascinated with the Internet that they make it their prime source for searching for a job. Well, newly inducted computer nerds, if you think the Internet is your answer, then think again. Nothing beats actually talking to employers and co-workers about available positions and nothing will take the place of casual conversation with an actual recruiter or interviewer. This is not to imply that you shouldn't use the Internet as a tool, but make it only a part of your search and not your only means for finding a job or making a career move.

By using the Internet, you can gather information much faster than conventional methods like the phone or by mail. If you call a company and request an annual report, for example, you might not see it for a couple of weeks. On the Internet, that information is immediately available to download and print out.

The Internet can be a tremendous source for learning about new industries without asking embarrassing questions to prospective employers. Unlike conventional methods of job searching, the Internet is available and accessible twenty-four hours per day, seven days per week. You can sit around on Saturday morning in your heart-covered boxer shorts and eat powdered doughnuts while you search for a job. Once you have located a particular company's Web site, it could be like reading a book about every aspect of the business. Imagine how well prepared you will be if you have all that information prior to an interview.

As the Internet grows and gains popularity, the amount of information will be proportionately more plentiful. Some companies even have Web sites that actually allow you to send your resume to them electronically by e-mail, maybe even directly to their human resource data bank.

If you are planning to move across state or across the world, the Internet can prove invaluable. Not only can you visit Web sites about prospective employers, you can also find out about housing, schools, and extracurricular activities at your place of relocation. This is a definite advantage. Imagine what it would cost to fly to those prospective cities just to gain the same information that's free on the Internet, not to mention the time savings.

Advantages of Taking Your Job Search Online

➤ You can search for a job any time you want, 24 hours a day, seven days a week.

➤ You can research jobs at your own pace.

➤ During your search you can discover other opportunities.

➤ You can find more information about jobs that you're interested in.

Getting Ready To Start a New Job

Few things are as intimidating as starting a new job. The looks you'll get from other people, the whispering, and the occasional cold shoulder are all part of those first few days. Focusing on the job and not your emotions is easier said than done, but for your sake, you have to do it. Before you start the new job, confront your uneasiness and be prepared to show your confident side. Don't be cocky or brash; instead, be confident and focused. You weren't just given the job— somebody selected you from all the other applicants. This should make you feel good about yourself, but not to the point of being obnoxious. Remember, you could be working there for a long time, so start off this new working relationship the same way you would start any new relationship.

If you have a report date, say two weeks from now, use that time to brush up on your computer skills. Read over any pre-employment information you may have been given and prepare questions. If you are entitled to benefits like medical, dental, 401K, or life insurance, take this time to fill out the required documents in advance. If time permits, take a quick job-related course at a vocational center or simply read up on your new job. You got the job based on your experience; however, what was current then may not be current when you start your new job. Try to stay on top of changes and approach them with enthusiasm and anticipation.

If you know what your first task will be on your new job, start preparing for it. Oh, by the way, if you do not own a day planner, buy one and use it. The more you have to do, the more likely you'll forget something. But planners are going to be useful only if you use them properly. Many people use planners for more than just work-related topics such as to record personal information like doctor's appointments, birthdays, and so on. Using a planner effectively will make your life a little easier and more organized.

When you interviewed for the job, you took a road to get there. Investigate alternative routes to work in case a road is closed, or perhaps to find a better way to get to work. Allow yourself ample time to get to work. If the drive is long, take a trial run at the same time of day you'll be driving once you start work. If you have to jockey for parking spaces on a daily basis or hunt down a parking meter, take that additional time into consideration. If you have to use a parking garage or parking meter, stash away some bills and change somewhere in your car.

The night before you embark on a new career, don't go out and celebrate with your chums; save that for the weekend. Instead, do a little exercise, eat a good meal, and go to bed early. Discipline yourself to get a good night's sleep and avoid partying during the work week. No employer likes to see an employee, especially a newly hired one, come to work with red, glazed-over eyes, shaking a cup of coffee. It's hard when you are young to not go out at night and have fun with your friends, but for the sake of your job, limit your time out. Remember, there's always the weekend.

On your first day, plan to stay as long as it takes to get situated. If you have an office space or cubical, move in but don't completely rearrange everything the first day. Gradually move in whatever personal items that seem appropriate to your new workspace. One day bring in some family pictures, on another bring in a few other things.

Many offices have a coffee fund, so if you indulge, be prepared to sign up the first day. Don't just get a cup with the intention of signing up another day. You don't need co-workers thinking you're cheap. As a matter of fact, why not bring in a can of coffee your first day? This first day is critical because, after all, you'll be making a first impression.

Be polite and friendly to everyone and avoid aligning yourself with anyone, regardless of whom they are. If you know someone there, don't spend a lot of time with him or her right off the bat. Instead, just say hello and focus on your job. Make a smooth, uneventful transition into your new job. Take the time to see what's going on around you and adjust accordingly. Make decisions carefully at first, unless, of course, you are expected to make an immediate impact on your department.

Over time, providing your work speaks for itself, you will become increasingly more comfortable with your job and co-workers. This relaxed atmosphere is conducive to an effective and efficient working environment, but it should not be a case of sit back and relax. Commit yourself to continuous improvement by adapting and conforming to the ever-changing job market.

Your Values Determine What's Important to You

Sit down in a quiet place and write out what your values are. You just might find out that your values determine what matters to you and what you truly care about. In short, your values are an excellent indicator of who you are. After you have carefully written out your values, develop a list of what is important to you about being an employee and working in general. Compare your list with the following topics:

➢ Having the ability to live wherever you want.

➢ Feeling like you are truly accomplishing something.

➢ Being recognized for your accomplishments.

➢ Having adequate time to give to family and friends.

➢ Having a reasonably stable job with a reasonably stable company.

➢ Becoming financially independent while you are young enough to enjoy it.

➢ Working with a good group of people.

➢ Looking forward to going to work because you enjoy it instead of dreading it.

What Bugs You Most About Work

For some people, just having to work at all is annoying enough. However, for the sake of this section, let's concentrate on more definable reasons. Many people hate their jobs or at least dislike them, not because of what they do, but because of whom they work with or for. How many times have you heard people say, "I really liked that job, but my boss was a pain in the neck." Each employee has his or her own story. Working with difficult people takes patience and concentration. But the fact is, you need to work, and who's to say the next job won't be worse? Trying to get along is your best bet. Why do you think that your job should be any more perfect than the rest of your life? With company downsizing, layoffs, unfair treatment, and low pay, it's no wonder working environments are stressed. It's true— many people find the working environment and not the work itself to be the worst part of the job. So, what can you do? Well, you can suck it up and try to block it out of your mind for the sake of a weekly paycheck, or you can quit. Not much of a choice, is it?

While co-workers and bosses can contribute to a less-than-desirable working environment, other issues can be equally as annoying. For example, how about those ridiculous rules; long, boring, ineffective procedures; and stupid policies. Who comes up with all that crap, anyway? You can try to change the rules, procedures, and policies or just live with them. However, a better suggestion would be to try to understand their purpose before you react.

As with any business, there is one definable mission: to make as much money as possible with as few people and resources as possible. When management introduces a policy or procedure, most likely many people have reviewed it. It was written with production, quality, safety, or operational objectives in mind. With larger companies, policies and procedures can also be implemented to cover human resource issues like benefits, promotions, salary, and disciplinary topics. If a business thought that policies and procedures would cause them to lose money, they would probably not issue them unless they were mandated by a federal or state agency. Don't be so hard on company-issued policies and procedures; they are usually in place to help the process along, not hinder it. Who knows, maybe one day you will find yourself writing or at least reviewing, one.

Whether it's the people or the rules, practically every job will have something you don't like, so get over it. Maybe, one day when you're the president of the company, you can fire all the buffoons, burn the stupid procedures, and tear up those silly policies. But guess what? No matter what you change as the new president, your employees are going to find fault with it, just as you did when you were a peon.

An Ideal Work Environment

 You arrive at work one day and the boss calls you over and says, "So, Mr. Employee, today's your lucky day. I have decided to let you design the ideal work place." Before you embrace this opportunity, consider these issues:

➤ The ability to be creative

➤ Being able to work at your own pace

➤ A free on-site child care facility

➤ Flexible work hours

➤ A better parking area

➤ A company fitness center

➤ The chance to be recognized and rewarded for your accomplishments

➤ More pay and benefits

➤ A greater opportunity for advancement

I'm sure you could add to the list; however, the point of this quick exercise was to identify what you desire most about a job and work environment. If you had to pick just one from the above list, what would it be? Some would pick creativity; others might choose pay and benefits. What's important here is to remember that, as a young employee, your ability to impact change is limited. With that in mind, you have to accept your surroundings at work and be able to adapt.

Coming to work every day with a poor attitude is not only unhealthy, it's useless. If you truly want to make changes in the work environment, become a respected, valuable employee. Suggestions from valued employees are taken seriously. Most companies want to keep their employees relatively happy because the cost of retraining new employees is expensive. Although you don't have the power to make changes, you do have the power to work together as a team and try to give the employer a day's work for a day's pay. That's all you can do.

Strong Personal Qualities

Whether you're working now or looking for work, know what your personal qualities are. Write them down and use them in your resume and cover letter. Your strong personal qualities will define who you are and what makes you tick. Most employers are looking for applicants who possess many of the following qualities. Understand what your personal qualities are and how you can work to acquire more of them.

Read the following list and circle those that apply:

Adaptable	Determined	Inspiring	Productive
Ambitious	Diligent	Intelligent	Resilient
Analytical	Disciplined	Intense	Resourceful
Appreciative	Efficient	Intuitive	Responsible
Articulate	Energetic	Loyal	Spontaneous
Assertive	Enthusiastic	Mature	Strong
Charismatic	Flexible	Organized	Supportive
Committed	Hard-working	Patient	Tenacious
Confident	Honest	Perceptive	Thorough
Cooperative	Helpful	Persistent	Trustworthy
Decisive	Imaginative	Persuasive	Versatile
Dedicated	Independent	Precise	

Most employers would agree that employees who possess many of these strong personal qualities are those worth hiring and keeping happy. However, unlike taking a class to improve your computer skills, strong personal qualities come only if the person genuinely wants them to. If you're not particularly efficient or organized, then only you can change that by truly wanting to improve yourself. In any event, look over the above list again and work to improve on those that you did not circle.

Developing Meaningful Goals

One of the best things you can do for yourself when you are considering a new job or career change is establishing meaningful goals. If you haven't already done so, now is as good a time as any to create goals for yourself, both personally and professionally. Your individual career success is a long process of discovery, with strategic steps being made against pre-established goals. The same is true for your personal goals. If you want to lose fifty pounds, set a goal of five pounds per month and work toward that end. If you want to be vice president of the company one day, lay out a plan for that as well, by establishing mini-goals along the way. An example of those mini-goals would be to set a series of intermediate goals, such as:

Goal 1: Become assistant manager within three years.

Goal 2: Make shift manager in five years.

Goal 3: Department manager, six years.

Goal 4: Division manager, eight years.

Goal 5: Vice president, ten years.

When setting goals, remember that they will have to truly be meaningful. Consider what inspires you and be specific about how you intend to achieve them. Be realistic in your approach toward goal setting, being careful to not be overly ambitions. Setting a goal to become vice president over a ten-year span is more realistic than a five-year span. The worst thing you can do is set multiple, unrealistic goals tied to specific dates and watch as they go by. On the other hand, don't set a five-year goal to become assistant night shift manager in charge of filling the ketchup bottles at a second-rate restaurant.

Aside from professional goals, set personal goals. If you are 20 years old with $250 in saving and an annual salary of $20,000, don't expect to be able to purchase a $400,000 house in two years. Furthermore, avoid setting goals that could make you uncomfortable. A prime example would be setting a goal to be married by age 25 and another to have 2 children by age 32.

Make goals obtainable and realistic. While you're working on them, be careful to build in contingency and room to modify. Once you have completed them, post them somewhere at work and at home so you can see them. Put a copy in your desk at work and place another copy on the refrigerator or the area where you sit down to figure out the monthly bills.

Goals are not made to be set and then forgotten; you have to be aware of them to achieve them. Establish whatever means you need to remind yourself of where you are in relationship to achieving them.

Realizing Past Accomplishments

In order to help you decide on a new job or career, you will likely need to build on existing accomplishments. Over the course of your young life, you probably accomplished some impressive things. They could have been at work or in your community. To help you recall these events, consider the answer to these questions:

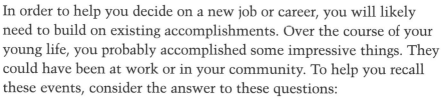

➤ Did you suggest new ideas, and then have the opportunity to implement them with good results?

➤ Have you ever identified a problem at work or in the community, offered a solution, and then witnessed the positive result?

➤ Have you ever organized an activity that resulted in a positive result?

➤ Did you ever suggest a cost-savings idea that proved successful?

➤ Have you ever improved the quality or reliability of a product or service?

➤ Have you been able to increase sales or production with documented results?

With the help of the above questions, you should have been able to create your own list. With that exercise out of the way, use some of the following words to complement those accomplishments when drafting a resume and cover letter:

Acquired	Developed	Improved	Prepared
Advised	Devised	Increased	Presented
Assisted	Diagnosed	Installed	Produced
Conducted	Directed	Invented	Provided
Constructed	Eliminated	Negotiated	Reduced
Coordinated	Expanded	Obtained	Saved
Created	Formulated	Operated	Sold
Delivered	Identified	Organized	Solved
Designed	Implemented	Planned	Supplied

The purpose of identifying these accomplishments was for you to understand what has made you successful and to assist in guiding your next career move.

Proper Behavior on the Job

Like it or not, times are changing, and nowhere is change more evident than at your local workplace. Companies are writing and implementing *code of conduct* policies to reflect changes in our society relative to language, sexual harassment, acceptable dress codes, and so on. These changes are due, in part, to society's move toward political correctness and the ever-increasing fear of lawsuits. Most of these newly introduced policies have been long in coming and are necessary to change an attitude and environment that were somewhat discriminatory and demeaning to minorities in the past.

To avoid trouble on the job, avoid talking in other than a normal tone of voice. There will certainly be times when you will feel the need to raise your voice, but try to control yourself. When you are at lunch or on a break you can relax somewhat; however, you should always be aware of your tone and volume. If this sounds like a lot of work, just think of it as good manners and proper work etiquette. Avoid at all cost the use of derogatory statements, sexual comments, and slang, and completely eliminate profanity while at work.

Aside from using proper verbal etiquette, avoid practical jokes and teasing. Jokes can not only get you in trouble; they can also backfire and hurt someone. It's one thing to hang a funny cartoon or calendar on the wall; it's quite another to pull a chair out from under someone. To be safe, avoid practical jokes involving any direct physical contact with co-workers if at all possible. Proper behavior on the job doesn't just apply to the side-by-side cubicle; it also applies when interacting with customers and clients.

Anymore it seems like so many completely innocent statements are taken out of context. What used to be acceptable behavior is now grounds for termination and lawsuits. This sad but true situation is played out in offices across the country every day. Like it or not, to survive in today's business environment, employees have to be aware of what they say and to whom they say it. Be smart and make your workplace a source of income, not a source of entertainment.

Can't We All Just Get Along?

It doesn't matter whether you like someone or not, you have to get along on the job. You don't have to believe in what is important to them, or respect how they live their lives, but you do have to work with them every day. Therefore you will need to get along, for your sake and theirs.

Despite what prejudice you might have toward another person, you have to keep it to yourself. The focus of prejudice is usually directed toward women, minority races, different religions, and homosexuals. To harbor a prejudiced opinion toward any one group is extremely shallow and immature. Preconceived opinions about other people are destructive to a healthy work environment and, hence, are disruptive to productivity.

Aside from any prejudice you might have to overcome, you will also have to be tolerant of others. If you do not agree with a co-worker's sexual orientation, you will have to learn to tolerate his or her sexual preference just as he or she will have to tolerate your lack of understanding. There are, however, situations where your tolerance does not have to be stretched. Let's say a new co-worker occasionally uses drugs on the job, and you simply tolerated the behavior because it seemed harmless enough. If that co-worker is going to be involved in an activity when his or her drug use could be harmful to another co-worker or to company property, then you need to report that individual to supervision. How would you feel if you said nothing and that co-worker operated a forklift and caused a serious accident? Clearly, there are limits to being tolerant.

In order to put prejudice and tolerance in perspective, consider your immediate family. If you strongly disagree with a brother or sister, you will still try to maintain mutual respect, will you not? How about an uncle who drinks all the time? Despite your feeling toward drinking, are you not somewhat tolerant of his behavior? This same type of individual respect for family members, regardless of your feelings or convictions, is required on the job as well. Therefore, your ability to look past your feeling is critical to survival on the job.

Sexual Harassment

Few things will get you fired faster than engaging in sexual harassment. Sexual harassment is behavior that is sexual in nature, such as making comments about a person's private parts, using sexually offensive language, telling dirty jokes, fondling, kissing, hugging, and touching. If a supervisor makes a job decision based on an employee's willingness to be involved on a sexual basis, he or she is guilty of sexual harassment. Supervisor or not, if any employee engages in or projects sexual behavior that makes another person feel uncomfortable, he or she could be guilty of sexual harassment.

If you are being harassed at work, tell the offender to stop. If he or she persists, try to remain composed and, as soon as possible, write down what happened and whether there were witnesses. Before you report the incident to your supervisor or manager, know what the company sexual harassment policy says and follow the steps exactly as detailed. Document any meeting(s) about sexual harassment and, as best you can, write down the entire conversation. If the situation persists and the company you work for has a human resources office, file a complaint if the policy calls for that next step. Keep referring to the policy if there is one, because, if you follow it and nothing happens, your case, if you decide to take it to court, will be much stronger. If the harassment persists, consider seeking legal advice. However, the decision to contact an attorney should not be taken lightly.

Regardless of how well documented you think your case is or how many witnesses you have, the legal process will prove to be embarrassing and revealing relative to your past and present sexual character. If you have a pending case, your employer, if he or she is smart, will not fire you. However, the work environment will most likely become uncomfortable, depending on the circumstances of the complaint. Be prepared to deal with that for a long time. Cases of this nature can take months before they come to court. After they are tried, regardless of the outcome, things will probably not be the same.

Know what your company's policy is on dating between co-workers. Some companies are explicitly against it, while others don't even address it. If you date someone on the job, avoid showing affection at work. If your company has no policy against dating, still be careful about asking someone for a date. If you are turned down, stop asking. If you don't, your persistence, although innocent on your part, could be construed as sexual harassment.

References

➢ 101 Great Answers to the Toughest Interview Questions, by Ronald W. Fry

➢ The Complete Resume & Job Search for College Students, by Robert Lang Adams

➢ Cover Letters for Dummies, by Joyce Lain Kennedy

➢ Dynamic Cover Letters for New Graduates, by Katharine Hansen

➢ Job Interviews For Dummies, by Joyce Lain Kennedy

➢ Resumes For Dummies, by Joyce Lain Kennedy

➢ Your First Resume, 4th Edition, by Ronald W. Fry

➢ Job Searching online for Dummies, by Pam Dixon

Part 2
Moving Out

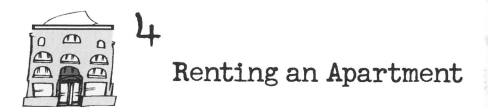

4

Renting an Apartment

Congratulations, you have decided to move out on your own. Of course, you will now have to start paying rent, buying groceries, cooking, washing dishes, defrosting the freezer, purchasing Tupperware to hold left-over meatloaf, filling ice trays, washing, drying, folding, and ironing your clothes, cleaning the bathroom—including the toilet—vacuuming the floor, sweeping the porch and deck, calling the cable repair man, taking out the trash, calling the landlord to complain about noisy neighbors, dealing with door-to-door salespeople, and putting a new roll of toilet paper on all by yourself! With that said, you might be wondering why you ever wanted to move out. Be that as it may, expect your decision to move out to be a life-changing experience.

Moving into an apartment is exciting and should be viewed as one of your first steps toward independence. Now you can walk around the house in your underwear, sleep late, and turn your stereo on whenever you want. You can leave the television on for days at a time and use the phone whenever and for as long as you want. When you leave and put the remote control down on the coffee table, it will still be there when you return. Sounds great, doesn't it? It is great, but as you will find out, there is much to do before you can move in and put your feet up.

Searching for an Apartment

So where do you look for an apartment? There are several places to find your new place, for example, the newspaper, the yellow pages, rental guides, or, if you can afford it, a fee-paid rental agent. Most large apartment and condominium complexes can be found in all of the previously mentioned sources. However, the best way to find a place is to get a pad and pencil and sit down with either the yellow pages, the newspaper, or a rental guide and start calling.

There's a good chance that you probably know where you want to live or at least which part of town. Knowing where you want to live will narrow down your possibilities and make the search much easier. However, if after searching through the yellow pages, you discover that your desired location has rentals that are out of your price range, you will have to look elsewhere. The newspaper, much like the yellow pages, will have listings that represent a full range of prices and accommodations. If you're in the market for a small apartment, a single room, a house to rent, or a duplex, the newspaper will be a much better source than the yellow pages. Newspaper advertisements reflect the latest available apartments, unlike the yellow pages, which are updated once per year. Whatever your preference is for living accommodations, you will most likely find them in your local newspaper. The paper will probably have several categories, such as furnished and unfurnished. This is quite helpful when you're deciding to rent or buy furniture. The newspaper, unlike a majority of yellow page advertisements, might also include the apartment prices, which is also helpful in narrowing down your choices.

Rental Guides

Rental guides, sometimes called apartment guides, are another excellent source for locating your new apartment. These guides are highly focused and detail oriented to specifically inform the potential renter of what is available. They are usually the most comprehensive resource that you can use. However, despite their comprehensiveness, they are usually printed monthly, which leaves the newspaper as your most current source for locating an apartment.

Rental Agents

If searching on your own isn't getting you anywhere, find an agent. Most agents can be found in just about any publication that lists apartments. Agents find apartments for a living and are usually very good at what they do. You tell the agent what you are looking for and for a small fee they will find it. For example, you have $250 per month to spend and you want a completely furnished, five-thousand-square-foot, tri-level, waterfront apartment with direct TV, private parking, maid service, an Olympic-size pool, with a state-of-the-art exercise facility, golf course, club house, and free lawn maintenance. Who knows? They just might find one, but don't count on it. However, on the outside chance they can't find this apartment, you should have plan "B" ready. Be realistic with your expectations. Talk to your parents and friends who have rented before. Remember, the rental agency will charge you a relatively small nonrefundable fee for their service. Nothing is free, but look at it this way: They did all the work; all you have to do is have enough money to cover the check.

Regardless of how you find your potential new home, you will need to drive out to see the place and talk to the landlord. Make a good impression by dressing appropriately for the occasion. I'm not talking about a tuxedo, but leave your University of Budweiser ball cap, lime green fishnet midriff shirt, the extra-wide three-times-your-normal-size-jeans, and fluorescent orange sneakers at home. Also, be prepared when you get there by having a list of questions ready for the landlord. Here are just a few to consider:

➤ How much is the monthly rent, and what day of the month is it due?

➤ Is there a late fee, and how is it calculated?

➤ How much is the deposit?

➤ Are children allowed?

➤ Are pets allowed?

➤ What kind of laundry facilities do they have?

➤ What is the parking situation?

➤ Do I have to pay extra for trash collection?

➤ Is cable included in the rent, and, if not, has the apartment been wired for cable?

➤ What have the utilities cost over the past year?

➤ Is the apartment heated and cooled with electricity or gas? Note: Historically gas is cheaper. However, you will still need electricity for lights and other appliances.

➤ Does the door have a dead-bolt lock and, if not, can you have one installed?

➤ Does the apartment have a refrigerator and stove?

➤ Have telephone wall jacks been installed?

➤ Can I get a blank lease to take home and review?

Now that you have finished asking questions, be prepared for what the landlord might ask of you. Most landlords want a credit report, a list of personal references, and the name of your employer, just to mention a few. Applications for renting an apartment are usually lengthy and should be filled out with care. Do not assume that if you have the money, you will be able to rent an apartment. Too many tenants have destroyed apartments and left without paying rent for landlords to trust anyone just because they have the first month's rent in hand. However, if you pay your bills on time and have good references, you will not likely have a problem.

If you are the first occupant to rent the apartment, some of the previous questions are very important. Some landlords make their first tenant (that's you) pay for the initial installation of telephone and cable. If you don't ask up front, don't be surprised if you find yourself paying for installation cost.

When you drive out to see your potential new home, notice how clean the area is around the apartment. If the area looks nice, this usually indicates that management cares about the complex, which is a good sign. Once you finally get in to look over your new apartment, don't spend your time trying to figure out where you will hang your paintings or how your 10,000 watt stereo will look on that back wall. Instead, stop and listen for the sounds around you.

Look for smoke detectors. Most apartments have them, but many times they are electric, which is fine unless a fire breaks out in your fuse panel. You can't always trust that electric smoke alarms have a battery back-up system. Even if the electric detectors have back-up systems, budget for at least two more battery operated detectors and more, if you can afford it. If you are not sure where to install them, the local fire chief will be glad to instruct you on the best locations. Smoke detectors are cheap insurance and well worth the peace of mind that they provide.

Also, while you are there, find out about your neighbors. Do they have nine children and five large dogs? Ask your landlord if you can come back at night to listen and to see how the complex looks under security lights. If you don't like what you see, find another place. If all this work seems time-consuming, consider the fact that once you sign the lease, you will be there for a long time. Do your homework before you sign on the dotted line.

Laundry Rooms

Many apartment complexes are equipped with coin-operated washers and dryers. This is not as convenient as having one in your apartment, but it's a heck of a lot better than loading up soiled underwear, sweaty shirts, and smelly towels into your front seat and driving to a laundromat. If you have to use the complex laundry, your next challenge will be to pick the best time to wash your clothes. Don't forget, when it's convenient for you to wash, it's most likely convenient for the other 5,000 residents as well. Once you decide to trot down to the laundry room, be prepared to have to wait for an empty washing machine and, just to be safe, bring your own change. You can never tell if the laundry room change machine, if they have one, will be working.

Apartments With Washers and Dryers

If you are lucky enough to have a washer and dryer in your apartment, then you're probably paying more for the convenience. But it's worth it! Consider—you're gobbling down a spicy burrito on the way out the door and you drip some taco sauce on your white pants. You can strip down and toss them in while you wait, standing in your underwear. This is well worth the extra bucks.

Some apartments are equipped with individual laundry hook-ups for each unit. However, this means that you will then need to either rent or purchase a washer and dryer that will fit in that allotted space. For the most part, these hook-ups are located in small areas within the apartment and are not conducive to full-size washers and dryers. When considering buying or renting, remember that most good brand-name washer and dryer units last around ten years. With that said, purchasing would be a better choice than renting, although that is entirely your decision. However, if you decide to rent these appliances, please read Chapter 7 before you make a decision.

Parking

Parking could prove to be an unexpected hassle, especially if you're not used to the endless competition for available spaces. On the other hand, you might be fortunate enough to be renting an apartment that has assigned spaces, usually two per apartment. Where those spaces are, and whether they are exposed to the elements, will vary. This type of assigned parking has its ups and downs. For example, you come home on a rainy day to offload sixteen bags of groceries just to find a car parked in your space. After temporarily subduing your anger, you pull into someone else's spot just to unload. While you're in putting up your refrigerated items, the owner of the space you just occupied calls and has your car towed off. This is legal and usually only requires proving to the tow-truck operator that the spaces are individually assigned. What a great way to end your day. If you are renting in a larger metropolitan area, parking could be a major hassle and expense. Unless you check into it up front, parking could be an additional fee, one for which you were unprepared. Parking is always going to be difficult in apartment complexes due to constant visits by other tenants' friends, relatives, and parties, so just learn to deal with it.

Recreation

Be familiar with the rules of your pool, clubhouse, golf course, or tennis courts. There could be a fee to use them; and fee or no fee, there are almost always going to be restrictions relative to the use of those facilities by you and your guests. Know what the restrictions are, including hours of operation and your responsibility for cleanliness. If you're planning to have a party, expect to pay a deposit on the facilities you use.

The Lease

The number-one rule is, if you don't have time to read the ENTIRE lease, don't sign it. If you are convinced that this apartment is right for you, request a blank lease in advance and read it front and back. Reading the lease slowly and carefully will be time well spent. Most leases have all the basic information, such as amount of rent, payment due date, the duration of the lease, number of tenants allowed, and so forth. However, there are some leases that are written solely in favor of the landlord. Be aware of these kinds of leases. The following are some terms and conditions commonly referenced, as well as some typical clauses which could appear in your lease. Be sure that you understand them, and if you don't, get clarification prior to signing.

Some Typical Clauses

1. Landlord (landlord's name) called "Lessor" leases to (your name) hereinafter called "Lessee" the following described property (name of apartment unit and unit number) hereinafter called the "premises," for a term of (typically one year) beginning on the __ day of_____month, _____ year terminating on the____ day of _____ month _____ year.

2. Rent is payable in monthly installments of $_____per month and is to be mailed to the following address (_____).

3. Lessee must notify in writing 30 days in advance prior to a premature departure from the property and is subject to the terms and conditions of the lease relative to early departure. (Note: Read and understand what this really means. This could be very expensive if you do not understand the obligation here. For example, if you sign a one-year lease and leave one month later, you could be responsible for eleven months' rent with no legal way out. Again, be sure you understand this condition of the lease.)

4. A walk-through of the apartment was conducted on the following date, _____, and the attached document reflects the condition of the apartment as witnessed by the lessor and lessee. The attached walk-through document will be used to compare conditions upon departure. (Note: If you don't leave the premise in the same condition you will have to pay for it, first with part of your deposit, and more if the deposit doesn't cover the damage. Make sure you notice and document little things like numerous nail holes, cracked tile, appliances that are not fully functional, the cleanliness of the stove, stains on the floor, missing screens and cracked glass, to mention just a few.)

5. For the purpose of this lease agreement, the premises shall not be deemed vacant until lessee has completely removed all possessions from the premises and returned all keys to the landlord.

6. The lessee shall deposit the sum of $_____ with the lessor as a security deposit against damage to the premises while the lessee is in possession and as security for the performance of all the provisions under this agreement. The security deposit may not be applied to or used for rental payments while the lessee is in possession of the premises. The security deposit will be withheld in the event that premises are not cleaned to the satisfaction of the owner or owner's agent, excluding reasonable wear and tear.

7. Lessee shall be responsible for all damage to premise, whether caused by lessee, guest of lessee, pets, or by children of lessee.

8. Lessee shall not make any alterations to the premise or change the paint color thereof without the written permission from the lessor. (Note: Understand that if the lessor gives you permission to paint any room, you could still be responsible for repainting that room to the original color.)

Although the previous list is incomplete, it does represent some of the terms and conditions that you could encounter on a lease. Aside from terms and conditions, understand what constitutes minor repairs and major repairs and who pays for them. For example, who pays to have a leaky faucet fixed? Understand the responsibility for pest control, because you could be expected to pay for periodic treatments. Ask such questions and document the answers. You also need to consider what will happen if you decide to stay longer than the lease stipulates, or if there is a work transfer clause which would allow you to leave early. All of these concerns should be considered prior to signing a lease. One last time, *get the lease early and read it over.* Get advice from those you trust, and seek outside assistance if necessary, but please understand it before you sign.

Packing Up

Getting ready to move can be an emotionally charged experience filled with excitement and anticipation. To temper some of those natural feelings and to help you focus on the task at hand, sit down and prepare a checklist. One of the first things on that list should be to file a change of address with the post office. This small task will require you to go to the post office and fill out the form. This change of address form tells the post office to start sending your mail to your new address. However, just to make sure you get your mail, contact businesses that currently send you mail like credit card companies, magazine subscriptions, and so on.

After your address change has been submitted, there are five other key tasks that, depending on how far away you are moving, need to be accomplished as soon as possible.

1. Cancel any local memberships to clubs and organizations.
2. Close checking and savings accounts.
3. Call and cancel phone service, cancel Internet service, and notify your long distance carrier.
4. Cancel electric, gas, water, sewer, cable service, and trash collection.
5. Cancel any newspaper subscription service as well (many people forget this one).

Things To Consider Before You Move

Now that your mail situation is taken care of, it's time to pack. Whether you are moving a little or a lot, across town, or across the country, whether you decide to do it yourself or hire the job out, there's much to consider. So unless your worldly goods consist of a portable stereo and a sleeping bag, you need to plan. Consider some of the following issues when making your moving decision:

➤ A professional mover can pack your possessions in one day. Plan on the job taking two or three days if you pack yourself. Packing yourself is economical but time consuming, so if you decide to take on the job, start early.

➤ Renting the right size truck is important. To get an adequately sized truck, call a mover and tell the rental agent how much stuff you have. (Note: Rental agents usually size the truck based on the number of rooms to be packed. Look at your possessions and have an estimate ready.)

➤ Unless you are renting a semi-tractor-trailer, you won't have to worry about obtaining a special license. In fact, most rental trucks have automatic transmission, power steering, and power brakes. You will nonetheless need to pay special attention while driving the truck. The biggest difference in driving a moving truck and your car is the height. Shaving the top off of a drive-in hamburger joint is very embarrassing and expensive.

➤ Rental costs vary from city to city and from season to season. Some companies charge a lump sum rate, while others charge for rental and mileage. Know what your charges are. (Note: Don't forget about a dolly rental, blankets/padding, boxes, and bubble wrap.)

➤ Trucks are usually equipped with either a built-in ramp or mechanical lift on the back.

➤ Use good boxes, even if you have to buy them. Those behind-the-grocery-store boxes are usually in poor condition.

➤ If you decide to pack, select an uncluttered area to stack your boxes, being careful not to block the doorway.

➤ Figure out in advance how to get your boxes to the truck. Consider steps, ramps, the condition of walkways, muddy areas, low ceilings, fences, gates, and tight corners.

➤ Take the time to label your boxes. You'll be glad you did.

➤ Don't over-pack, and don't mix glassware with hard objects.

➤ Save newspaper for packing material. Buying packing material is really expensive.

➤ Load heavy items first and securely tie them down. If you're not sure how to tie them down, get help.

➤ Prepare an inventory of your possessions and come up with an estimated value in case of damage.

➤ Take this opportunity to sell or discard unwanted things.

➤ If you move yourself, ask only dependable friends and relatives to help you.

Hiring Someone to Move You

If you can afford to hire a mover, this is the way to go. Someone else will pack, load, unload, and then unpack. It's great, but it's also expensive, especially if you want them to move any outside items, like a satellite dish, picnic table, or an extra car.

Before you sit down and start calling movers, consider the adage *You get what you pay for*. Select a well-known nationwide mover and your chances of having problems will be greatly reduced. If you don't select a reputable mover, you could have trouble if you need to file a damage claim. This is not at all to say that a local or small-time mover can't do a good job. It's just that, if you don't have firsthand knowledge of a smaller agent, use a national mover. While you are on the phone with a moving agent, request a brochure on how to prepare for the move. These brochures are filled with good common sense advice and can help you during this difficult time.

Prior to packing day, make sure you have prepared an inventory of your possessions. This will come in handy when you're looking through your stuff at the other end of the move. Make sure you've made arrangements to be there when the mover is boxing and loading, because that's when they note what is scratched, torn, dented, or broken. This will be your opportunity to agree or disagree with their assessment of your goods. Once your items have been delivered, you will once again need to look at the condition of your possessions and assess any damage that may have resulted from the move. Most professional movers, to reduce claims, take good care of your possessions and are very good at what they do.

Regardless of who moves you, it's unrealistic to think that there will be absolutely no damage. If you find something that has been damaged during the move, save the packing material and the box for the insurance adjuster to examine. Don't call the insurance company or moving company until you have unpacked everything. This will keep the adjuster from scheduling multiple inspection visits to see the damage.

Before you move, call for an estimate. Some companies will give you an estimate over the phone while others will want to come out and look the job over. Regardless of what the estimate is, remember that it's just that, an estimate. Be prepared to pay more. The final bill is rarely the same as what was originally estimated. Many things can change the price. For example, when the mover arrives at your new home or apartment, they discover they have to park a great distance from the front door, or you live on the fifth floor and there is no elevator. These unexpected inconveniences can cost extra.

Take the stress out of your move by doing your homework, asking questions, seeking advice, and reading the mover's agreement if you decide to hire the job out.

Additional Information on Renting an Apartment

What To Consider When Selecting a Roommate

For many people, living alone represents ultimate freedom and independence. Living alone means you decide when and if the laundry needs to be picked up and when the dishes need washing. You have ultimate supreme control over the much-coveted remote control, you don't have to wait for someone to get off the phone before you use it, and if you want to take a forty-minute shower, well, that's okay, too. You need not consider anyone else's feelings or plans. If you want to stay out all night, you'll have no one to check with. You essentially have no responsibility to anyone for any reason once you are home alone in your apartment. Living alone is quite an experience, especially if you have never done it before.

Now that you have read about some of the advantages, perhaps you would like to consider a few other realities about living alone. Living alone means you will have to pay *all* of the rent, buy *all* the groceries, cook every meal, wash *all* the dishes, and pay *all* the utility bills. Living alone means you will have no one to help you clean the kitchen and bathroom, rearrange the furniture, or take out the trash. The biggest downside for many, however, is the financial side. Having someone to split the $700 rent and $175 utility bill would be a tremendous benefit, don't you think? However, as with any benefit, it carries a price, one that can easily outweigh the financial benefit if you're not careful.

An obvious solution to your financial burden would be to find a roommate. But before you decide to let someone move in, there's much to consider. First of all, friends do not always make the best roommates. Don't let your desire to have someone pay a portion of the bills override your need for comfort and relaxation. For example, if you sleep between 10:30 p.m. and 7:00 a.m., consider what an inconvenience it would be to have a roommate who works the second shift and gets home at 11:30 p.m. Your roommate will most likely wake you up every night as he or she arrives home in search of his or her own rest and relaxation. Your roommate will be taking a shower, playing music, cooking, and watching TV. If you can sleep through all of that, then don't worry about it. If you can't, look for a roommate who works a compatible shift.

Some of us are relatively clean and organized, while others are quite the opposite. Nothing will drive a clean, organized person crazy faster than walking into a dirty cluttered kitchen or bathroom day after day. Avoid a roommate who does not share the same need for cleanliness. Conversely, don't bring in a roommate who is a neat freak if you are not that concerned about such things. Life is too short to have to deal with the "Odd Couple" syndrome. If you know the person, chances are you will have an idea of how clean they are. Washing towels once a week is very different from once a month. This is not to drag the issue of cleanliness too far, but it will make a bigger difference than you think. Just wait and see.

Do you drink, smoke, use drugs, or gamble excessively? If you do any of these, consider the habits of your roommate prior to working out an arrangement. Nonsmokers can tolerate a lot of things, but the smell of stale cigarette smoke lingering throughout the apartment is not one of them. Sharing your apartment with someone who gets obnoxious and loud when they drink is another situation that is hard to overlook. Remember, your decision to have a roommate was probably due to financial matters. With that in mind, don't compromise your standard of living and don't allow for things to get out of hand just to save a few bucks. Take your time and select a roommate you can live with. Even if money is not the reason for wanting a roommate, don't let your desire for companionship overshadow your fundamental ethics and values.

How about hobbies? If you enjoy snowboarding, hiking, canoeing, and beach volleyball, that's great. Getting outside is healthy and it allows you to get exercise while doing something you enjoy. The point here is to consider the hobbies of your proposed roommate. For example, after a long day outside, you probably don't want to come home to a satanic ritual being performed in the living room. You would also probably not prefer to hear your roommate practice his "In-A-Gadda-Da-Vida" drum solo at 4:00 a.m.

Compromise is the key to any relationship, but some things cannot be overlooked. If your roommate confined his or her drumming to the hours between 2:00 and 4:00 p.m. on Saturday only, that would be a compromise. However, few of us could deal with the burning candles and ritual chanting on the floor.

When considering the values, attitudes, and personal habits of a proposed roommate, do not overlook the rules of the apartment complex. Check to see what is allowed and what is not. You don't want to be evicted because of a poor roommate.

Let's talk about pets. Depending on your lease, pets are either allowed or they are not. If they are allowed, and you have a small cat, don't bring in a roommate with a pit bull. Compatibility of pets is as important as compatibility of people, especially if you have the smaller pet. How about snakes, iguanas, or loud-mouth parrots? Roommates are one thing; their pets are quite another. Have you ever met someone you really liked that had an obnoxious pet? Not only would an obnoxious pet drive you crazy, but the pet's owner would probably take offense to your dislike of their pet. Avoid this situation by knowing what kind of pet they have and, if they don't own one, what kinds of pets they are considering to buy.

Roommates are not just some "thing" you acquire to help offset expenses. They are individuals just like you who have their own needs. How well do you really know this person? Do you agree with or tolerate his or her sexual orientation or behavior? If you are the reserved one, do you want a roommate having a multitude of sexual partners over all the time? Does this person enjoy dating many different people, or is he or she content to stay home and read a book? How would you react if your new roommate stepped in the shower with you one day? Set some ground rules early and establish what is going to be acceptable behavior for the both of you. It could be that you are the wild one and have to tone down in order to get a good roommate. Are you prepared to make those changes? If not, ask your proposed roommate to reconsider his or her request. If he or she is insistent on having you change, then keep looking. An individual's sexual behavior is one of the biggest obstacles to overcome when looking for a roommate, yet it is probably the least discussed because it is such a personal matter. However, failure to resolve this situation could prove devastating to the relationship between you and your roommate, not to mention your friends and lovers.

Just as sensitive as sexual preferences is the individual's religious conviction. Your roommate may want to live with someone whose religious lifestyle or lack thereof is somewhat compatible. If confronted with a situation that challenges a person's religious beliefs, most people will side with his or her own. This may or may not be a problem, but the subject should come up when interviewing a potential roommate.

If you are selecting a roommate to help pay the bills, ask about their job. How long have they been working there? How stable is their job? You don't want a roommate who is unstable and apathetic towards work. If you have a roommate who is always calling in sick and going to work late, they are not going to be working for long.

This kind of information is hard to find out, but it is nonetheless critical to know. If you feel strongly about the person, but you need more financial information, ask to see a copy of his or her credit report. Although not always a true indicator of a person's character, you can learn a lot about a person's commitment to paying the bills from reviewing a credit report. If you don't want to ask for a credit report, or your potential roommate doesn't want to let you see it, inquire about other places he or she has lived and call those former roommates. If the person has lived with other people, but doesn't want to give you any references, that should tell you something. Keep looking.

Things To Consider in a Roommate Agreement

Once you have made a decision about a roommate, it's time to nail down the particulars of who, what, when, where, and how. After all, the work of finding a roommate isn't done until you have worked out the details. Take your time and think out how you plan to share expenses and responsibilities.

Who is going to pay the rent is different from how the rent will be divided. If you both share equally in the rent, whose checking account will the check be drawn against? Whose bank account is used doesn't really make any difference if the account has sufficient funds to cover the check and the person sends it in on time. However, if you give your roommate half of the $700 rent and he or she forgets to deposit it, or doesn't pay on time, there could be a problem. The check could bounce, causing additional fees from the bank. A returned check means your rent is not going to be paid on time. The lease probably provides for the addition of late fees, bringing the total cost of rent from $700 to maybe $775. Is your roommate going to pay for the extra money and accept responsibility? Are you going to tolerate late rent checks and nasty letters from the landlord?

The simple matter of who is going to send out the check should be given sufficient thought. The person who is better organized should be the one who collects the rent from the other and takes responsibility for paying it on time. As far as sharing the fees is concerned, if the rent is late because one of the roommates is late in paying, then the roommate causing the fee should accept that financial burden. How are you going to address the situation if one roommate cannot pay his or her share of the rent? You ought to think about that scenario and have a plan. The two of you should set aside an emergency rent payment to cover an unexpected problem. Pulling together extra monthly rent might be hard to do, but if you don't set aside an emergency rent payment, you could be sorry.

If you have not moved into an apartment yet but you will be doing so with a roommate, decide on whose name will be on the lease if only one is required. In some cases, the landlord will let both of you sign the lease. If not, decide on who is going to sign on the bottom line. This same decision also applies when deciding on whose name will be on the phone, cable, sewer, water, gas, and electric accounts. This is a big decision because, despite what you may be thinking, creditors will be after the person who establishes the service if anything happens.

Before you sign the lease and move in, decide on how you are going to handle the cost of utilities. Are you going to share the cost? If so, consider what that could be like. If your roommate is hot all the time and you're not, you may resent splitting the $300 utility bill generated from the constant usage of the air-conditioner. Work it out ahead of time.

How about the phone? If you enjoy long phone calls to family and friends, do you think it's fair to tie up the phone all the time? If you really enjoy talking on the phone, consider having two lines. The additional expense is minimal and well worth the added benefit of using the phone whenever you want. Separate lines will also eliminate debate over who made the long distance calls. If you're not going to get separate lines, work out times and limits on phone usage. If you have Internet service, consider the phone line usage and plan accordingly.

Some people really like their movies and sports. If one roommate wants all the cable channels but the other is content with having just basic cable service, work out a fair compromise. But first consider that the roommate who wants only basic cable could also be the person who watches the most television. This is unfair to the other party, who is paying extra for a wide variety of channels but can't seem to get the remote to watch them. As with anything else, compromise is in order.

Although the television is a small part of living together, it could get ugly on the weekends when one wants sports and the other wants MTV. A simple but expensive solution would be separate televisions. If two televisions is the answer, who is going to buy the new one, and who gets the existing TV in the big living room?

The place is a mess and you cleaned it only last week. Do you have to clean it again or do you share those duties and responsibilities as well? Make a list or at least verbally divide the workload. One week you take out the trash; the next let the other roommate do it. If you cook, let the other clean up. You'll wash, your roommate will dry, and so on. Living together is a partnership in the sense that you both share the rewards of companionship and reduced expenses.

How about food? Will you buy only what you want, leaving your roommate to fend for him or herself? If you buy a six-pack of Pepsi, how will you feel if you go to get one and see six empties in the trash? Just like the TV situation, resolve the potential conflict before it arises. One roommate eating the other's goods could be unpleasant. Avoid this unfortunate situation by deciding how you plan to handle the grocery bill.

When you signed the lease, you accepted full responsibility for paying rent and assuming costs for damage. If you both split the security deposit, make sure you know how to get your half back after you move out. How about if you decide to move out early? Will you get your half of the deposit from your roommate or will you have to wait? Don't forget the deposits on utilities, phone, and cable. If you had an apartment and then found a roommate, talk to them about his or her financial responsibility for any damage he or she causes. These delicate issues should be treated as simple business decisions; nothing personal should get in the way.

Talk to each other about overnight guests, privacy, pets, and the volume of the television and stereo, parties, rules on smoking, drinking, drugs, and who will get the big bedroom with private bath. How about the extra storage space? Who will get that? If there is a covered parking spot, who gets that?

Last but not least, you should consider furniture and other possessions. Will a roommate be bringing over a six-piece dinning room set or a couch with end tables? Have you talked about what possessions they can bring and what you would prefer they didn't? If you need to rent furniture, be very careful about the rental lease. (Note: Renting furniture is covered in Chapter 7). If you decide to rent, whose taste in furniture will ultimately decide on what is rented? If you plan to buy, will you both share the cost and, if so, who will own it when either moves out?

How about damage to each other's possessions while in the apartment? Renter's insurance is covered in another chapter; however, the issue of insurance should come up when talking with roommates. Whatever you decide, be fair and be willing to compromise.

If you were going to be together for only a week or two, you could put up with just about anything. However, signing a lease and moving in together is a long-term commitment. Take whatever time you need to discuss and work out all of these issues in advance.

Roommate Problems and Conflicts

When two roommates sign a lease for $700 per month, they are really signing a lease for $8,400 per year. With that in mind, defaulting on a lease can be very expensive. Signing the lease is not only a legal promise to pay the landlord; it's also a promise between roommates to share the cost. In many states, if you have a roommate who did not sign a lease but shared your apartment with a verbal commitment to pay, that verbal commitment could be viewed as an implied agreement and, therefore, enforceable in court.

If a landlord wants only one person to sign the lease knowing that four people will be sharing the apartment, that's up to him or her. The landlord looks for the one who signed the lease to pay the rent, while you'll be looking for the other three to share the expense. If one or more roommates cause damage to the apartment, the landlord will be expecting the name on the lease to pay, regardless of who was at fault. There are multitudes of problems that can emerge from renting an apartment. The best way to deal with them is to draft a document detailing individual liability and how it will be resolved. If you think you are immune to problems and conflict just because your roommates are friends or lovers, you are in for a real surprise. Nothing will end a friendship or relationship faster than being sued or evicted because of one roommate's disregard for the lease and its content.

Avoid trying to break the lease if you and your roommates start to have problems. Even if you know that the landlord will not have any trouble renting the apartment, you are still obligated to pay any remaining rent, whether you lived there or not. In many states, the landlord has no obligation to mitigate or reduce your obligation to pay unused rent. If you sign a year's lease at $700 per month and move out after two months, you will still be obligated to pay the balance of $7,000. Your other roommates will also be liable for their portion as well. So don't think about breaking the lease early, because it won't solve anything but the immediate conflict. The long-range effects will easily be worse to deal with. Take control over the situation and try to keep it from getting out of hand.

The more roommates you have, the cheaper it will be to live, and there's no denying that. However, the more roommates you have, the greater the chance for conflict.

Steps to Follow when Encountering a Conflict

➤ Despite your initial desire to react with a verbally offensive or defensive tone, stop and control your emotions for everybody's sake.

➤ As best you can, identify the problem or conflict, even if it has been long in coming. Who is at fault? Who contributed to the situation? What triggered the conflict?

➤ If tempers are hot, leave for a short time and come back to discuss the issue.

➤ As best you can, have the other roommates there to help ease the situation and allow for their input.

➤ Whether it be a financial or a personal issue, try to work it out. Don't let something like one roommate's snoring or a dirty kitchen cause you to break up a good thing.

➤ Listen to each other and try to relax despite the level of emotions.

➤ Arrive at an alternative or compromise and apologize if necessary.

➤ If the conflict cannot be resolved, or you are just too angry, seek the help of a family member or friend. Remember, the cost of breaking the lease and ruining a relationship at the same time is high. Take your time and try to resolve your problems well before they reach this point.

Roommate Finder Services

A roommate finder service is helpful, especially if you have moved to another city. Most services operate the same by allowing the one seeking a roommate to fill out a very detailed questionnaire and then looking through their data banks for a match. These questionnaires are very thorough, asking about sexual preference, personal habits (like smoking and drinking), money, pets, profession, and so on. Finder's services match roommates according to personalities and living preferences. Some roommates want only first-floor accommodations, with private parking and a doorman, while others may prefer a simple room to rent no matter where it is.

Fees charged by finder services vary from state to state, with some charging a month's rent while others charge a percentage of the annual rent. However, the cost is well worth it if they can find a compatible roommate that will save you half of the $700 monthly rent for a year. As with any service or business, if you are concerned about a particular finder service, check with the Better Business Bureau for complaints.

One of the biggest advantages of using a roommate finder's service is the screening process. If the finder's service has a good reputation, it's most likely because of many satisfied customers. Trying to find a roommate on your own is really tough because, as mentioned earlier, friends don't always make the best roommates. If you were to place ads for a roommate on the bulletin board at the local drug store or food chain, you might get flooded with weirdo phone calls. This is especially true for women. What woman wants to put up, in clear view, "Roommate needed to share an apartment with a single woman?" The number of prank and indecent phone calls that might follow is simply not worth it.

Can I Afford To Live Alone?

Before you start your apartment search, calculate how much you can afford to pay. The best way to do that is by first totaling your existing monthly payments and then estimating the new expenses you will have once you rent an apartment. Once you have that dollar amount, subtract it from your take-home pay. The amount left over will be available for rent. Some experts say that you should allow your rent payment to be only 25 percent of your take-home pay. The following list represents most of the expenses you might encounter when renting an apartment:

- ➤ Utilities: phone, cable, gas, water, sewer, and electric
- ➤ Moving expenses (one time)
- ➤ Renter's insurance
- ➤ Food
- ➤ Trash collection
- ➤ Apartment association fees, where applicable
- ➤ New furniture and appliances purchased or rented

Once you have assigned a dollar amount to these expenses, don't forget to allow for clothing, medical and dental, entertainment, auto payments, gas, auto insurance, and miscellaneous. Although this exercise is fairly simple, if you are unclear about how to do this, sit down with a relative, family member, or good friend and ask for help. As a closing note, if you know any prior tenants, ask them about their utility cost. While you have them on the phone, inquire about the landlord and why they left. Be sure to ask if they felt safe there and what, if anything, to be aware of.

What's The Landlord Suppose to Do?

The landlord is essentially running a business, and, like any business, there is much to do. For example, either the landlord or building owner is responsible for assuring that all state and local fire, housing, and health codes are met. Inspections take place from time to time, and fines are issued if any code is found to be out of compliance. So how does all of that affect the tenant? Well, if the landlord is fined for failure to comply with the fire code, you may be inconvenienced by the repair or installation of a sprinkler system, fire pull boxes, additional smoke detectors, or fire doors. The same inconvenience would apply to remodeling due to structural violations, like steps that are unsafe to walk on or handrails that are loose and pose a danger to the occupants. There is little you can do; however, the corrections are made for your benefit as well as the other tenants.

Landlords are responsible for making sure that each apartment has utilities such as water, gas, and electricity. If the water main breaks outside your apartment parking lot, the landlord is responsible for coordinating the repair. This, of course, would be an unfortunate situation, but it should not cost the tenants a dime. If the central air-conditioning unit were to fail in August, that would be the responsibility of the landlord, but it would also be an inconvenience to you and the other tenants.

If your lease stipulates that you are responsible for routine bug spraying, then so be it. However, if the vacant apartment next door is infested with rats and roaches and they are invading your space, then the landlord is responsible for taking care of that. If the landlord is unwilling to do anything, follow the rules of your lease relative to your responsibility and then contact the local health department. This also applies to rodents in the lobby, clubhouse, and laundryroom. This disgusting problem, if left alone, can and will get out of hand quickly, so don't feel bad about calling the health department if you have to. If you fear retaliation from the landlord, look into making the call anonymously or ask the health department if they would not reveal your name.

Laws vary from state to state, but many landlords are required to repair broken windows and any other unsafe conditions, whether it be in your individual apartment or not. One gray area has always been the repair of the parking lot. Potholes get deeper and cracks seem to get wider by the week, yet rarely is anything done. On occasion, you can get together with other tenants and try to force the landlord to make the repairs. However, if the landlord is of the type that would allow such a condition to deteriorate to that point, good luck in forcing the needed repairs.

One of the biggest complaints from tenants is the return of their security deposit. Landlords are required to return the security deposit usually within thirty days and, in some states, with interest on the original amount. Your chances of getting your deposit back are greater if you move somewhere local. However, if you are moving out of state, and the landlord will know that by the forwarding address you are required to leave, the task of getting your deposit back will be greater. Read your lease carefully, making sure you have documented evidence of the condition of the apartment before and after you vacate. Unfortunately, landlords all too often have to be forced by letters from attorneys and small claim court rulings to return the security deposit. Again, your best defense is documentation of the apartment's condition signed by either the landlord or the landlord's representative when you moved in and again when you moved out.

If you are having problems with your landlord, start documenting every call and follow the call with a certified letter. Try as best you can to work it out. Read your lease and know what your responsibilities are. If nothing happens, or the problem gets worse, contact the local housing authority, health department, or fire inspector. You have the right to live safely in your own apartment, and the landlord has the responsibility to follow the codes and regulations of the city, state, and federal government.

Sample Check Sheet
Used for Moving In and Out

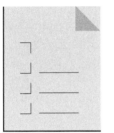

Every apartment is different, but the process of moving in is the same. Walk throughout the apartment with the landlord or his representative and make a list of damages before you move in so you will have something to compare to when you move out. Some apartment landlords make this process a part of the lease, others do not. It would not be a good idea to move in unless this check sheet, or one you create, is filled out. Use the following as a guide:

➤ **Outside entrance to your individual apartment:** Walls, ceiling, paint, scratches, dents, dings, locks, window(s), etc.

_____

➤ **Foyer:** Walls, floor, lighting, paint, window(s), scratches, ceiling, carpeting, stains etc.

_____

➤ **Kitchen:** Appliances, condition of each and cleanliness, walls, stains, floor, lighting, paint/wallpaper, ceiling, window(s), plumbing fixtures, garbage disposal, etc.

_____

➤ **Dining room:** Wood floor/carpet, lighting, holes in walls, stains, ceiling, window(s) etc.

_____

➤ **Living room:** Wood floor/carpet, lighting, holes in walls, stains, ceiling, window(s) etc.

_____

➤ **Bedroom No.1:** Floors, stains, holes in walls, window(s), closet doors, lighting fixtures, ceiling, etc.

➤ **Bathroom No.1**: Cracked tile, ceiling, floor, plumbing fixtures, glass mirror, window(s), shower curtain, caulking, etc.

➤ **Bedroom No.2:** Floors, stains, ceiling, holes in walls, window(s), closet doors, lighting fixtures, etc.

➤ **Bathroom No.2:** Cracked tile, ceiling, floor, plumbing fixtures, glass mirror, window(s), shower curtain, caulking, etc.

➤ **Heating and air-conditioning:** Overall operation, thermostats, hot water heater (if in apartment), etc.

➤ **Security system and smoke detectors:** Total number of detectors and operation, key pad for security system, dead-bolt or chain locks, etc.

➤ **Insects:**

➤ **Fireplace, gas or wood burning:** Burn areas, flue operation and cleanliness.

Tenants' Responsibilities

Most of what you have to do is spelled out in the lease. But just to make sure, let's review a few key points. Most important is the rent: Pay it on time and keep a record of your payments. Consistently paying the rent on time will make the landlord happy and more lenient if you have an occasional late payment or shortage one month. If the lease prohibits pets, don't try to sneak one in. Follow the lease and you will have no problems.

Notify the landlord in writing before you make any alterations to the apartment, such as painting or putting up wallpaper. Landlords want to be notified, because they are concerned about property damage and shoddy workmanship. If you wish to paint the walls, the landlord could agree but will probably insist that you change them back to the original color prior to moving out.

Once the lease runs out, notify the landlord of your intentions. If you want to stay and you have made prior commitments with the landlord, then let him or her know out of courtesy. If you have not made plans to stay, but would like to, you will need to discuss that with the landlord as soon as possible. There could be someone ready to move in on the last day of your lease, so check it out. If you are smart, you will send a letter to the landlord months in advance requesting an extension. If you are not planning to stay, you should still send the landlord a letter out of courtesy. In that letter, you should request a date to meet and walk down the apartment, comparing notes on damage. If you have been a good tenant, paying each month on time, the landlord could be a little more lenient towards the occasional picture hole in the wall.

The tenant's responsibility to make certain repairs has always been subject to certain important limits. The responsibility does not apply to major structural items like walkways and handrails, but only to relatively minor items like curtains, venetian blinds, and so forth. Major or minor, the tenant has the responsibility to make emergency repairs to protect the premise from severe weather conditions like a driving rain. For example, if a windstorm blows an object through the window, as soon as it is safe, you should try to cover the window to keep rain out, thus preventing further damage to the walls and floor. If you just sit back and say, "Hey, that's the landlord's problem", you could find yourself paying the bill as a result of your lack of preventative action. This does not require anything heroic, just an attempt to mitigate any further damage.

The last thing you'll need to do before you move out is provide the landlord with a forwarding address. Without a forwarding address, you may have a problem getting the security deposit back. Where is he going to send your deposit if you don't give him an address? If you don't have a forwarding address because you don't know where you are going, give him your parents' address or ask him to hold the check until you do have one.

Covenant of Quiet Enjoyment

The landlord has an obligation not to interfere with the tenant's lawful possession and use of the premise. This obligation, called the *covenant of quiet enjoyment*, is usually stated in most leases. This covenant may be breached by the conduct of the landlord, someone acting under the landlord's authority, or someone having better title to the premise than the landlord has.

Eviction

Eviction rules and procedures vary from state to state. Generally, an eviction occurs if the landlord padlocks the premises, changes the lock on the door and refuses to give the tenant a new key, or in some way physically bars the tenant from entering the premises. If this happens, the tenant may sue for damages or treat the eviction as a *breach of condition* and be relieved from further obligations under the lease. However, if the tenant has violated the lease in some way the eviction could be perfectly legal with no recourse.

Another form of eviction, called *constructive eviction*, occurs when the landlord's action or inaction causes the property to become uninhabitable. An example would be failure by the landlord to make badly needed repairs to the furnace and thus allowing it to break down in January. As with the other form of eviction, the tenant has a couple of options. The tenant can stay and continue paying rent and then sue for damage or vacate the premises due to bitter cold and treat the landlord's failure to act responsibly as a constructive eviction, thus having no further obligation to pay rent.

The Much Coveted Security Deposit

Most leases provide for a security deposit. Depending on the apartment complex, the deposit could be quite high. If you are planning to move to an exclusive complex with lavish accommodations, expect to pay for the privilege both in monthly rent and security deposit. The more expensive the apartment, the greater the repair bill if damage occurs. As a rule, expect the equivalent of one month's rent as a security deposit. The purpose of the deposit is to provide the landlord with a quick and sure remedy when the tenant damages the property and fails to pay for the damage, breaks the lease, or refuses to pay the rent.

By law, landlords are entitled to keep only the amount needed to compensate for needed repairs resulting from a tenant's damage. If a tenant spills grape juice on the carpet and it has to be replaced; the cost will be deducted from the security deposit. If the kitchen was left in a mess, and the walls have been damaged, the landlord will deduct for that as well.

Most landlords try to be fair, but just for a moment, look at it from the landlord's standpoint. For years, a small percentage of tenants have damaged apartments far beyond what their measly security deposits could pay for. They steal appliances, mirrors, curtains, doors, and even lighting fixtures. It's no wonder that on occasion landlords can be hard and uncompromising. If you were treated that way, wouldn't you be suspicious and overly protective from time to time? Landlords can never figure out who is going to take advantage of them next, so on occasion they react by taking a little extra for a repair just to get some of what they have previously lost.

Be Prepared By Having a Toolbox in Your Apartment

To be ready to tackle those small repair jobs around the apartment, put together a toolbox. Don't wait until the kitchen faucet starts to leak to run to the hardware store for a wrench. You are going to be hanging pictures, installing ceiling fans, and putting up curtain rods.

Remember, most leases require that you make some repairs, so be prepared. The following tools will get you started, so make sure you have them:

- ➤ A metal and a rubber hammer
- ➤ An assortment of screwdrivers
- ➤ A small hand level and a few pencils
- ➤ A caulking gun and a tube of waterproof caulk
- ➤ A putty knife and assorted paint brushes
- ➤ A 25-foot measuring tape
- ➤ A 6-foot step ladder and, if storage allows, a small step stool
- ➤ A hand saw, sand paper, and a file
- ➤ Masking tape, scotch tape and teflon tape
- ➤ A 6-inch and a 10-inch adjustable wrench
- ➤ An assortment of washers, nails, and screws
- ➤ A pocket knife and a utility knife

Assignments and Subleases

On occasion, tenants want and need to transfer their rights and obligations under the lease to a third party. This type of transfer is either an assignment or a sublease. An assignment of the lease occurs when the tenant transfers the entire remaining portion of the lease to a third party. A sublease occurs when the tenant transfers the lease for only part of its remaining duration.

A situation for an assignment and sublease would be, for example, a tenant who has fourteen months left on a twenty-four month lease and needs to move, or needs help with the rent. If the tenant transfers the entire remaining fourteen months to a third party, this would be considered an assignment. If the tenant allows a third party to move in for say twelve of the fourteen months, this is a sublease.

Under an assignment, the landlord-tenant relationship, with all its rights and responsibilities, transfers from the original tenant to a new third party. Of course permission to do so, and the entire transaction itself, has to be approved by the landlord. The landlord and assignee each have the right to legally enforce the lease obligations of the other. However, the original tenant is bound to the new agreement unless the landlord expressly excuses them from such responsibility. If the assignee fails to pay the rent, the landlord can proceed against them or the original tenant, or both. If the original tenant has to pay, then he or she is entitled to recoup the loss from the assignee.

If you are considering assignment or subleasing, do so only when you know exactly what you are getting into. What if your lease doesn't address assignment or subleasing? In this case, it's best to check with the landlord; you definitely don't want any hassles. If you think you want the option to assign or sublease, ask to have that right included in the original lease before you sign it. If you want the option after you have signed, ask the landlord to amend the lease.

How about just taking in a roommate to share expenses? Taking in roommates isn't the same as subletting. The original tenant whose name is on the lease is still solely responsible for maintaining the contents of the lease. If you want someone to move in to share expenses, or just provide company, be aware of the potential consequences—one of which could be eviction due to the unruly, obnoxious behavior of the roommate. If your landlord allows you to have a roommate after you have moved in, understand that your roommate's behavior is your responsibility.

5

Renter's Insurance

Now that you have made the decision to move your "stuff" to a new apartment, condo, or house, you will have to consider how to protect it in case the joint burns to the ground. Did you know your landlord's insurance does not cover your personal property? In fact, the only way to get your landlord to cover your property loss is by suing for negligence. For example, if the security gate was broken or the smoke detectors didn't work, you might have a legitimate claim. A landlord has insurance that covers only the building structure; it does not cover your personal belongings. If the apartment building burns to the ground, the landlord owes you nothing. Just think of it—your complete set of Burger King Disney glasses, your oil-on-velvet Elvis painting, your $200 sneakers, your disco anthology CD collection— gone, all gone. How do you stop this from happening? Answer: Get renter's insurance.

Personal Property Coverage

Personal property coverage pays to repair or replace belongings such as your television, furniture, clothing, appliances, some of your jewelry, and other personal items, if damaged, destroyed, or stolen. Claims can be filed for the following hazards: fire, smoke damage, burglary or vandalism, riot or civil commotion, explosion, electrical surge damage, lightning, windstorm or hail, falling objects, and other hazards as defined by your policy. Also, some of your personal property is covered anywhere in the world. To find out what is covered and for how much, read over the policy before signing. If your policy does not protect your possessions outside the home and you want that type of protection, ask an agent about the additional cost to provide such coverage.

Personal Liability Coverage

Personal liability covers claims or lawsuits resulting from bodily injury or property damage to others caused by an accident on your property or as a result of your personal activities. Many standard policies are written to pay up to $100,000 per claim. Of course, you can get higher limits if you are willing to pay.

Medical Expenses for Injury to Others

This type of coverage pays for the cost of others accidentally injured on your property or through your personal activities, regardless of who is at fault. It also pays for any necessary medical expenses for approximately three years from the date of the accident, depending on the policy. As a rule, medical payments usually do not apply to your injuries or those household members living with you.

Additional Living Expenses Coverage

This type of coverage is provided to pay for expenses associated with temporary living conditions. If your rented house, condo, or apartment is damaged to the point where you cannot live there while repairs are being made, this additional living coverage will pay for some of the extra out-of-pocket expenses. Some of these expenses include storage fees, the extra cost of living in a hotel, and the extra cost of food. The coverage pays only for the difference over and above your normal expenses.

Here's an example of when extra living expenses would be available and how they would pay. If your apartment were damaged due to fire, you would have to move out while repairs are made. The cost of moving and storage of possessions not destroyed by fire would probably be paid in full, because moving and storage is not considered a normal expense and the cause was directly related to the fire. If your rent was $450 per month and the hotel cost $1,250 per month, the extra $800 would be above and beyond and, therefore, paid by the insurance company. How about food? While in the hotel, you had to eat out three meals a day for a month at a cost of $600. If your normal grocery bill were $300 because you cooked at home, the difference of $300 would be reimbursable. Keep every receipt associated with your temporary move, including coin laundry expenses. However, if you did not have the use of a washer and dryer in your apartment and you had to use an outside laundry, don't expect to get reimbursed for the cost. The reason the cost is not covered is simple: You were already using an outside laundry before the fire.

Optional Coverage

In addition to your standard policy, you can purchase separate policies or endorsements. Most good personal property policies cover your jewelry and art objects. However, they are covered only up to a certain value. If you have any expensive jewelry or art objects that are worth more than the standard policy allows, you should consider purchasing additional coverage. Your insurance agent can tell you about this type of extra insurance. If you do not have a current appraisal of your jewelry or art objects, the insurance company could request that you get one in writing and give them a copy. This documentation protects both parties in case of loss and ensuing debate over the value of the damaged or missing piece.

How Much Coverage Should I Buy?

The best way to determine the value is to make a detailed inventory of your possessions and estimate their value. Many insurance companies have work sheets that you can use for this purpose. After you have completed this list, take photographs and, if possible, take a video of all your possessions. From that point on, when you purchase items for your apartment, save your receipts, especially for large purchases. Remember, when putting your insurance estimate together, be sure you write down the current value, not what you paid for it six years ago. If you don't know the current worth of a particular item, estimate the value. Rest assured that the agent would let you know if the value is out of line when and if the time comes for you to settle a claim.

Replacement Cost Coverage
vs. Actual Cash Value

When you're shopping for a renter's insurance policy, make sure the policy has replacement coverage. Many policies insure the contents of your rental home, condo, or apartment on an actual cash value basis. However, by paying approximately 20 percent more, you can purchase *replacement coverage insurance*. The difference is drastic in some cases. For example, under an actual cash value policy, if you purchased a complete living room, dining room, and bedroom set three years ago for $2,000, you might expect a check for $1,200 if fire destroyed them. The lower amount is due to wear and tear since the original purchase. On the other hand, with replacement cost insurance, you would get the cost to replace the furniture at today's prices. If you found similar furniture to replace what you lost in the fire and it cost $2,700, you would get that amount, not the original or depreciated value. There's a big difference, especially if you lost everything you own. Still, replacement value does cost more, but if you can afford it, by all means look into the extra coverage.

Do I Really Need a Policy?

If you're wondering whether you need a policy, consider having to replace your clothes, linens, sports equipment, and so on. Even if you own very little, replacing everything you have can be very expensive. If you own a lot of furniture, the cost could get serious really quick. Here's the deal: A good renter's insurance policy will pay to replace your loss at today's cost, not when you bought it. A good policy will also cover losses when you're not at home. For example, depending on the policy, coverage could include protection against loss from robbery, pickpocket theft, credit card loss, forged checks, and counterfeit money.

Renter's insurance policies are relatively inexpensive, usually around $10 per month per $10,000 of personal property. However, if you have installed smoke detectors, dead-bolt locks, and fire extinguishers, you could be paying less for being safe. Living in a complex that has a security gate and lighting can also help reduce your rate. To find out if any of these safety features qualifies for a deduction, ask an agent.

As with most insurance policies, there will be some form of a deductible required. After your out-of-pocket deductible is paid, the insurance will kick in. The standard amount for a deductible is $250. If you purchase a policy with a higher deductible amount, your monthly policy premium will most likely be lowered.

6

Having the Utilities Turned On

Electricity and Gas

Now that you have selected an apartment, having the ability to see what you are doing at night might come in handy. The only way that is going to happen is if you have your utilities connected or, in some cases, just transferred over to your name. To start the process, look up the phone number of your local electric company. Most electric company suppliers will have several numbers. You are looking for the phone number under the heading "New Service" or "Customer Service." Once you've called the customer service department, they will walk you through the process step-by-step, which takes only a few minutes.

If you're moving into a new apartment, there's a chance that the electricity and/or gas has never been turned on. If that's the case, your landlord could expect you to pay the first-time connection fee. If that happens, the fee will be added to your regular bill; if so, request that the cost be spread over several payments to make it easier. First-time connection fees vary from state to state and from company to company, but expect around $100 to be billed to your account. The customer service representative will tell you what those costs are and then request information like your name, apartment address, and employer. This is standard information requested by creditors. Yes, creditors. The local electricity and gas company is a creditor and should be considered as such when it comes time to pay the bill. If you're just starting out in the world of credit, paying your utility bills on time will be viewed by other potential creditors as a sign that you intend to pay your bills. Although not the greatest credit reference, it's better than no reference at all. If you have credit established, keep it in good standing by paying your bills on time. A credit report is an extremely valuable or damaging tool, depending on how you develop it over time.

After taking your application, the customer service representative will have your power turned on very soon—in some cases the same day. Remember, the sooner they turn it on, the sooner they can start making money. It's usually not necessary to keep calling them; they want to make money just as badly as you do. Oh, by the way, on the outside chance you're not 18 yet, you'll need a parent, legal guardian, or older roommate to take responsibility for having the power turned on in their name.

If you are moving into an apartment that was occupied up until the time you moved in, the customer service representative will simply transfer the service over to your name. This is much faster than having new service installed and can usually be done the same day. This is how the transfer takes place: The prior tenant will get a bill for service up to the day he or she moved out, and your service will start the day you request it to be turned on.

Water

Now it's time for some water! Having the water turned on is about the same as getting your electricity going; however, it is almost always a different company, so get out the phone book and look it up. From there, you know the drill. In some cases, there will be a sewer charge included on your water bill. The same company usually provides sewer and water, and the cost is minor and quite mandatory. Check with your landlord and review your lease, because sometimes water and sewer are included in the rent.

Telephone

As with your electricity and water, the procedure for new telephone service is much the same. Again, you are probably going to have to be 18 years old. Once you have provided customer service with all the standard information, you will be ready to start running up the bill. Having your phone connected is about the same as the electricity in that, if service has never been installed, you could be paying a first-time installation fee. Note: The telephone installation technician will not provide your phone. That purchase is up to you and is best made prior to his arrival. By purchasing the phone first, the installation technician can check out the service after connection and you can make sure the phone works.

Cable TV

Saving the best for last, it's now time for *MTV, VHS-1, ESPN, HBO*, and *Comedy Central*. Now you can enjoy both Eric and Cartman along with Ren and Stimpy. Certainly, by now you can figure out how to get in touch with the company and what to do when you find them. Unless you live in a heavily populated area that has enjoyed cable service for some time and offers more than one cable carrier, you will probably have only one cable provider to chose from. This is normal; however, if you're not satisfied with the cable company, look into a satellite dish provider.

Credit Checks

In some cases, creditors such as your utility company request that a credit report be provided prior to service being installed. Don't worry if they request the report; it's standard procedure with some creditors. If you have lived somewhere else and have had utilities, be assured that the company will know. If you have any unpaid balance, be prepared to pay it off up front, and also be prepared to pay a deposit prior to new service. Previous bad service reported on your credit report could also increase your deposit amount. On the other hand, if you were a good customer, expect no problems at all. Good luck.

7

Furniture and Appliance Rental

The Advantage of Renting

Eating off a cardboard box and sleeping on the floor, although very cost effective, will soon lose its appeal. So unless you have saved up a lot of cash, or your relatives have given you everything you need, you will be faced with a crucial decision. Do you rent or do you buy? Renting allows you to try out different types of appliances and furniture. You can rent a 1000-watt-per-channel stereo with separate sub woofer only to find that your neighbors will tolerate only 10 watts. You can rent a big-screen television, bring it home, and then figure out that you need to be 15 feet away in order to get a good picture, which is hard to do in an eight-by-ten-foot room. How about couches? You could rent one that has removable back cushions, only to find out that your friends are constantly relocating them throughout the rest of the apartment and doing who knows what to them.

Finding a Rental Company

The telephone book is usually full of companies that rent furniture and appliances. You should have no trouble finding one close by. As a rule, the national chains are your best bet and will usually have the largest advertisements. If you have heard suspicious things about a particular rental business, call the Better Business Bureau and inquire. Either way, stop in and check them out for yourself. Some locations may not have what you are looking for, and that will help you eliminate businesses from which to choose. When you have narrowed down your choices, get a copy of their rental purchase agreement to take home with you. Don't try to read and understand the agreement while the sales person is writing up the order. As with any legal document, take the time to read and understand it before signing.

Typical Terms & Conditions

The following is a representative sample of typical terms and conditions found on rental purchase agreements, although you should expect them to vary among rental companies:

1.   Typically, "you" and "your" refers to the person signing the agreement and "we," "us," and "ours" refer to the rental company.

2.   The agreement will detail how much the payment is, when it's due (weekly or monthly), processing fees, delivery fees, taxes that are due, and the duration of the agreement itself.

3.   "This agreement is for (_____) weeks/months, and you are not obligated to renew the agreement after the designated period. However, you may renew this agreement by sending or delivering a weekly or monthly payment to us before the end of the originally stipulated rental agreement period."

4.   "This agreement terminates automatically if you do not renew it." (Note: Give this condition careful consideration long before the original term runs out, and understand what is expected relative to getting the appliances and/or furniture ready for pick-up if you choose to let the agreement run out.)

5.   "We offer insurance on the property and you are required to purchase insurance; however, if you elect not to buy insurance from us, you are totally responsible for any damage to the property beyond normal wear and tear." Regardless of what happens to the property, or how it happens, you are financially responsible for any damage. (Note: Some rental companies give you the option to purchase their insurance, but it is usually expensive). Before you make any decision relative to insurance, read the chapter on renter's insurance. If, after considering your insurance options, you elect not to purchase it, at least ask how the rental company calculates any damage. Some companies will expect full-market value; others might accept some depreciated value. You need to know what the real costs are. This could very well change your mind about purchasing insurance.

6.   "If you have complied with the terms and conditions of this agreement, you can purchase the property at any time during the first month of the agreement. If you choose to purchase, we will transfer any manufacturer warranties that are still in effect." (Note: Prior to making a purchase decision, understand how this "pay-off" is calculated and what other, if any, fees are included.)

7.   "You must keep the property at the address that the property is delivered to. If you move the property without written permission, we have the right to terminate this agreement immediately."

Most agreements will calculate the amount and number of payments necessary to own the property. For example, to own the dining room table, you will have to make weekly payments of $12 for 50 weeks, which totals $600. However, if you stop the agreement on week 49, you own nothing, you have built up no equity in the property, and you have voided the agreement. You will not own the dining room table unless you make all 50 payments, as specified by the agreement.

Making the Decision

When you are just getting started, the natural tendency is to acquire as much as possible as soon as possible. Don't let this materialistic desire to fill your apartment with "stuff" lead you into an undesirable financial situation. In many cases, acquiring a credit card and purchasing a dining room table is a better choice. Take the time to decide what is best for you. It will mean so much more if you figure it out on your own. (Note: Rental agreements are regulated by state law and may be enforced by the attorney general of that state or by any other private legal action).

Alternative Sources

There are other alternatives to furnishing your new apartment, one of which boggles the mind of every adult male in the United States: "The Yard Sale," sometimes referred to as a garage sale. To take advantage of this alternative source, you merely have to choose from the tens of thousands that are held every day in every city in every subdivision across the country. You can pick up a six-piece dining room set and seven-piece living room with matching lamps for only $100, or $75 if you're good at haggling. All kidding aside, you might be amazed at the selection and quality of stuff you can pick up for a fraction of its regular cost. So don't let the sarcasm keep you from driving out and taking a look for yourself.

Four other alternative sources remain: the Salvation Army, Goodwill, thrift shops, and pawnshops. Pickings are usually slim for large items, but they should not be completely overlooked, especially if money is really tight. To find these facilities, simply get out the yellow pages and look them up.

References

Finding an Apartment, by Stuart Schwartz
Leases & Rental Agreements, by Marcia Stewart
The New Apartment Book, by Michele Michael

Part 3
Getting a Ride

8

Buying a Car

Aside from buying your first house, buying a car will probably be the second-largest purchase you'll ever make, so let's get right down to business and think this process out. There are four basic models of automobile: full size, intermediate or midsize, compact, and subcompact.

The Basic Models

Full-size cars are roomy, with large seats and large trunks. Full-size cars usually have a smoother ride and are better equipped to accommodate long road trips. They are also usually very expensive and not particularly economical relative to fuel efficiency. *Intermediates* offer a good compromise between roominess, comfort, fuel efficiency, and overall cost. They usually seat around five people comfortably and are slightly less expensive than full-size cars. *Compact* cars are excellent for commuting back and forth to work. They usually seat four with relative ease and come in a variety of styles like two-door, four-door, and hatchback. The last of the four basic models is the s*ubcompacts*, which are well suited for short around-town travel. Historically, they are noisier and stiffer to drive than larger models; however, they usually cost less than the other models and are by far the cheapest at the pump.

How to Select a Car

When selecting a new car, don't forget about the dealer. Buying a car from the wrong dealer could make your life miserable, especially if there are initial problems with your car or you need to have warranty work performed. Ask around and find out who the good dealers are and, more importantly, who the bad ones are. Buying a new car, especially your first, is very exciting, so to make your purchase a pleasant one, consider the reputation of the dealer.

If you're new to an area and don't know anyone, you'll likely have to find a good dealer on your own. Call the local Better Business Bureau to inquire about a prospective dealer and jot down whatever information they have. Another way to find a good dealer is to inquire about their Customer Satisfaction Index (CSI). The CSI is a form of customer service rating conducted by the auto makers and applies to all but those very small dealerships who, for whatever reason, seem to get left out. To find out about a particular dealership's CSI rating, ask a salesperson. If they have a good rating, they'll be glad to talk about it; if it's not so good, they will probably want to change the subject.

If you want to research the customer service rating for a particular model of automobile, purchase a consumer magazine that has a *J.D. Power Auto Survey* in it. These surveys for automobile customer satisfaction are relatively accurate and unbiased.

To help you narrow down your new car choice, consider some of the following questions before you get to the dealership:

> ➤ What is the upkeep on your existing car and what have you learned from it?

> ➤ What are the weather conditions like in your area? For example, is there snow on the ground seven months out of the year? If there is, you might want to consider an automobile that offers four-wheel-drive.

> ➤ List in descending order what is more important to you: overall looks, luxury, economy, prestige, performance, and so on.

> ➤ What is the primary use of the car?

> ➤ Do you need room for two people, or six?

> ➤ How often will you be traveling? Does it have adequate power and cargo space?

> ➤ If you plan to do routine maintenance such as oil changes and tune-ups, are those areas relatively accessible?

> ➤ How much does the insurance cost for the model you want? Depending on the make and model, the rates could be very expensive.

> ➤ What kind of down payment and monthly payment can you afford?

There are numerous questions to ask and only you know what's really important. So prepare your own list and start answering them.

The Best Time to Buy

For the most part, the best time to buy a new car is when most people are, unfortunately, strapped for cash—the end of the year. In most of the United States, the winter months usually mean winter clothing and high fuel bills. The winter months also brings Thanksgiving and Christmas, which usually redirects income toward holiday gifts and travel. However, if you can afford to buy, this would be a good time. The end of the month is another good time, because it's the dealership's final attempt to increase monthly sales figures. Another good time is when the new models come out. For example, you can get a great deal on a 2001 model when the 2002's start rolling off the trucks and on to the showroom floor.

Avoiding the Hype

I'm by no means an expert and I don't proclaim to have documented evidence on the following information. However, I've purchased enough new cars to be able to read between the lines of many of the more popular automobile advertisements.

If you watch television and listen to the radio, you've heard these claims in the ads a thousand times: "We beat any deal in town!" "We will not be undersold!" "We undersell all our competition!" "We are having an inventory reduction sale!" "Push it in or tow it in!" "One dollar above invoice!" Have you every stopped to consider how these claims could possibly be true? Think about it—if there were a dealership that undersold every other dealer on every car, every time, all the other dealers would be forced out of business. How could they stay in business if the other guy sold *all* the cars? How many towns do you know of that have only one auto dealership? Time's up—there are none, and if there are such towns, the total population is probably fifty or less.

Unfortunately, these types of advertising gimmicks suck thousands of people in every day. For those buyers, the bottom line is usually much different once the salesperson's calculator has finally stopped smoking. This sad but true scenario is played out every day in every town. Don't get lured in by their deceptive advertisements.

Test Drive

Once you've decided on a car, it's time to take it for a spin. But before you do, make sure that the car you're about to test drive is essentially the same as the one you want to buy. Don't test drive the eight-cylinder, supercharged X10 luxury edition with all the options if you're going to buy the X1 four-cylinder economy model. Make sure the interior, exterior, and options packages are also the same, if possible.

When you open the door and sit down, check for headroom and look over the instrument panel. Make sure the wiper controls, lights, cruise control, and radio are easy to find and operate. Check out the seat adjustments and find the best setting for your legs. Adjust the rear view mirror, including the one on the passenger side. If air bags are important to you, see if there is at least one.

The salesperson is probably going to ride along with you to answer questions and to try to downplay or explain away any deficiencies that you may notice on the test drive. Once you're on the road, try to avoid statements like, "Man, I've got to have this car." Instead, try to remain neutral even if you love the car. Maintaining your composure and remaining neutral will help when trying to negotiate for a better price.

While driving the car, try to focus on the car's capabilities, not its looks or how excited you are; there will be plenty of time for that later. Take this opportunity to really check the car out by considering the following things:

> ➤ Start the car twice. How does the car start?
> ➤ How well does it accelerate when passing?
> ➤ Is the engine powerful enough, or should you consider a larger engine?
> ➤ How does it handle in turns and does it have a tight turning radius?
> ➤ Can you control the lights, wipers, radio, horn, and cruise control easily?
> ➤ Do the breaks work smoothly, or do you have to really push on them?

➤ How quiet is the car when stopped at a traffic light and while driving?

➤ How is the overall visibility? Can you see all around you in traffic?

➤ Check the vanity mirrors. Do they have lights?

➤ How accessible is the glove compartment?

➤ Try to parallel park. How is the visibility?

➤ If the vehicle has four-wheel-drive, how easily does it shift into that mode?

Now that the test drive is over, check out the trunk space and exterior features like hide-away lights and the antenna. Finally, if you are buying a full-size model, will it fit into your garage or parking space?

Lemons

It would be unrealistic to think that, during the mass production of automobiles, a small percentage wouldn't be less than perfect. The mass production of anything routinely turns out *lemons.* Just look at the return counter at virtually every store you walk into. However, when the lemon turns out to be your car, it can be a really serious problem. Fortunately for you and other consumers, there are lemon laws on the books, which give manufacturers an ultimatum: Repair it or replace it.

Most state lemon laws are written in such a way that, if a major defect in a new vehicle cannot be repaired within a few attempts, a reasonable time, within the first year of operation, or within less than 12,000 miles, the manufacturer must either replace the vehicle or provide a refund. Naturally, there will be much to do if you are unlucky enough to buy a lemon. But just remember that lemon laws are in force to protect you. This is when selecting a reputable dealer from the beginning really pays off.

Trading in Your Car

Before you drive your car to the dealership, call your bank's auto loan department and get the current market value of your car. This is very useful information when negotiating with the dealership about your trade-in allowance. But no matter what your car's value, the dealer will most likely be offering wholesale, which is going to be less than you expected. You'll get even less if your car has high mileage or is in need of repairs like new tires, a break job, a new muffler, or extensive body work.

If you stop and think about it, in order for the dealer to make any money off your trade-in car, they'll have to give you less than what they can expect to get for it. Don't spend a lot of time riding around looking for the dealer who'll give the most money. Most dealers are very good at estimating what they can realistically get for used cars and will probably offer about the same amount for it, no matter where you go. Be leery if you find a dealer who is willing to give you substantially more, because they will most likely be adding the extra cash to the bottom line of your new sales contract.

Negotiating the Best Price

Buy your car from a respected dealer that has a good customer service rating and is offering a reasonably good deal. Don't base your buying decision on finding the dealer with the lowest price, because you might be buying from a dealer that will make your life miserable when a problem with your car comes up and you need warranty work performed.

Buy the car you really want, not just the best one you can find. If the dealer has the model you want, but not the options package or color, they can have exactly what you want delivered to them from another dealership for a small fee. The little extra cost will be worth it if you get what you really want.

Start your negotiating by knowing in advance what the dealer's invoice costs are. Take a good look at the window sticker and look for the manufacturer's invoice price. Another source for finding out the price is one of several good consumer magazines that list the recommended prices for all the major automakers by a breakdown of types, models, and options. With this information in hand, you will enter the showroom armed with a better idea of what the car should be selling for.

When you first meet your salesperson, don't start your conversation with "Hey, let's cut the crap, just give me the bottom line." Nobody likes that attitude and it usually doesn't work. Instead, simply convey to them that you are serious about buying and you would prefer not having to look all over town for a car. This tells them that, if they are reasonable, you can do business. Offer a few hundred over invoice and go from there. The salesperson will probably react to your offer in a less than positive way, but at least you've made the first offer. If you're wondering if making the first offer is a good idea, remember that their offer will be considerably higher than just a few hundred over invoice. Don't think that making the first offer of a small amount over dealer invoice might preempt an even smaller price from them. Their first offer would be considerably higher.

Once the salesperson has countered your offer with a higher offer, you can suggest to them that if they can explain why you should pay more, you will try to work on getting the extra money. Try this tactic at several dealerships if necessary, and if no one bites, you just might have to come up with the extra cash.

You can expect that some models will sell for the advertised price with no margin for negotiation and some will sell for even more. This is sometimes due to a manufacturer introducing a new body style or the popularity of the car. For example, when the new Volkswagen Beetle design came out in 1998, dealers were getting considerably more for the cars than the advertised price, and consumers were lined up and happy to pay.

Consider the following items when you're finally ready to sit down at the salesperson's desk:

➢ How much, if any, are the rebates worth?

➢ What is the final price of the car?

➢ If you are trading in a car, what is the allowance?

➢ If you have a payoff balance on your trade-in, what is that amount?

➢ How much are the taxes?

➢ What are the miscellaneous fees?

➢ What kind of down payment is required? (If you can pay more, do so.)

➢ How many months are being financed, and what is the monthly payment? (Note: Get the shortest term you can afford. The shorter the term, say, 48 months instead of 60, the less interest you will pay).

Extra Warranties

In general, extra warranties are a bad investment. You rarely recover your investment and the cost for such questionable protection is usually high. The quality of most cars today is very good and a majority of the repairs are already included in the manufacturer's warranty. However, the dealership makes a healthy profit on warranties, and their sales staff will try to sell you one. If you are insistent in buying one, at least take the time to read it over and see what you're really getting for the extra money.

Arranging Financing

When you start looking for financing, look for the best annual percentage rate (APR). The most common places to look are credit unions, banks, and the dealerships themselves. Most places are competitive; however, an employee credit union historically has the best APR. When you start asking around, be sure you know what all the fees are and ask if there is a pre-payment penalty, just in case you want to pay off early to save interest.

Used Cars

When you start your search, have two things in mind: price and reliability. Price is usually the biggest concern, so set a limit and stick to it. As a rule, you should buy the newest car possible and finance it for the shortest term possible. You should also try to select a car that you think will *live* longer than the time it takes to pay it off.

This is really crucial, especially if money is tight. The worst thing that could happen would be to buy a car based solely on the price and then find out you have to dump another $1,500 into it just to drive it. With that in mind, make every effort to resist letting price be the determining factor. You'll be glad you did.

If at all possible, have the used car inspected by a mechanic prior to closing the deal. New or used, reliability is a major issue. If you're buying a used car from a dealership, you will have some recourse if there are major problems. However, recourse is essentially nonexistent when buying from a private party through the local paper or auto trader. Many cars are sold as is, with a handshake and a title transfer. If the seller has a hand-written sales receipt, he or she will more than likely have <u>as is</u> written on it. This is the epitome of "buyer beware," which simply means that if the car's transmission falls out two weeks after you buy it, the loss is yours to absorb.

Where to Look

The most common places to look for used cars are new-car dealerships, used-car dealers, and private owners found through the *Auto Trader* and the local paper. New-car dealers are the best sources for finding used cars that still have some type of warranty. They have a reasonably good selection and, for the most part, check out the cars prior to selling them. Their selection is good because many new car buyers usually trade in their older models in exchange for a better deal on a new one.

Used car dealers, as the name implies, specialize in used cars and know what the customers are likely to be looking for and how to finance them. Used car dealers usually have less overhead than new car dealerships and therefore can offer you a better deal most of the time. However, unlike the service departments of new car dealerships, a used car dealership's service department, if there is one, will be generally smaller and less equipped to handle repairs.

Private owners have no sales staff, no display area, no service shop, and no wealth of knowledge about cars. Instead, private owners have a car for sale and about $20 to spend on advertising it. Private owners want to make as much money as possible; that's why they're selling directly to you and not some dealership. When you buy from a private owner, you are entering their turf and usually buying on their terms. So, once again, buyer beware.

How to Determine the Price

After you've been out looking for cars, make sure the price is fair by either calling the auto loan department at your bank or by going to the library and finding a *NADA* guide for used car prices. If you are calling a private owner in response to an advertisement, get the particulars on the car and look up the information before you drive out to see it.

Whether you are talking to a loan officer or researching at the library, make sure you are comparing apples to apples. Make sure your search reflects the same year, model, options, mileage, and general overall condition. Armed with the loan and retail values, go back to your private owner or dealership and start negotiating.

When You See the Car, Ask Questions

Make your mind up ahead of time that when you see the car for the first time, you will be able to suppress your true feelings and remain neutral. The best stance is always to be relaxed and appear nonchalant. This attitude will not tip off the seller to your intentions and will come in handy when negotiating. The less positive the body language and comments, the better price your apt to get.

If you have previously inquired about a car over the telephone and you still want to see it, ask these questions when you arrive at the seller's location:

> ➤ If your city requires an emissions test, see if the car has passed.
> ➤ Does the seller owe money on the car?
> ➤ Has the car ever been involved in an accident?
> ➤ How much body and/or mechanical work does it need?
> ➤ Is there any current warranty on the car?
> ➤ Does the owner/seller have the legal title?

If you are serious about the car, have a mechanic check it out and make sure the following items are considered:

> ➤ Paint job—look for signs of rust or prior body work
> ➤ Interior—look for cracks and tears
> ➤ General condition of upholstery and carpet, including the headliner
> ➤ Odometer—check for possible tampering
> ➤ Check out accessories to make sure they work
> ➤ Look at the tires—are they in good shape?
> ➤ Are there holes in the exhaust system? How does it sound?
> ➤ Check out the on-board computer, the fan belts, seals, the charging system, and the cooling system.
> ➤ How are the brakes, pads, and the master cylinder?
> ➤ How is the steering?
> ➤ Does the car start okay every time?
> ➤ Are the maintenance records in order and up to date?

Negotiating Points and Tips

When getting ready to make an offer, explain to the dealership or owner that some things were found to need repair and thus should be deducted from the price. This form of negotiating is standard and reasonable and therefore should be anticipated by the owner. Some of the items that could reduce the seller's price are excessive mileage, mechanical repairs, bodywork, tires, and brakes. If the owner is insistent on selling you the car as is, then simply adjust your offer accordingly and wait for the counter offer. Don't let your desire to own a car blind you to inevitable repairs.

If you have been tipped off that the owner is anxious about selling, then make a low initial offer and go from there. If the car has been on the lot or in the paper for some time, your chances of getting a real deal are good. If you expect this to be the case, be ready to act by either having cash or being pre-approved at the bank. Try to remove any emotional feelings you have toward the seller. Just because they seem nice doesn't mean you have to fold under and give them a better price. This is nothing more and nothing less than a business transaction and should be treated that way. Besides, once you drive away, you'll not likely to ever see or be in contact with that person again.

Leasing in General

If your credit is exceptionally good and you plan on owning a new car every few years, then leasing could be a good option. If you are in business for yourself, leasing could be a good tax deduction as well. There are as many pros as there are cons relative to leasing, and the transaction requires a careful reading and thorough understanding of the terms and conditions. For example, many leases have predetermined mileage allowances per year and stiff per-mile charges for exceeding them. Leasing in general usually requires a smaller down payment and carries smaller monthly payments. This combination is rather attractive, don't you think? However, don't be lured by the financial aspects alone. Leasing is not for everyone, and you should conduct extensive research prior to considering this option.

9
Automobile Insurance

One of the crowning highlights of young adulthood is the day you get a driver's license. However, this auspicious occasion is also the beginning of potential accidents, arrests, and injuries. With that unpleasant thought in mind, remember two things: drive defensively, and purchase a good automobile insurance policy.

Chances are your current policy, if you have one, was purchased by your parents or legal guardian. When you first got your driver's license, you were probably added to your parents' automobile insurance policy. This would have been much cheaper than getting a policy on your own. By adding another car or driver to their existing policy, your parents would have probably been entitled to a discount for multiple cars under one policy.

However, now that you're out on your own, it's time to get your own policy. So let's get a quick education on the basics of a policy so you can select what's best for you.

But before you get started, review the following definitions and then move on to the standard policy classifications. Understanding standard auto policy terminology will greatly enhance your ability to converse with insurance agents in your quest for the right policy.

A Few Definitions
- ➤ **Acts of God:** Perils that cannot reasonably be guarded against such as floods, volcanic eruptions, and earthquakes.
- ➤ **Actual cash value:** The replacement cost of property less allowances for depreciation.
- ➤ **Actual cash loss**: Loss occurring when property is completely destroyed.
- ➤ **Carriers:** In the context of this section, carriers refer to an auto insurance company or agent.

> **Collision:** Upset of the covered auto and non-owned auto and/or its impact with another vehicle or object. Simply put, a crash!

> **Compensatory damages**: A monetary sum awarded for the actual loss a person has sustained for a wrong committed by another person. If another driver collides with you and puts you in the hospital, compensatory damages are paid to reimburse you for repair of your car, lost wages due to being out of work, and medical bills.

> **Comprehensive personal liability:** Liability coverage for individuals that includes bodily injury and property damage.

> **Covered auto:** In general, covered auto includes any vehicle listed in the *Declarations* page of a policy, such as a private passenger auto, pickup, or van purchased during the policy period, provided the insured requested coverage within 30 days of ownership.

> **Declarations page:** Usually the first page of a policy that provides, among other things, information such as the policy coverage, limits, and vehicles covered.

> **Exclusions:** Restrictions of the coverage provided by an insurance policy.

> **Insured:** The individuals covered under the policy and any individual using a covered automobile.

> **Punitive damages:** A monetary award as punishment for a certain wrong usually awarded by the courts. Punitive damages are not covered in policies. If you sue another at-fault driver for emotional pain and suffering, the cash award is called punitive damages.

> **Trailer:** In the context of this section, a trailer is a vehicle designed to be pulled by a private passenger car, pickup, or van. It also includes a farm wagon towed by a car.

> **Underwriter:** An individual accepting risk under specified terms. It is the underwriter who usually grants you your policy. For example, when you complete your application for insurance, the agent will probably say that it will now go to underwriting for review. The underwriter usually verifies all the information on the applications.

➤ **Uninsured motorist:** Insurance that pays for the insured's bodily injuries from an accident with another vehicle if the other driver is negligent and has no insurance or has less than the amount required by law.

➤ **Youthful driver:** An unmarried female driver under the age of 25 or an unmarried male driver under the age of 30.

General Classifications

Liability insurance is protection for the cost of damage you cause to the property of others. Insurance carriers will pay damages for bodily injury or property damage for an auto accident you cause. Carriers will also defend or settle as they deem appropriate for any damage you cause. The policy agreement states that any prejudgment interest awarded against the insured is covered and included in the policy limits. In addition, they will pay all legal defense costs incurred while defending the claim. There is no per-person limitation coverage, and coverage is on a per-accident basis. It is common that coverage applies to each insured separately. However, regardless of the number of insured, the limit of liability is not increased.

Comprehensive coverage covers damage to your automobile from other than an automobile accident. Insurance carriers will pay for these damages minus any applicable deductible shown on the declarations page. Damage considered under this type of coverage includes fire, theft or larceny, explosion or earthquake, windstorm, hail, water or flood, vandalism, contact with animals, and broken glass. (Note: These classifications are a representative sample and should not be counted on with every policy.)

Uninsured motorist insurance pays for injury to you, your family members, and passengers in your car if an at-fault driver who does not have insurance causes the injury. Insurance carriers pay compensatory damages for your bodily injuries that result from an accident with another vehicle if the other driver is negligent and does not have any insurance or has less insurance than required by law. Insured persons include the named insured driver on the policy, family members, any person occupying your covered auto, and other persons who are entitled to recovery as described in your policy.

Underinsured motorist insurance coverage provides protection similar to uninsured but applies only when the at-fault driver's policy has insufficient coverage to pay for the loss.

No-fault insurance provides for the payments from one's own insurance company without the need to establish that someone else was at fault. No-fault means that the insured does not have to prove another persons negligence before compensation can be paid.

Selecting a Policy

The best way to select a policy is to first know what you're looking for and then to call around for different rates. When comparing policy rates, make sure they are quoting the same coverage. To assure you are comparing apples to apples, make sure the deductible amount, limits of coverage, and amount of coverage are the same between policy quotes. As a rule, the higher the deductible amount, the lower your monthly payment will be. However, when you need to file a claim, expect to pay considerably more out-of-pocket if you have selected a higher deductible. For example, a policy with a $250 deductible might cost $80 per month while a $500 deductible would only be $60 per month.

There are many variables that determine the cost, such as how many tickets or accidents you have had, your age, the type of car you own, and what city you live in. However, there are also some things discussed later in this chapter that can reduce the cost of your policy.

When you have gathered the different quotes, sit down and compare the bottom line. Seek advice from friends, relatives, and co-workers who have insurance, and learn from their experience.

Ways to Save on Your Policy

If you can answer yes to some of these questions, then you could be entitled to potential savings on your policy. Consider the following tips for lowering your cost:

> Have you successfully completed a driver education course?
> Does your car have antilock brakes?
> Does your car have an anti-theft device?
> Do you have more than one car to be insured?

➤ Does your car have motorized safety belts?

➤ Is your car equipped with at least one air bag?

➤ Have you successfully completed any accident prevention or defensive driver course?

Common Questions

If I have an older car, should I buy collision insurance? This is a personal decision that should be based on the value of the car and the amount of loss that you can reasonably afford. If you have a twenty-year-old car that cost you $900 four years ago and looks like it has cancer, you should probably not pay for the extra insurance. However, regardless of how old or how many repairs are needed, once your only source of transportation is gone, you are on your own if you haven't purchased collision insurance. You will now have to buy another auto without any help from the insurance carrier. This is a difficult decision to make. Some people would rather pay for the extra insurance just to keep from having a major expense in case of loss.

What is the difference between bodily injury and medical payments coverage? Bodily injury coverage pays for injuries you cause to others for which you might be held at fault in a court of law. Medical payments coverage pays for injuries suffered by you or your family while occupants of the auto. It also covers other passengers in any car you may be driving, regardless of fault.

What happens if I am driving someone else's auto and become involved in an accident? The terms and conditions relative to this type of question are specifically addressed in your policy. However, in general your liability for bodily injury to others or property damage to other autos will be covered under your liability coverage.

May I cancel my policy with my carrier? Yes, you can cancel at any time and the portion of unused paid premium will be returned to you. In addition, you are not obligated to tell your existing insurance carrier why you are canceling the policy. However, if you decide to secure another policy, make sure the replacement policy is approved in advance before you cancel your existing policy.

May my insurance carrier cancel my policy? There are provisions for a carrier to cancel your policy. However, the most frequent reason is for non-payment. Insurance companies must have good reasons to cancel a policy and are required to give you ample notice to purchase another policy prior to the cancellation of the existing policy.

What does depreciation really mean? Depreciation is a decrease in the value of your automobile due to age, wear, and tear. The insurance payment is based on the depreciated value of the auto at the time of the accident. However, many policies offer full replacement value, which pays for repairs at current cost, not depreciated cost. Check with your carrier about full replacement value coverage.

What is actual cash value? This term refers to what it would cost to replace your damaged auto with one similar in condition and mileage. It also refers to the replacement of components, parts, and bodywork.

You should now have enough information to call a carrier and have an educated conversation on the subject of auto insurance, so shop around, select a good policy, and pay the premium on time.

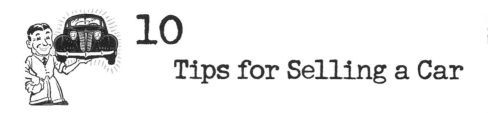

10
Tips for Selling a Car

Regardless of whether you own a car with a clean title or have it financed through the bank, the following tips will assist you in preparation for the sale. So, where will you get the best offer for your car? If you sell to a dealership, expect to get the *wholesale value* or *trade-in value*. This price is less than *retail* because, in order for the dealer to make a profit, they will have to sell for a higher price than what they paid you. Your best bet is selling the car through the local paper or *Auto Trader*. Before you decide to advertise, remember a private buyer will be calling the bank and inquiring about the *loan value*. The loan value is the amount that the bank is willing to give them toward the purchase. The loan value is almost always less than the retail value, so if the buyer finances the car, the balance will have to come from their pocket.

Setting the Price

Setting the price is key to getting interested people to call or come by. To find out how much to ask for, contact a bank's auto loan office, give them the description of the car, and then ask for the loan and retail value. If you have made significant improvements to the car, you can add to that retail price. For example, if you have installed a $2,000 stereo system and expensive wheels, reflect those upgrades in your price. On the other hand, the bank's value does not take into account, say, significant body rust, so you will need to reflect that in your price as well.

Setting the right price is critical, because prospective buyers will have to come up with the difference between the loan value and your selling price. Some prospective buyers have little money for this purpose, but if you're convinced that the car is worth it, be firm. However, the down side to being firm is potentially losing the sale due to overpricing. Be reasonable and realistic about your price.

If you give the description of your car to the bank and they tell you the value is, say, $9,500, and you list it for $13,000, you will probably not get many calls. Most people looking for a car can get the same information from the bank that you can. They know what the car is worth and will not likely be interested in paying more.

Setting the price is essential, especially if you still have a balance due with a bank or some other financial institution. If you sell the car for more than the payoff, that's great. On the other hand, selling the car for less than payoff means that you will have to come up with the difference between what the buyer is offering to pay and the payoff balance. Not exactly a happy time—you now have no car and have to pay out of pocket to sell it. What a deal.

A Bad Situation

Everyone's decision to sell is based on his or her own set of circumstances. Some people sell their existing car in order to buy a newer model or to simply upgrade in quality. They plan to use the proceeds from the sale toward a down payment on another car. This is a normal reason for selling a car, and it happens every day for positive reasons. Unfortunately, there is another reason for selling that's not so positive. If, for example, you are out of work and can't afford the payment, your decision to sell and sell fast is based on your desire to get out from under a payment you can no longer afford. If the bank or lending institution is not willing to help you through this tough time by restructuring your loan, sell the car quickly, even if it's less than what you owe. Taking a small loss is better than not making the payments and damaging your credit report. It's also much better than having the car repossessed. If you have to sell your car for less than payoff, you will obviously have to work that out with your lender, but at least they will see that you are serious and in desperate need of help. Although not a good situation, it is better than having your lender call you about late payments. Don't risk ruining your credit report by not making payments on your car. A bad credit report will haunt you for many years to come. Finding a job when you don't have a car is difficult, but it is child's play when compared to re-establishing your credit once you ruin it.

Checklist for Preparation of Sale

Once you have made the decision to sell, spend the necessary time to get your car ready to show, because it will be time well spent. A clean, well-maintained car tells a prospective buyer that the car has probably been well cared for. Review the items listed in the following checklist to make sure you've got the car ready to display:

1. If the car needs to have the oil changed, do it prior to selling.
2. Clean out the trunk and make sure the spare tire and pieces to the jack are there.
3. Replace badly worn tires and inflate the others if necessary.
4. Clean out the glove compartment, and lubricate squeaky joints.
5. Shampoo the carpets and empty the ashtrays.
6. Make sure all the glass is cleaned and the chrome, if any, is polished.
7. Get all records ready and organize them for the prospective buyers to see.
8. Clean the upholstery, and wash and wax the body.

Writing the Ad

Now that you have prepared your car for sale, it's time to write the ad. If you plan to run an ad in the local paper or list your car in some kind of trade publication like an *Auto Trader*, you will need to keep your ad short and to the point. Most publications only allow a specific number of words per ad, so you might want to call first. For best results, be brief, descriptive, and honest. If you say the car is in excellent condition when, in fact, it is actually in poor condition, you will be wasting your time as well as the caller's time who comes by to take a look. If you are dishonest about one aspect of the car, in the eyes of the prospective buyer you are probably not telling the truth about the rest of the information in your ad. Make a good impression by being truthful and accurate in your advertisement.

When writing your ad, include the model, make, year, color, and body style. Then list some of the major options like: V-6, air-conditioning, automatic transmission, four-wheel drive, power windows, and so on. If your car has low mileage, include that as well. If you can be reached only after a certain time of day or night, put that in your ad. Be sure to state the price; this will eliminate those callers who are just calling to find out how much you want for it. If you are not willing to negotiate on price, be sure to include the term *"firm"* in your ad; however, if you are willing to negotiate write *"OBO"* meaning "or best offer."

If the publication in which you advertise requires that you provide the photograph, don't try to hide any obvious exterior damage. This will only aggravate a potential buyer who sees a flawless car in the ad, only to walk around to the other side to see a huge dented fender. Remember, you want only interested buyers to come by, buyers who will see what is in the ad and not some trick just to get them out to see it.

Showing The Car

Make no mistake about it, selling a car to someone without telling them about known problems is wrong and could mean legal action against you. Once again, be honest. Give the buyer all of your records and tell them about any known problems. If you do that and they still want to buy, include on a sales document the words "*as is.*" If you have followed the guidelines in the section entitled "Checklist for Preparation of Sale," you'll be ready to show the car.

Negotiating Tips

Everyone likes to feel like they are getting a good deal, so leave a little room in the price to bargain with the buyer. If the buyer makes an offer that is low, don't turn it down right away. If they are really interested, you should be able to tell and make a counter offer later while they are still looking over the car. Be confident and be fair.

If you are selling your car in the winter, scrape any ice from the windows, and just before the prospective buyer comes by, start the car and turn on the heater. If selling in the summer, turn on the air-conditioner for a short while. This will make their first impression much nicer. Be honest, don't try to hide anything, and treat the buyer as you would like to be treated.

Transferring the Title

There are two possible scenarios here: You own the car with a clear title or you still have a balance due at some financial institution. If you own the car, the entire proceeds from the sale go to you. If this is the case at the time of the sale, accept only cash or a cashier's check; this is just good business. If someone wants to give you anything but that, for example a personal check, it's best to just say no. During the sale, you give your title to the person buying the car, and they give you cash or a cashier's check. Requirements for transferring the title may vary from state to state, so call the Division of Motor Vehicles or the License Bureau for any specific questions you might have.

If you still have a balance due at the bank, the transaction will take place at the bank and your proceeds check will be the difference between the payoff balance and the selling price. This transaction is done at the bank because the bank has the title and they want to make sure they get paid. The bank, if that is where your car is financed, will walk you and the buyer through all the steps involved in transferring the title.

SAMPLE SALES AGREEMENT

BILL OF SALE: This is to certify that I have sold the below described automobile to **NAME(S)**_____and the price is $_____.

AUTOMOBILE DESCRIPTION

TITLE_____MAKE_____MODEL_____VIN _____
As of **(DATE)**_____the odometer reading was_____.

SPECIAL CONDITIONS IF APPLICABLE

_____

_____

NOTARY: The foregoing instrument was acknowledged before me this _____, 20___by_____, who is personally known to me or has produced_____ as identification and who did/did not take an oath.

_____

Signature of person taking acknowledgment

_____

Printed, typed, or stamped name of person taking acknowledgment

_____

Notary seal/commission exp. date or serial number, if any

11

Caring for Your Car

Putting your car on a good preventive maintenance schedule and being consistent with regular oil changes and tune-ups can help your car run smoothly for years to come. So, whether you own a Porsche or Pinto, the key to mechanical longevity is directly proportionate to how dedicated you are in maintaining a consistent habit of taking care of your car.

Checking and Changing the Oil

Practically every car has an oil light and oil pressure gauge that, when lit, indicates that you are low on oil or losing oil pressure. If you are driving and the light comes on, quickly find a safe place to pull off the road and immediately turn the engine off. Failure to stop when the light comes on could mean serious damage to the engine. When you do pull over, look for a level surface to stop. You should always check your engine oil on a level surface with the engine turned off.

The next time you get in your car, look for the oil light and gauge. If you cannot find them, look in the operating manual. Some indicating lights and gauges are illuminated for only a few seconds when you first turn the engine on and are visible after that only when there is a problem. Know where they are in case they do come on.

Before you check the oil, let the engine cool. If you have been driving for, say, only twenty minutes, your wait will be only a few minutes. However, if you have been driving for more than an hour, wait about five minutes. In order to check the oil, you need two things: some sort of rag and the knowledge of where the oil dipstick is. If you can't find the dipstick, look it up in the manual. While you're looking through the manual, find the location of the oil cap as well, just in case you need to add oil. Once you pull out the dipstick, wipe it off from the bottom up and look for a small mark that indicates where the proper oil level should be. If it's low and you have a quart in the trunk, add it and then check again.

If you don't have any oil in the trunk and the engine is empty, call for road assistance on your cell phone or place some kind of flag on the antenna. If you are the bold type, flag down a police officer or, if you feel up to it and a service station is in view, start walking. If this sounds like a drastic measure, consider the consequences of driving without oil.

To add oil, remove the oil cap and pour it in, being careful not to spill any on the engine. Depending on the oil cap location, using a plastic or paper funnel could be necessary. If you don't have a funnel and a couple of quarts of oil in the trunk, get some soon. When adding oil, be careful to check after each quart. Too much oil is bad for your engine. After adding the oil, be sure to securely replace the oil cap (Note: While checking the oil, look at the color. New oil that hasn't been in the car long will look kind of like honey; old oil will be black or very dark brown. If the latter, have it changed as soon as possible.)

Once you get back in the car, start the engine and look for the light. If the light does not go off, recheck the oil level and, as soon as you can, find a service station or quick oil change business and pull in for an inspection.

On occasion, your oil light or oil pressure gauge might come on as a result of losing oil from a blown valve cover gasket, oil-drain plug, oil filter, oil-pan gasket, or front engine seal. If it's the valve cover gasket, you should see oil all over the engine and the underside of the hood. The other problems are slightly more difficult to determine. Regardless of which of these problems is at fault, adding oil will not help, because the pressure of the engine will just blow it out again as soon as you start the car. You need to have your car towed at this point.

An automobile engine is designed to operate with oil and lubricants. Without lubrication, the engine will quickly seize up and when it does, it's time to get a small loan for the ensuing repair bill. The single most important preventative maintenance item you can perform for your car is changing the oil approximately every 3,000 miles. Your best bet is to find one of those quick oil change companies that not only changes the oil but performs other vital lubrication checks as well. Sure, you could change the oil yourself, but knowing where to inspect, and how to fill the other lubrication fittings is another thing.

Besides, if you do change the oil yourself, you will then need to find out how to properly dispose of it as well as the filter. Each state has specific rules for disposal of oil, and I can assure you they don't include dumping it in the back yard or pouring it down the storm drain. Be environmentally conscious if you decide to make changing your oil yourself a routine event.

If you are going to change the oil yourself, make sure you know what kind of oil to use and how to do the job. Your operating manual will most likely list the approved oils and show you the location of the oil cap, filter, dipstick, and drain plug. If this will be your first time, or you just need a refresher short course, use these few tips the next time you change the oil:

1. If the engine is cold, start it up and let it run for a few minutes. This will allow the oil to circulate and warm up. Warmer oil drains faster (Note: Never run the engine in an enclosed area without proper ventilation).

2. Make sure the car is parked on a level surface and the engine is turned off.

3. Position a container under the drain plug and filter sufficient in size to hold the old oil.

4. Remove the plug and let all the oil drain. Usually a small crescent wrench will do the job.

5. If you have a good grip, you can remove the filter. Sometimes wrapping a dry rag around the filter will help. If you have any doubt about your ability to remove the filter, purchase a filter wrench. Being under the car with the oil plug off and no means of removing the filter is bad news.

6. Just before you put the new filter on, apply a small amount of new oil to the o-ring of the filter. This will help it seal better.

7. Be careful not to overtighten the replacement filter.

8. Once all the oil has drained out, thoroughly clean the drain plug before replacing.

9. With the filter and plug installed, begin pouring new oil in the fill cap hole. The operating manual should indicate how many quarts to add. Check the dipstick level before and after the last quart goes in.

10. Put the oil cap back on and start the engine. If the oil pressure warning light does not go off in about five seconds, turn the engine off and start looking for leaks. If the light does go off, let the engine run for a few minutes and then check the oil level. Add, if necessary.

11. Now that you're done, remember to dispose of the oil and filter properly.

Tune-Up Time

Tune-ups consist of minor adjustments to the engine to help it start more easily, run better, and burn fuel efficiently. What is included in a tune-up and how much it costs depends not only on the year, make, and model of your car, but how well you have been taking care of your car in the past. A tune-up for a 1990 model and a 2001 model are very different and what is included also varies. However, the following replacement parts and minor adjustments are standard on most cars: replacing spark plugs, filters, rotor, replacing the positive crankcase ventilation (PCV) valve, and adjusting the timing and idle speed. On occasion, belts and hoses will need replacing.

Most cars need major service inspections and/or tune-ups after every 30,000 miles or so. Of course, don't just assume that you need to spend $150 for repairs the second you've reached 30,000 miles. It's always best to be safe and make an appointment for service at this mileage interval. But unless your car is running badly, having trouble starting, or is experiencing some other obvious problem, expect a reasonable bill for service inspections and repairs.

If you plan to perform relatively simple tune-up related repairs yourself, make the investment in the service manual for the car and purchase the right tools for the job.

Tires: Balancing, Alignment and Rotation

If you've ever looked at the side of a tire and noticed some sort of hieroglyphics like (P 185 75 R14), you've probably wondered what they mean. Well, here's the answer:

➤ P: Passenger car

➤ 185: This is the tire width in millimeters

➤ 75: This is the ratio of the width to the height

➤ R14: This is the rim diameter

The other letters and numbers found on a tire refer to the tire manufacturer and the proper air pressure in PSI—pounds per square inch. If you are going to periodically check your own tire pressure, and it is recommended that you do, make the investment in a good tire gauge, or at least frequent a service station that has a good gauge attached to its air hose. The correct air pressure is printed on the side of the tire. If you can't find it, look in the owner's manual. While you are checking the tires, on occasion open the trunk and check the pressure in the spare.

When it's time to buy new tires, buy good ones. You'll be glad you did. However, before you make a purchase, get the prices up front and make sure everything is included, such as alignment, balancing, and valve stems. Shop around, because it seems like someone is always having a sale.

Balancing & Alignment

If you start to experience a shimmy, or mild vibration, when you drive, stop in for a wheel-balancing inspection. The shimmy, or vibration, could be the start of a serious problem, so it's best to have it checked out. If you're lucky, it's something minor, like one tire is really low on air. If you experience a vibration only at certain speeds, chances are it's a balancing problem. If this is the case, have your tires balanced right away. Riding on wheels that are out of balance can cause other problems, and the shimmy/vibration problem will only get worse. If the car consistently pulls or drifts to one side, take it in for what will most likely be an alignment problem. As with balancing, alignment problems should be taken care of right away.

Tire Rotation

Another way to prolong the life of your tires is by having them rotated about every six months. To be more precise about the frequency, check your owner's manual. If you don't rotate them regularly, expect two of them to wear out early. This little inconvenience will send you shopping for two new tires. To correct this potential problem, rotate them and save yourself an unnecessary shopping trip. If rotation is done regularly, then all four tires will wear the same.

The Art of Changing a Flat Tire

So, you're driving along and then—POW!—there goes $75 bucks. That is, there goes a tire. Do you know what to do? If you have a phone, AAA, and two hours to kill, you have nothing to worry about. However, in the event that you have no such luxuries, you should know how to change a tire. Here are a few tips that will help you do it right:

1. If you are driving along and have a flat tire, try to maintain control of the car while you pull off the road. Do not panic and slam on the breaks; instead, gradually apply pressure to the break and slow the vehicle down while turning on the blinker. Once off the road, turn on your emergency flashers.

2. Do not pull off onto a bridge or overpass and always look for a relatively flat, hard surface, with enough room to change the tire. Remember, if the left tire goes flat, you will be closest to the road while you change the tire, so pull as far to the right as possible.

3. Leave the emergency flashers on, turn off the engine, and set the parking break.

4. If you have passengers, have them get out and stand in a safe place, or make sure they remain still throughout the changing process.

5. If you have flares, set them out or open the hood to indicate you are in distress.

6. If you have never changed a tire on that car before, check the owner's manual for any special instructions.

7. Before you get started, lay out everything you need—a fully inflated spare tire, all parts to the jack, a tire iron, and a screwdriver to remove the hubcap if the tire has one. (Note: Some tire iron/lug wrenches have a chiseled end for removing the hubcap. You might also need a rubber hammer for replacing the hubcap).

8. Just to make sure the car doesn't roll, place a rock under the tire on the opposite end of the car.

9. Position the jack in place, but do not start to lift the tire off the ground. If you lift the car before you loosen the lugs, the tire

will most likely start to spin in place once you try to loosen them. If you do not know where to position the jack, check the owner's manual. If you do not have the manual, position the jack under the car's frame. Avoid areas such as under a fender, because the fender will not support the weight of the car. Select a location that will likely support the weight. (Note: Not positioning the jack in the proper location can cause harm to the person changing the tire and can damage the fender or a weaker area. Know where to put the jack).

10. Remove the hubcap, then loosen the tire lugs, but do not remove them completely. Remember, counterclockwise to loosen.

11. Once the lugs are loose, jack the car enough to allow the flat to be pulled off. At this point, remove the lugs and place them close by. You will notice that it doesn't take much jacking to lift the car high enough to remove the flat. However, to get the spare on, you will have to jack much higher. To get an idea of how high to jack, occasionally place the spare next to the lug rim and eyeball the height.

12. When you have the right height, line up the lugholes with the rim and push the spare on firmly. Start replacing the lugs by pushing the tire on the rim at the top and putting that one on first. Placing the top lug first will help hold the tire in place. Then, in random order, hand tighten the remaining lugs.

13. Take the lug wrench and start tightening the lugs, moving from top to bottom and from side to side, alternating them as you tighten. This alternating/tightening technique will assure that the tire is being evenly secured to the rim. Tighten the lugs to about 90 percent capacity.

14. Lower the jack, putting full weight on the tire. At this point, finish tightening the lugs using the same alternating method.

15. If the tire had a hubcap, replace it by lining it up on the lugs and the tire's air stem hole. You will understand when you look at the tire. This is when having a rubber hammer would come in handy. However, if you don't have one, make a fist and use the side of your hand, or carefully use the heel of your shoe to gently tap the cap in place.

16. If you placed a rock under the tire, remove it. Also, completely stamp out the flare and take it to the closest waste can.

17. As soon as it is practical, have the tire patched or replaced with a new one. Don't be driving around without a spare.

18. There is one other alternative to changing a flat tire that does not require calling AAA or doing it yourself. This alternative costs about $6 and is available in many stores like Wal-Mart. This wonder product is *Fix-A-Flat*, made by SNAP Products, Inc. Fix-A-Flat comes in a container about the size of a large can of bug repellent. The product operates by screwing the hose connected from the can to the flat tire's air stem and then pressing the button. It's that simple. The entire process takes about five minutes.

Belts and Hoses

Belts and hoses develop cracks over time. If you check them out while you are performing other engine maintenance, you might save yourself a breakdown one day. Unless you have the right tools and know-how, leave the replacement of hoses and belts to an automobile technician. As a rule, these items are relatively inexpensive and best installed by professionals.

Air Filters

Check out the owner's manual for the location of your car's air filter. If the car you own has a carburetor, the air filter will be located on top of the engine in a round compartment. Air filters are flat and located on the side of the engine if you have fuel injection. Either way, the best time to replace the filter is when you have a tune-up or routine oil change. However, if you live in a particularly dusty area, you might have to change it more often. Dirty air filters can damage the engine and waste fuel. Reusable filters are on the market and available for most cars, but they require periodic removal for cleaning.

Your Battery

Most batteries last about three to four years, if maintained properly. One key maintenance tip is to keep corrosion from building up around the terminals. Corrosion looks like a whitish powdery material around the battery post and cables. To clean the terminals, you will need a box or crescent wrench, a small wire brush, a couple of clean rags, a bucket of water and baking soda solution, and a small amount of petroleum jelly. Armed with these items, make sure the engine is off, then follow these steps:

1. If the terminal cables are not visibly marked positive (+) and negative (-), do so before you remove them. This will keep you from accidentally reattaching the wrong cable. Using the wrench, loosen the nuts at the end of the cable next to the terminal post.

2. Gently remove the terminal from the battery, applying just enough pressure to lift it up and away from the post. Depending on the condition of the terminal, you might need to slide a straight-end screwdriver underneath and pry the terminal away from the post.

3. Take a small wire brush and clean off the inside of the cable, and then clean the battery post. Thoroughly clean them to the point where they appear shiny. Warning: Make sure you put on safety goggles before you start wire brushing the corrosion off the terminal.

4. Clean the top of the battery with a rag dipped in the water/baking soda solution. This will clean off excess corrosion and remove any tiny pieces of wire brush that may have fallen off the brush.

5. Reconnect the terminals to their correct posts, applying the positive first. Now securely tighten the nuts.

6. With the terminals in place, rub a small amount of petroleum jelly around the outside of the terminals. This should help prevent the buildup of more corrosion.

Fuses

Fuses are used to protect electrical components in your car. Fuses are also very inexpensive and easy to replace. If you do not know where the fuse box is, get out the owner's manual and look it up. If the fuse box has a cover, remove it and look inside for a diagram that indicates what each fuse is used for. For example, if your clock is out, look for the fuse located next to the word "clock." It's just that simple.

When replacing a fuse, remember that you have to replace it with the same amperage fuse. If you use a smaller amp fuse, it will blow out; if you install a larger one, you risk damage to the component. In

short, never replace a fuse with a fuse of a different size. If you have a plastic fuse-puller, use it. If not, gently pry the fuse out with something plastic and look for damage to the fuse, such as a broken internal wire or burn mark on the fuse itself. If the fuse is bad, replace it and be happy. If the fuse is good, get on the phone, because you just might have a bigger problem. While the fuse cover is off, look at the other fuses and check their amperage. Once you know what the other amperages are, you can stop in and pick up some the next time you are near an auto supply store.

Radiators, Water, and Antifreeze

You will be hard pressed to find a car without a temperature gauge. Do you know where yours is? The cooling system uses a mixture of water and antifreeze to keep the engine running cool. Never continue to drive if you notice the temperature gauge indicator is pointing to the red/danger zone. However, if you notice the gauge starting to climb and the air conditioner is on, turn it off and find a safe place to pull off the road. Turn the engine off and lift the hood. CAUTION: Never remove the radiator cap when the engine is hot. The radiator is pressurized, so if you open it before the engine has enough time to cool, about twenty minutes, you could be badly burned.

After the engine has cooled, place a rag over the cap, press down, and then turn counterclockwise until it opens. If the car has a safety cap, you should still allow the engine to cool before you place a rag over it and release the pressure. If you are thinking about pouring cold water in, DON'T. Adding cold water to an overheated engine could crack the engine block. If you have a gallon of water in an old milk container in the trunk, chances are the temperature will be just right, so pour it in. If you do not have any water, call for road assistance. You need water to continue driving. After you add water, put the cap back on and pull over at a service station to recheck the level and have the antifreeze checked.

While you have the cap off, look in the radiator and take note of the water color. If it looks cloudy and dirty, it's time to have the engine flushed. There are three different ways to have the radiator flushed: (1) take it to a service station; (2) buy a flushing kit and do it yourself the right way; and (3) cram a garden hose down inside the radiator, turn the water on, and let the crap run all over the driveway.

No matter what method you choose (preferably one of the first two), you need to keep the water/antifreeze mixture fresh. Also, check the radiator solution from time to time, regardless of whether the indicator gauge reads high or not.

How to Jump-Start a Car

Before you open the trunk and pull out the cables, make sure the battery is your problem. If you turn the key on and the radio, lights, and wipers work, chances are the problem lies somewhere else. You did buy an AAA membership, didn't you?

If the battery is very weak or dead, check for excessive corrosion or loose cables. If there is little corrosion and the cables are tight, find someone with a car that starts and proceed with the following steps:

Make sure the ignition is off on both cars before you get started

➤ Align the cars so the batteries are close enough to be able to attach the jumper cables.

➤ Starting with the good battery, attach the red-handled cable to the positive terminal. Move it around a few times to assure a good connection. The positive battery terminals should be marked in red and/or with a positive (+) symbol stamp.

➤ Now connect the other end of the positive cable to the dead battery positive terminal, assuring a good connection.

➤ Again starting with the good battery, connect the black or negative cable to the negative (-) terminal and the other end to a ground on the car with the dead battery.

➤ Start the engine of the car with the good battery, and then try to start the other. If it starts, let them both run for a few minutes. If the car does not start, recheck the connections and try again. If it still doesn't start, call a repair shop.

➤ To remove the cables, start with the negative, then remove the positive cable.

If you are not going to drive to a service station to have the battery checked out, recharged, or replaced, at least park in a place that is conducive to having another jump. In some cases, the battery could have been drained because you left the lights on. If that's the case, let the engine run and the battery will charge itself. If that was not the case, buy a new battery.

Use the Right Kind of Gas

The owners' manual should list the proper octane for your car. If it doesn't, ask a service station mechanic to look it up for you. Octane levels range from 87, which is regular, to about 93 for premium. If your car doesn't require premium, save your money. However, if you hear a pinging or knocking sound when you accelerate or climb a hill, you could need to upgrade from regular to a mid-octane fuel.

Don't Forget to Check the Fluids

Aside from oil and radiator fluid, which were covered earlier in this chapter, check the fluid levels of these other components on a routine basis:

➤ Windshield

➤ Automatic Transmission

➤ Manual Transmission

➤ Battery

➤ Differential Fluid

➤ Clutch

➤ Break

➤ Power Steering

Parts That Just Wear Out

Despite every effort you make to prolong the life of your car, some parts are going to simply wear out. To keep from having them go out while driving, check the inspection and replacement frequency schedule in the owner's manual. If you can afford it, have them replaced early. Here are a few parts to consider:

➤ Tires, Headlights, Fuses, Wiper Blades, and Battery

➤ Wheel Bearings, Brakes, and Clutch

➤ Muffler and Exhaust Pipes

➤ Thermostat, Fuel Pump, and Fuel Filter

- Alternator, Starter, and Air Filter
- Timing Chain or Belt and Water Pump
- Transmission, Belts, and Hoses

What to Put in Your Car's Emergency Tool Box

You can never tell what's going to happen when you are on the road, so be prepared. As a rule, always try to keep at least a half-tank of gas, and be sure you have a spare tire that actually has air in it. Depending on what part of the country you live in, the following list of essentials could change; however, the following items are highly recommended:

- A small basic first aid kit, and a container of drinking water.
- Car jack, a rubber hammer if you have hubcaps, gloves, and a straightedge screwdriver.
- A gallon of water for the radiator.
- Flares and/or emergency triangles and a flashlight.
- Jumper cables, a crescent wrench, and spare fuses.
- One can of Fix-A-Flat.

To help your car last longer, read the owner's manual section on preventive maintenance. Also, be consistent about taking your car in for regular oil changes and tune-ups. If something sounds odd or if the car starts to handle differently, have it checked out. You might just be heading off a serious and very expensive problem.

References

- *Car Buying & Leasing 101*, by Charles DeVorak
- *The Chilton Series*, (Depending on the type and model they will have a repair book for you)
- *The Complete Idiot's Guide to Buying or Leasing a Car*, by Jack R. Nered
- *How to Insure Your Cars: A Step by Step Guide to Buying the Coverage You Need at Prices You Can Afford*, The Silver Lake Editors; Paperback
- *Sold: How to Sell Your Private Car Yourself (Even if you Hate Selling)*, by Eric White
- *Take Care of Your Car The Easy Way*, by Michael Kennedy and Carol Turkington
- *Understanding Personal Auto Insurance*, by Sheryl Lilke
- *Used Cars: How to Buy One*, by Darrell Parrish

Part 4
Money Matters

12

Personal Investing

If it seems like you're living from pay day to pay day, join the club. Millions of people both young and old live this way, with little hope for change. This sad but true reality is inescapable for many older citizens; however, you can avoid this destiny by making the decision to start saving NOW. This is much easier said than done, but failure to discipline yourself could prove devastating down the road.

Ask any retired person what they would have done differently in their earlier years and you will likely hear, "I wish I would have started saving much earlier." As a young person, you have the opportunity to change the outlook, for you're future years by starting to save just a little now.

Many financially restrictive lifestyles are due to insufficient financial planning for one reason or another. Take a look at an older relative who is doing well, if you know one, and a relative who is living on the edge of poverty. Now, which one do you want to be? The one doing well either maintained a really good income over their working life or was smart enough to invest early. Most likely it was a little of both.

Some of you are thinking, "I'll wait until I start making more and then start saving." This is a dangerous approach for a variety of reasons. Do not make this choice. Inevitability, when one starts to make more money, one starts to buy more of the material things that were previously out of financial reach. For example, if a person is making $18,000 a year at age 19, they will probably be living in a small, sparsely furnished apartment, driving an older car, and saving no money. Over the next ten years, the same person will move into a much larger apartment, acquire a spouse, have kids on the way, and will be driving a newer car, but still not saving a dime. By the time that same person is 39, making $80,000, he or she will have purchased a home for the spouse and 2.3 children, acquired a pocket of credit cards, several loans, a healthy mortgage, and will still not have managed to save anything.

How can this be? Simple—people spend proportionately more money as it becomes available. It is very hard to make more money and not spend it on something you have waited on for years, like a bigger apartment or home and a newer car or second car. If you don't think this can happen to you, ask the millions of others who thought the same thing. So, whether you are living on $18,000 or $80,000, if you are not saving, you are going to be in trouble.

People gradually increase their lifestyle and the cost that goes with it. I remember reading about a very wealthy real estate tycoon who lives in New York. This particular tycoon was experiencing hard times and was forced to put himself on a meager $450,000-per-month allowance. Think about it: He had progressively acquired a lifestyle that took $450,000 per month just to make ends meet. Poor guy. The point is, the more you make, the more you spend, and the more you seem to need, with "seem" being the key word. Make the decision now and start saving something, even it's only $20 per month.

Goals and Commitment

If you have been living at home and you thought having extra money for yourself was tough, then wait until you are faced with all the expenses of living away from home. Trying to manage money for the first time is tough for anyone. Trying to manage your monthly living expenses will prove to be a difficult and ongoing process. However, if you do not make a commitment early in life to save, you will be doing yourself a grave injustice.

The longer you do anything, the easier it becomes. Saving is a good example. If you start saving, say, 5 percent of your take-home pay now, then two years, five years, and ten years from now, the process will become routine and the benefits will become obvious.

Everyone's financial situation relative to savings is different; however, the end result should be the same. Start saving early. The how and where of saving and investing will be covered later in this chapter, but for now let's concentrate on making the commitment and setting financial goals. Only you know how much you can afford to save, so establish some short-term financial goals that will help you work towards your long-term goals. For example, if you set a goal to save $500 per year—that's less than $10 per week—make your long-term goal to have $5,000 in ten years. Of course, there will be interest involved, and as you make more, you should save more, but the connection between short- and long-term goals is the point to be made.

If you don't think saving for the future is important, consider stashing away a little money as protection against hard times. Put away some cash and call it emergency funds. This way, you will be putting away money for unexpected times like unemployment or unexpected medical bills. As you start to save, you may or may not need to dip into those emergency funds. If this happens, consider what would have happened if you had not saved a little. Aside from saving as a form of risk protection, don't forget insurance. Make sure you have an adequate mix of automobile, medical, and renter's insurance to cover unexpected losses.

Make a commitment to save something from every paycheck, no matter if you're paid weekly, bi-weekly, or monthly. Deposit your savings in the same bank where you have your checking account established. This will make the transaction much easier and, thus, less noticeable. Opening a savings account is quick and painless, so the next time you're at the bank, allow another fifteen minutes to open an account. The reason for opening an account at the same place you have your checking account is simple. If you cash your check at one place, it's easy to make a savings deposit at the same time.

If your company has a savings plan that automatically deducts from your paycheck, sign up for that plan. This will make the process of saving a little less noticeable and will therefore reduce any anxiety relative to physically writing out a saving deposit slip and watching the teller take it from you. Having the money deducted from your check eliminates the emotional tie you have to your hard-earned money. As time goes by, you will find the process less noticeable and you will want to designate even more to be deducted as you start to see your account grow.

Moving from Saving to Investing

After making the commitment to save, and after setting some short- and long-term goals, it's time to withdraw your money from some 3.2 percent savings account at the bank and deposit your fortune in one of a variety of places, such as mutual funds, bonds, or stocks. Don't worry about your current lack of knowledge on investing. Before you finish this chapter, you will have the tools you need to make reasonably good investment decisions. But before learning about stocks, bonds, mutual funds, and 401(k) plans, let's get familiar with the terminology.

Financial Terms and Definitions

➤ **Bear Market:** A market in which prices are declining.

➤ **Bid**: The price that the market participants are willing to pay.

➤ **Bond:** A long-term debt security issued by a borrower, usually a public or private institution.

➤ **Bull Market:** A market in which prices are rising.

➤ **Call:** An option contract that gives the holder the right to buy the underlying security at a specified price for a certain fixed period of time.

➤ **Callable Bond:** A bond that can be redeemed by the issuer prior to its maturity.

➤ **Convertible Bond:** A bond which is convertible into stock.

➤ **Contract:** Unit of trading for a financial or commodity future.

➤ **Coupon:** The stated interest payments made on a bond.

➤ **Date of Record (Dividend):** The date set by a firm's directors on which every person whose name is recorded as a stockholder will at a specified future time receive a declared dividend.

➤ **Discount Bond:** A bond that is valued at less than its face value.

➤ **Dividend**: A return on an investment, usually in the form of cash or stock.

➤ **Dividend Reinvestment Plan**: An option to have any dividends automatically reinvested in the company.

➤ **Face Value:** The stated principal amount of a bond.

➤ **Futures:** A term used to designate all contracts covering the purchase and sale of financial instruments or physical commodities for future delivery on a commodity future's exchange.

➤ **Future Value:** The value of an initial investment after a specified period of time at a certain rate of interest.

➤ **Hedge:** A conservative strategy used to limit investment loss by effecting a transaction which offsets an existing position.

➤ **Inflation:** A general price increase in the economy.

➤ **IRA**: Individual Retirement Account

➤ **Offer**: The price at which an investor is willing to sell a futures or options contract.

➤ **Option:** The right to purchase stock at a specified price.

➤ **Par Value:** The face value of a bond.

➤ **Preferred Stock**: A kind of equity whose owners are given certain privileges over common stockholders, such as a prior claim on the assets of the firm.

➤ **Present Value:** Today's cash value of future returns.

➤ **Principal:** The amount originally invested.

➤ **Prospectus:** A legal document required by the Securities and Exchange Commission detailing a firm's operating and financial position and available to any potential buyer who requests it. In general, a prospectus is used to research the company.

➤ **Put Option**: An option that gives the holder the right to sell.

➤ **Return:** The gains or losses incurred by the owner of an asset over a period of time.

➤ **Risk:** The degree of uncertainty associated with the outcome of an investment.

➤ **Securities:** Company assets guaranteed to lenders to ensure repayment of loans.

➤ **SEC:** Securities and Exchange Commission, a federal regulatory body that governs the sale and listing of securities.

➤ **Stock Dividend:** A dividend in the form of additional shares of stock, issued in lieu of a cash dividend.

➤ **Stock Split:** The issuing of more shares of stock to current stockholders without increasing stockholders' equity.

➤ **Yield:** A measure of the income generated by a bond.

➤ **Yield to Maturity:** The rate of return anticipated on a bond if it is held until the maturity date.

➤ **Zero Coupon Bond:** Bond issued at a discount from par value that pays no coupon and promises to pay par value at maturity.

Stocks in General

So, what is stock, and why do companies sell it? If a company wants to raise money (capital), one of its options is to sell (issue) stock. Companies sell stock as opposed to getting a loan from a bank because, unlike a loan, selling stock does not create debt. Stocks are essentially pieces of paper that indicate a percentage of ownership. The more money a company has to invest in the research and development of new and existing products, the more profitable they will likely become, thus increasing the value of the company. As a rule, if a company's earnings go up, so does the price of their stock. People buy stock for a number of reasons, among them the desire to make more money on their investment. Shareholders, including you once you buy a company's stock, expect their investment to grow.

As with any form of investing, there is risk. For example, if you buy 10 shares of a stock for $20 per share and the stock drops to $4 per share, you just lost $16 per share, or a total of $160 if you sold the stock at $4 per share. Many advisers would recommend holding on to the stock instead of selling at $4, because the value could eventually increase beyond its original purchase price of $20. Remember, if the price of stock drops, you only lose money if you sell. On paper, you have still lost the money, but if you hold on to it, the loss is strictly a paper loss. Of course, many investors would be very nervous watching their money dwindle from $20 to $15 to $8, and then to $4 per share.

At what point should you make a decision to sell or hold on? That, my friend, is a difficult question to answer and should be considered long before you decide to buy your first share of stock. Some people will sell their stock as soon as it drops below its original value, while others will hold on to it with hope that it returns to at least its original value.

For example, decide up front what percentage is going to be your cut-off amount. For example, if you decide to sell when the price drops below 15 percent of its original value, stick to that decision and be ready to sell if need be.

Conversely, establish a selling value when the stock starts to rise. Decide on what value above original cost you are going to sell to make a profit. There are just as many people who have lost out on potential profits because they held their stock and didn't sell at the right time, just as there are people who have lost money because they did not sell before the values really dropped.

Stock Dividends

Dividends are funds divided between shareholders of common stock resulting from a company's good financial fortune. The payments are made out of a firm's earnings to its owners, either in the form of cash or stock. The most common type of dividend is a cash dividend. However, dividends come in several different forms: regular cash dividends, extra cash dividends, special dividends, and liquidating dividends. *Regular cash dividends* are paid directly to shareholders and are viewed by the company as a routine practice with no reason to be discontinued. On occasion, a company will pay a regular cash dividend and an *extra cash dividend*, calling part of the payment "extra." The board of directors usually indicates whether or not this extra dividend will be repeated in the future. The *special dividend*, as the name implies, is very special and is very unusual. A special dividend is likely to be a one-time deal for a company. The last major dividend type is the *liquidating dividend*. This type of dividend is usually a result of the liquidation from the sale of a portion of a firm's business.

The board of directors decides when and if dividends are to be paid. If dividends are to be paid, they could be sent out quarterly, semi-annually, or annually. To be eligible to receive a dividend, you must have purchased the stock at least three days before the board announces the dividend. This *record date*, as it is called, of at least three days is due to the time it takes to settle or make a typical trade. You can sell your stock the next day, but you must have owned it for at least three days prior to the announcement. If you are entitled to receive a dividend, then the company will mail you a check. However, if you are taking advantage of a *dividend reinvestment plan*, your dividend proceeds will be credited to your account.

On occasion, some companies may be temporarily prohibited from paying dividends on their common stock because they, for whatever reason, have missed payments on their bonds and/or preferred stock. In general, earnings are always calculated first and then the board of directors decides what to do with those earnings.

Dividends are not always paid to shareholders. Sometimes the board elects to hold on to the funds or to reinvest the would-be dividend on other facets of the company. Companies make the decision to hold on to earnings so they will have the capital to expand, develop, or refine existing products or services. By paying dividends, a company reduces its ability to make the money work for them. Regardless of what circumstances drives a company's decision to pay out dividends, many investors are attracted to their stock solely for that reason. Some companies pay dividends, some don't. If receiving a dividend is important to you, make sure the company you are considering pays them.

Stock Splits

A stock split is a method commonly used to lower the market price of a firm's stock by increasing the number of shares belonging to each individual shareholder. In general, a stock split occurs when a publicly held company distributes more stock to its stockholders of existing stock. For example, a typical stock split would be 2-for-1, in which the company would essentially be giving one share of stock for every share owned. If you owned 100 shares of stock worth $20 per share, you would end up with 200 shares worth $10 per share. The amount of money is the same, only the quantity of stock has increased. The reason the dollar amount is the same is because the company's assets haven't increased, only the number of outstanding shares.

In many cases, an ordinary stock split often drives the new price per share up as more potential investors are attracted by the now lower price per share. On occasion, a company may decide to split when the existing price has risen to a level that individual investors cannot afford. This would probably not be a big deal if people were buying five shares at a time, but many traders and investors buy and sell in lots of one hundred, so a stock selling at $200 per share is a big deal when you consider how many shares you could buy of a comparable stock selling for $100 per share.

Bonds in General

Bonds are like IOUs; they promise to repay a sum of money at a certain interest rate and over a certain period of time. Most bonds pay fixed rates of interest to their holders for a fixed period of time. Companies sell bonds for many of the same reasons they sell stock. However, the process is different for the company, as well as for the bondholders.

Unlike purchasing stock from a company, when you purchase corporate bonds, you do not own any part of the company. But if the company falls on hard times, bondholders must be paid off in full before stockholders get a dime. Corporate bonds are issued by a variety of companies and range in price, duration, and interest repayment terms. *Municipal bonds* are issued by states, cities, and other local agencies and may or may not be as safe as corporate bonds. As a rule, the taxing authority of the state or town backs municipal bonds, while others rely on earnings income to pay bond interest and principal.

United States bonds are issued by the Treasury Department and other government agencies and are considered to be the safest form of bonds. In exchange for the maximum security, expect to get slightly less interest. Remember—the greater the risk, the higher the return on your money. Also, depending on the type of bond, the tax ramifications will differ, so check it out when and if you decide to buy.

Bonds with a maturity of less than two years are generally considered to be a short-term instrument or short-term note. Medium-term bond notes range from two to ten years and long-term notes are greater than ten years. The shorter the term, the less exposure to bond volatility, better known as risk. Also, shorter-term bonds give you the comfort of knowing that you will be getting your principal payment back sooner.

Bonds are normally an interest-only loan, meaning that the borrower will be paying only interest every period, making the principal payment at the predetermined end of the loan. There are many different types of bonds, so shop around and decide what best fits your situation.

If you like the idea of stock, but want the greater security of bonds, consider a *convertible bond.* Convertible bonds are securities that can be converted into shares of the company that issues the bond if the bondholder so desires. However, this process must take place before the bond matures.

As with any investment, there is risk, and bonds are no exception. In general, when interest rates rise, your bond's value declines; when interest rates fall, bonds perform well. If you own a bond during falling interest rates, you might not reap the full benefit because of a little thing referred to as a *call.* Their issuer can call bonds before maturity, paying only a slight premium over par value. If your bond is called, you will have to reinvest in a new bond paying you less interest. The ultimate risk of owning a bond is associated with the defaulting of the bond by its owner. Although rare, defaulting does happen and usually with devastating results for bondholders.

Mutual Funds in General

Mutual funds are an easy way to participate in the stock market by allowing potential investors the opportunity to diversify risk and obtain professional management. The advantage of diversifying helps to reduce overall risk while enhancing your total return.

Mutual funds pool money from many different investors and use it to pursue a specific objective. Funds comprise a multitude of investors whose money is pooled by funds managers to purchase securities. A common variety of mutual funds invest in stocks and bonds of U.S. companies. But don't expect to take your $27.50 and buy into the action. Most funds require a $1,000 minimum. Once you have saved the minimum amount, this would be a good place to put that money you have been stashing away in your less than impressive 3.2 percent savings account at the bank.

To learn more about a particular mutual fund, request a *prospectus* by calling the fund directly or by searching on the Internet. Calling them is better than just opening up the business section and blindly selecting one. Most of the time, you are considering a fund because you know of a friend or relative who thinks highly of it or is making money on the fund's performance. You might even hear about the fund on the news or by reading about its performance in the paper or in a trade magazine. In any case, you can usually find a phone number with little effort and then request a prospectus.

All funds are either *closed-end* or *open-end*. Closed-end funds issue a fixed number of shares and are traded like a stock on the different stock exchanges. You can buy and sell shares through a broker just like a stock. Prices fluctuate due to public perception of their performance. For example, if you read or hear about some fantastic growth fund, the price will likely rise in response to the article. Open-end funds are considered to be the most popular and, unlike closed-end funds, they have no limit on the number of available shares. When you buy into an open-end fund, you are essentially purchasing a fraction of all the securities that the fund owns. An open-end fund may be either a *load* or *no-load* fund. Load funds charge a fee to purchase their shares, no-load funds do not.

A major fund category is stock funds, which can be broken down into specific classifications. In general, stock funds invest in all sizes of companies in the U.S. and overseas. Stock funds are characterized as follows:

➤ **Income Funds:** These funds buy shares in companies that have little prospect for growth; however, they have reasonably good dividend yields.

➤ **Aggressive Growth Funds:** Purchase shares in companies that have large growth potential. Some consider these to be high gain/high risk funds.

➤ **Growth Funds:** Buys shares in companies that are growing very quickly and are considered to be good investments.

➤ **Growth/Income Funds:** Purchase shares in companies that exhibit some growth potential and also pay a dividend to their shareholders.

Two other major funds are *money market* and *bond funds*. Money market funds offer liquidity, which simply means your cash is easily accessible. Money market funds invest in short-term securities from companies or governments that are highly liquid and have relatively low risk. Money markets are a reasonably safe place to store short-term money while you are waiting for other opportunities or you just need access to your cash. Bond funds tend to be more conservative when it comes to risk and growth. Bond funds invest in medium- to long-term securities.

Certificates of Deposit

Certificates of deposit are loans to commercial banks in exchange for relatively small interest repayment terms. These safe, but low-interest bearing, deposits come in a variety of options, ranging from initial deposit to maturity duration. The next time you're in the bank, look around. You are sure to see information posters and advertisements relating to these certificates throughout the bank. Most banks even post the going rates, depending on amount and duration. There are usually stiff penalties for early withdrawal;

however, if security and relative liquidity are what you're after, go for it. For more information, stop by your local bank. They will be more than happy to talk to you.

Buying Stocks, Bonds, and Mutual Funds

Now that you have read about stocks, bonds, and mutual funds, and you are convinced that you are ready to buy, it's time to decide on whether you are going to use the services of a broker or try to manage things on your own. If you decide to seek out a broker, ask around, see if any of your friends or relatives have any first-hand dealings with a broker, and go from there. If this option turns up nothing, look through the phone book or consider the Internet or the local library for information on brokers.

Once you have found a broker, preferably a local one, stop in and set up the account in person. Although the process is somewhat more difficult than opening a checking account, opening a brokerage account takes about the same time. When you open the account, you will most likely be given written information, which details the fees and restrictions of the account. Don't expect a broker to provide you with anything for free. Remember, they are in the business to make money. Make sure you know what the fees are, when they are paid, and how. If you think the fees are high, look around at some other brokerage firms and compare.

There are three main types of brokerages: Full, discount, and deep discount. Full service, as the name implies, does practically everything for you. You give them your cash and they make money for you. Sounds great if you trust the guy, but remember— each time he buys or sells "for you," he is making a commission. The full-service broker is actively managing your account and is well compensated for his time. Discount brokers, on the other hand, offer you the opportunity to service your account yourself. This type of direct involvement allows you to make decisions on your own, with limited guidance from the broker. However, if you need a tip or piece of advice, the broker is there to help. Like a discount broker, a deep discount broker can save you even more, but you had better know what you are doing. When starting off, I would suggest that you either seek some outside advice from a friend or relative or use a discount broker.

Before you decide on the type of broker, ask yourself a few questions. Do you know what you are doing and how to do it? Do you want control over your investments at all times? Do you like knowing that someone else is handling your money for your benefit? The answers to these questions will likely guide your decision. Of course, you don't have to open an account with a brokerage firm to invest. For example, if you want to purchase shares within a mutual fund, you can contact the fund directly. You can also use the existing services offered through the Internet.

Another way to invest without involving a broker would be to take advantage of any program offered by your employer. For example, some companies that are traded on the exchanges offer employee stock purchase plans. This would be a good opportunity to get involved without being intimidated by an outside brokerage firm. You could learn the ropes of investing and then move on. Other investment opportunities through your employer, such as 401(k) plans, will be discussed later.

Planning For the Future

Planning for the future isn't just a good idea, it's an essential part of your overall financial plan. Every smart young person like you should be thinking about "the big picture," even if it seems so far away. So don't bank on that "I'm depending on Social Security" line. Even if Social Security was fully intact, it hardly pays for a comfortable lifestyle.

Since we are on the topic of Social Security, let's take a quick look at the program. In general, the amount you would receive in Social Security benefits is based on your average earnings during your working life. You are eligible to collect benefits if you are fully funded, which by definition is 40 calendar quarters, or 10 full years of work. In the early years of Social Security, the ratio of workers paying into the program and those receiving the benefits was sufficiently large compared to today's and future calculations. Despite the optimism of government officials, don't base your retirement on the plan of receiving any money from Social Security without some financial wizardry being performed over the next 30 to 40 years.

When it comes to financial planning, don't just say, "I'll need about a million bucks to retire" or "I can live pretty good off of $80,000 per year." Do you know what that money is going to be worth when you retire? If you do, that's great. If not, seek advice and read up on the multitude of investment opportunities. Who knows? You might just learn something from this book.

Start off by setting realistic goals and figure out how you intend to make them happen. Sure, it's tough, but if you don't at least start to think about it, time is going to creep up on you like tight underwear. There are many financial planning books that go into exhausting detail on how to calculate what you'll need. However, you can log on and do it yourself on the Internet through a host of free informational sites. Establish short-term and long-term goals and make every effort to stick with what you have planned.

Take full advantage of any program offered through your employer. They are usually good and assistance from them is less stressful than dealing with an outside firm. However, if you are the adventurous type, or you just don't like what the company plan has to offer, consider doing it on your own. The key point is to do something. In general, the stock market has the highest returns of any investment option. But don't think, "Hey, all I have to do is buy low and sell high, so how hard can it be?"

Outside of winning the lottery, there are no true, legal, get-rich-quick plans. Financial planning takes two things: commitment and time. If you are not ready to accept this fact, all is lost. You might as well blow your savings on the local lottery as soon as you get your check. Think about it, if financial planning was easy, everybody would be doing it. The sad but true fact is that many people are just not able to save, or so they say, and thus completely avoid the topic until it's too late. Those unfortunate souls should hope Social Security can survive the next fifty years.

The Almighty 401(k) Plan

A 401(k) plan is a retirement savings plan that is funded by contributions from you, the employee, and often by your employer's matching contributions. Some companies match a portion of their employees' contributions, some don't. These plans are attractive because employees can choose to have their contributions deducted on a pre-tax basis. If you sign up for the plan, and it is a good idea to do so, you can authorize your employer to deduct a certain amount from each paycheck and have that amount deposited in your plan.

The money deducted is invested with that of many other employees into a variety of investment funds. These funds usually include a money market, bond funds, company stock, mutual funds, and others. Historically, stocks have outperformed all other forms of investment and will likely continue to do so. Given the longevity of your invest-ment, twenty, thirty, even forty years at your age, the compounding effect of consistent periodic contributions over a long period of time is incredible.

Early on, you can select the very aggressive funds and then, as you move into your later years, you can move some or all of it into a safer investment option. Diversifying your money across different industries, stocks, and foreign countries is a good way to approach a progressive financial plan. While you are young, take advantage of the dynamic opportunities offered by aggressive funds and stocks. You can always become conservative later in life. However, no matter how good the 401(k) plan is, the decision to direct the funds to the variety of options remains yours. Stay on top of your investment options by checking your quarterly statements and tracking where you are and what the funds are doing. If need be, make a change, but don't continually be switching, trying to outsmart the market. Remember, you are in this for the long haul, so be patient, but be aggressive.

The tax advantages of a 401(k) are also good. When you participate in your company's plan and select the pre-tax option, you will save fed-eral taxes. How? Because the money is considered deferred compen-sation, meaning the money deducted does not appear on your annual W-2 form. Therefore, no taxes are paid on the deducted funds, because they do not show up as income. The money remains tax-free until you start to make withdrawals. For example, if you make $25,000 per year and invest 8 percent of your salary and the company matches another 3 percent, you can save 11 percent each year. The beauty of the tax advantage is that the $25,000 salary normally listed on your W-2 will now be recorded as $23,000. Why? Because the $2,000—your 8 percent contribution—is calculated as follows: 0.08% x $25,000 = $2,000; and $25,000 - $2000 = $23,000. You are not enti-tled to deduct the company-matched percentage—sorry.

Employees have the option of making all or part of their contributions pre-tax or after-tax. After-tax contributions are much different from pre-tax contributions. If you elect to contribute after-tax money, the money comes out after you have paid taxes on it. Although the tax advantage is gone, it will make removing those after-tax funds easier. When distributions are being made from the 401(k) plan, no tax is due on those contributions that were made with after-tax money.

Some Major Advantages of Participating in a 401(k) Plan:

➤ Some employers match all or a portion of their employees' contributions. This is free money, so don't miss out on it.

➤ The automatic withdrawal of the contribution is less noticeable from week to week, making saving much easier for those who would normally have to sit down and write out a check to invest.

➤ Pre-tax contributions are tax-free.

➤ All growth, including company matched, is also tax-free.

➤ The employee can decide when and where to put the money.

➤ Unlike a pension plan, 401(k) money can be moved from one company's plan to another.

➤ Unlike an IRA, the 401(k) has the advantage of employer-matched money.

A few disadvantages are that the money contributed by your employer is not really yours until you are vested, which will be discussed soon. Also, it is difficult to remove money from a 401(k) unless there is a dire reason. On occasion, you will find companies do not allow their employees to manage their money, so check it out up front. Although many people say 401(k) plans are good, ask to see the history of the companies that your particular company invests in. Although unlikely, you may find that you can put your money to better use somewhere else.

One last disadvantage, if you can call it that, is insufficient vesting. Most companies require that you stay with them for five years before you are 100 percent vested in their program. If you leave before you are fully vested, you still take with you your personal contributions, but the company's match money stays behind. For example, if the company has a typical five-year vesting program, you own 20 percent each year, or you are 20 percent vested each year. If you leave after three years, you are only 60 percent vested and only 60 percent of the company match goes with you.

The 401(k) plan is a very good investment; however, removing money can become difficult unless you can prove a hardship that meets your human resources plan guidelines. Two of those hardships are excessive medical expenses and a first-time home purchase. Many plans, even though there is just cause for the hardship withdrawal, will not allow the participant to continue in the program for approximately one year after the withdrawal.

There are many plans that allow their participants to make loans from their plans. However, the restrictions and guidelines should be understood before making the decision. When and if you do borrow from your plan, you will be paying yourself back, not some bank, and the interest and principal are funneled back into your account. On the other hand, if you make a withdrawal from your 401(k) as money other than a loan, not only will you have to pay tax on the money, you will have to pay an early withdrawal penalty of 10 percent to Uncle Sam.

What happens to money in a 401(k) plan if an employee leaves the company? Regardless of the reason, you can take the money with you, providing you are vested. The stipulation is that you have to reinvest the money in another qualified plan within sixty days or face stiff penalties. When you *roll over* the money from one 401(k) to another, the check is issued directly to the other account. Because you never physically take possession of the money, no tax is withheld or owed on the direct rollover amount.

Ordinary Individual Retirement Accounts

IRAs are types of investment accounts. The IRA allows a person, whether covered by an employer-sponsored pension plan or not, to contribute money for use in retirement while allowing the savings to grow tax-free. Slightly different than other investment plans, you can contribute money from January 1 of that year to April 15 of the following year. Because of the extra time, if you send in a contribution to your IRA manager from January 1 to April 15, make sure you let them know what year the money is for. You can deduct IRA contributions from your gross income if you meet eligibility requirements. Before you consider an IRA, consult your manager or human resource adviser and the IRA carrier/provider.

If you are employed, and your company doesn't offer another investment opportunity or pension plan, and you are not self-employed, you should consider an IRA. However, if there are other options available to you, by all means consider them before making a decision. Anyone with an income can contribute up to $2,000 of his or her income per year. If married, a couple can contribute up to $4,000 per year, providing the spouse makes at least $2,000 per year. If married and the spouse does not work, the couple can contribute $2,250 annually.

Getting money from an IRA may not begin until age $59\,^1/_2$, and payout from an IRA must begin prior to age $70^1/_2$, or the participants may face penalties. Participants have two basic payout options. The first option is the one most people take, which is the monthly check, taxed as ordinary income. The other option is a lump sum that Uncle Sam loves, because he gets a big piece of the pie all at once.

When leaving a job where you have an IRA, consider what you are going to do with the IRA. To avoid the 20 percent withholding, you must arrange for a direct rollover, known as a trustee-to-trustee rollover. This simply means that the distribution check from the retirement plan at your old company must be made payable to the trustee or custodian of the new IRA account. Before you leave your existing employer, notify the IRA plan administrator, fill out the proper forms, and follow their instructions.

Roth IRA

On occasion, our government will do something totally unpredictable. In this case, that unpredictable event was the creation of the Taxpayer Relief Act of 1997. From this act the Roth IRA was born. The Roth IRA allows taxpayers, subject to certain income limits, to save for retirement while allowing their savings to grow tax-free. There are no tax benefits associated with contributions, because all contributions to a Roth are made with after-tax money.

Unlike an ordinary IRA, the Roth IRA contributions are never deductible from gross income on your federal tax return. You can contribute up to $2,000 annually and may be restricted based on your individual income and filing status. The annual $2,000 contribution limit for a Roth is reduced by contributions to any traditional or non-Roth IRA for a given year. Investors can establish and add to a Roth IRA two different ways: first, by direct contributions and, secondly, by conversion or transfer of money from an existing IRA to the Roth.

One of the biggest differences between a Roth and an ordinary IRA comes into play when it comes time to withdraw past age $70\frac{1}{2}$. Unlike a normal IRA, the Roth IRA does not require the owner to ever make withdrawals. The treatment of withdrawals is what distinguishes the Roth IRA from other IRAs. Because the contributions to a Roth IRA are nondeductible, withdrawals of contributions are tax-free and penalty-free and are permitted virtually any time without restriction. Withdrawals of accumulated earnings are entirely tax-free if you hold the Roth for a minimum of five years and meet one of the following qualified exemptions:

➣ Take up to $1,000 for the purchase of a first-time home
➣ Reach the minimum age of $59\frac{1}{2}$
➣ Disability
➣ Death

One final thing to remember is the holding period. There is a five-tax-year holding period to satisfy. However, by making a small contribution, say $250, to a Roth IRA account now, you will have started the five-year time clock. So even if you can't save the maximum, save something just to start the five-year clock. The Roth is not intended to replace a 401(k) plan, but if you still have money to invest after contributing to other plans, the Roth is an excellent financial planning instrument.

Keogh Plan

The Keogh plan is a tax-deferred retirement savings plan for self-employed individuals and their employees. In general, self-employed means sole proprietorship or partner in a partnership. The main difference between an IRA and a Keogh is the limit on contributions. The limit depends on the type of Keogh; however, in general, a self-employed individual may contribute a maximum of $30,000 to a Keogh plan each year and deduct that amount from his or her taxable income. Wouldn't it be great if you had an extra $30,000 to invest each year?

Keoghs, like IRAs, allow the individual to grow their contributions tax-free until they begin withdrawing from the plan. Keoghs, like other IRA-type plans, have similar restrictions relative to withdrawal guidelines. For example, distributions cannot be made without a penalty before age 59$^1/_2$ and distributions must begin before age 70$^1/_2$. Although those restriction ages seem like forever from now, they should still be considered.

One of the biggest differences between IRAs and Keoghs is the contribution limit. However, the downside of a Keogh is the unfortunate amount of required paperwork that you will have to fill out. Questions about the business, your Keogh's vesting schedule, and the appointment of an administrator can be difficult to set up without help. But the benefits far outweigh the initial inconvenience.

Final Note on Investing

While you are young, look into some aggressive stocks or other equally dynamic investment options. If you're not sure which stocks to buy, stick with those industries that interest you so you can keep up with them without falling asleep while you are reviewing their performance. However, if you are not ready to venture out on your own, consider mutual funds or one of the IRAs previously discussed.

If you enjoy tinkering with the Internet, look at the many different investment brokers and do-it-yourself options available to you at your fingertips. The Internet will allow you to get market analysis and comprehensive market coverage twenty-four hours a day, seven days a week. If you are comfortable with trading and giving out personal and financial information online, give the Internet a try.

Finally, take full advantage of any company-offered plans, like 401(k) or stock options, because they are generally considered to be good financial planning tools.

13

The Truth About Credit Cards

Credit cards are instruments that identify their owners as individuals who are entitled to credit wherever their cards are accepted. Most places, especially retailers, accept not one but a variety of cards. When credit cards are used, the retailer scans the card, which identifies the name, account number, and total to be charged. This information is then forwarded to the credit card billing office, where approximately every thirty days, statements are mailed out to cardholders reflecting charges and recent payments. Statements will also show over-limit fees, late charges, and returned check fees, if any of those apply. To know what the credit card company charges for these items, read the cardholder agreement, which comes with your card.

Liability

It is important to remember that you may be liable for the unauthorized use of your card if it is lost or stolen. To find out what that financial responsibility is, read your agreement. However, you're most likely not going to be liable for unauthorized use if your card is missing and you've called to report it as lost or stolen. If this is the case, shortly after you contact the card company, take the time to write them a letter explaining when you realized the card was gone and if it was lost or stolen.

If you give out your credit account number to make a purchase such as calling the Home Shopping Channel to buy a fake diamond engagement ring, or you authorize someone else to make charges to your account, your obligation to pay will be the same. The point here is being responsible with your card and knowing the consequences of using it and giving out the number.

Cash Advance Option

If your credit card company, at their option, gives you a personal identification number (PIN), you may use your card to obtain cash advances from any automated teller machine (ATM) that bears the name of your card, such as Mastercard or Visa. For security reasons, your card issuer (the company that gives you the card) has the right to restrict your access to any ATM at any time or otherwise limit the number or amount of purchases or cash advances that may be made with your card. When your card company gives you a PIN, remember the number and store it in a separate place, away from your card. Never keep it in the same place as your card, because if you lose your wallet or purse, your account can be accessed very easily. If you believe that somehow another person has gained access to your PIN, you should advise your credit card company immediately by following the instructions on your agreement for lost or stolen cards. They will most likely cancel the current PIN and assign you a new one. Remember, while you're waiting for your new PIN, you will not be able to use your card for ATM withdrawals.

Always be careful when using an ATM, paying particular attention to anyone standing around the machine. Always cover one hand with the other while entering your PIN. If you need cash at night and you're walking, think safety by using an ATM in a well-populated area that has adequate lighting. If you are driving, find one that doesn't require you to get out of the car.

Credit Limits

Credit limits are usually established after reviewing a potential customer's credit rating and annual income. Combining a good credit rating with a $100,000 annual salary will usually result in a high credit limit. So unless you have managed to acquire a good credit rating and big salary, don't expect your first credit card to have a $100,000 limit. If you're filling out an application for your first credit card and you have not been working long enough to have a long credit history, expect your limit to be around $1,000.

With the exception of American Express, which requires the full balance to be paid each month, practically all other credit cards have a minimum due regardless of the balance. The minimum due will be printed somewhere on your statement. However, you should always try to pay a little more each month. The smaller your balance, the smaller your minimum payment.

When using your card, be aware of what your *maximum credit limit* is, which can also be found on your statement. For the most part, making charges over your limit is difficult, because your card company monitors your balance. However, if your purchase exceeds the limit by a few dollars, it will usually go through, but you will still get charged for being over the limit. That's why it's important to know what your balance is and what your credit limit is. For example, if your credit card limit is $2,000 and you've charged $1,950, you will probably be approved if you charge a dinner for $55, ($5 over the limit). On the other hand, if you're in a stereo shop, you'll not be able to purchase $400 speakers with a $1,950 balance. Trying to do so will surely cause you frustration and embarrassment. Once again, make an effort to be aware of your balance and your limit.

Returns

If you make a purchase with your card, remember that the credit card company is extending credit to you for that purchase. It is not the same as cash. For example, if you purchase a $500 television from Sears with your credit card and you wish to return it, you will be given a credit on your card for $500. The Sears salesperson will ask for your card and electronically return that $500 back to your account. You will not receive cash back. When you use your card, understand what the store policy is relative to returns. For example, if you purchased that same $500 television from another merchant, you could be stuck with only receiving an *in-store credit* if you decide to return it. That's right, an in-store credit, as the name implies, can be used only in that store. This is very important, especially for large purchases.

Annual Membership Fee

Many cards have an *annual membership fee*, which is usually around $35. The fee is simply a charge for the privilege of using the card. This fee is charged to your account whether or not you use your account at any time during the year. The annual membership fee is charged to your account in the same manner as a purchase, and it will be reflected on the monthly billing statement for the month in which the account anniversary occurs. (Note: Unless otherwise notified, the renewal terms, annual membership fees, and general conditions will remain the same.)

If you don't want to renew the card, you have the option to cancel the account. If you elect to cancel, notify them by mail and include your name, account number, and a brief statement. If you think you will be tempted to use the card, cut it up and include it in the same envelope as your cancellation letter.

Grace Periods

The best way to manage your account and save interest charges is by paying on time. The *grace period* is the time the card company allows you to pay on your account before additional fees are charged. You may avoid interest charges on purchases by paying the entire new balance in full by the payment due date shown on your statement. Remember, this is the new full balance, not the minimum due amount. This is by far the best way to manage your account, if you can afford it. Grace periods vary from card to card, however; expect around 10 days before the bill is considered late.

Finance Charges

All purchases and cash advances are subject to finance charges from the day they are posted to your account until they are paid in full. However, the card company will not charge a finance charge on new purchases if you paid the new balance shown on your prior monthly billing statement in full by the payment due date. For example, if your balance was $150 and you sent in a payment for $150, there will be no finance charge. Paying in this manner would be like having an American Express card, which requires the full balance every month.

Finance charges are calculated on your account by multiplying the *daily periodic rate*, which is a percentage of the annual percentage rate, by the number of days in the monthly billing cycle to the average daily balance of cash advances in your account, including current transactions. This may sound a little complicated, but it simply means that your finance charges are calculated on a daily basis.

The daily periodic rate is based on the annual percentage rate, which is usually slightly less for purchases than for cash advances. For example, if the APR for purchases is 8.9%, the APR for cash advances could be 12.9%. These charges are significant, especially if you pay only the minimum payment due each month. When you pay only the minimum, you are just barely paying enough to cover the finance charges. Let's say you have a $1,000 balance and the minimum payment is $25. If you made the $25 minimum payment, depending on your APR, you could be paying $15 in finance charges, leaving only $10 to be applied toward your principal amount. At that rate, it will take a very long time to pay off a $1,000 balance. If possible, always pay more than the minimum due.

Average Daily Balances

To determine the *average daily balance* of your purchases and cash advances for a monthly billing cycle, card companies separately add up the daily balances of purchases and cash advances in your account for each day of the billing cycle and divide each sum by the number of days in the billing cycle. The daily balance is calculated separately for purchases and cash advances by taking the beginning balance of your purchases and cash advances each day, then adding any new purchases and cash advances. There is one exception: New purchases are not included if you paid the new balance shown on your previous statement in full by the due date on your previous statement. The card company now subtracts unpaid finance charges and any payments or credits allocated to your purchase balance or cash advance balance, as applicable. Confused yet?

Annual Percentage Rate

Selecting a card with a low *annual percentage rate* (APR) should be a key factor, especially if you are planning to just pay the minimum payment each month. When you're comparing APRs, try to find one with a low fixed rate. Some credit card companies offer fixed APRs, which means that your rate stays the same. You will also see cards that have variable APRs. Having a card with a variable rate means that, when lending rates go up, so does your interest rate; but when rates go down, you pay less. Know the difference and select accordingly. If you are going to just pay the minimum due each month, it would be wise to select a card that offers the lowest fixed rate.

Low Introductory APR Offers

When you see advertisements for low introductory rates, be cautious. Many companies are mailing out card applications touting very low rates. Read these over carefully. For example, a low 3.9% rate is an introductory offer designed to get you to sign up right away. These card offers also allow you to transfer other credit card balances with higher rates to your new 3.9% card with no transfer fee. If this offer sounds good, get out your microscope and continue to read. The 3.9% rate applies to purchases, not cash advances. Cash advances on many of these cards have an APR of 19.99%, so be careful. The 3.9% introductory rate is going to increase to approximately 9.9% in six months. Of course, this is just one example of a card offering a low introductory offer. Other offers may vary depending on the company.

If you already have a card with a good fixed rate, avoid these marketing schemes. On the other hand, if you're convinced that you want to switch, at least take your time and really understand the terms and conditions before signing up.

Billing Disputes

The best advice for credit card users is to keep a copy of each receipt. This will come in handy, especially if there is a discrepancy with your monthly statement. If you discover a billing error, try to settle the dispute as soon as possible. Send your credit card company a letter detailing the charge in question and a brief explanation of why the charge is wrong. Be sure to include your name, account number, and address as it appears on your statement. The card company is required by law to either make the corrections or to investigate the complaint and explain why the charge is valid. If the charge is judged valid, you will have to pay. For more information, read the applicable sections of the Fair Credit Billing Act, which can be found at your local library or on the Internet.

How to Protect Yourself from Theft and Fraud

Consider the following advice in your defense against theft and fraud:

➢ Sign the back of your card as soon as you get it.
➢ If you have more than one card, make a list of their names and numbers.

➤ Never leave your card(s) unattended.

➤ Do not lend your credit cards to others.

➤ Unless you know to whom you are talking, never give your card number over the phone.

➤ Always check your monthly statements for suspicious charges.

➤ Make sure you get your card back from the merchant after a purchase.

➤ Never sign your card sales slip if it's not totaled up.

➤ Keep your cards in a visible place in your wallet so you can tell if they're missing.

➤ If you make purchases over the phone, deal only with reputable companies.

➤ Destroy any cards that you do not use.

➤ If you don't plan on filing your receipts, at least destroy the carbon copies.

➤ Report questionable charges as soon as possible.

➤ Notify card companies in advance of an address change.

➤ Carry your cards only when you plan to use them.

➤ Report a lost or stolen credit card as soon as possible.

➤ While on vacation or in a hotel, never leave your cards in your room.

Be Responsible

If you haven't already acquired a credit card, you will soon be faced with that decision. Having a credit card will either be a real convenience or a financial disaster. Using credit cards is as much a part of life as pumping gas in you car. Be aware of what you're doing and be responsible. Having a credit card is a privilege and should be viewed as such. Paying the bill on time will assure your continued use of the card as well as helping to maintain a favorable credit standing. Don't underestimate the value of a good credit rating; it will follow you around for the rest of your life. So, if you are having trouble with the card, cancel it as soon as possible and learn to live without it until you're in a better financial situation.

 **14**

Filing an Income Tax Return

Each year around January, the Internal Revenue Service (IRS) mails out federal income tax booklets to those who need to file. The booklet contains, depending on your last year's tax return, a Form *1040EZ*, *Form 1040A*, or *Form 1040*. Form 1040EZ is the simplest form to use; however, there are many different qualifiers that have to be met in order to use it, and you must meet all of them. The specific pre-qualification items are listed in the booklet, so read it over. This same pre-qualification process is applicable to the other forms as well. If you do not meet the requirements for one particular type of form, the booklet will direct you to the right one.

If you do not receive a tax return booklet by mail, or if you need additional forms, check your local post office, town hall, or library. If those locations do not have blank forms (although they should), then get the phone book and call for the IRS office in your area.

Filing Status

Life is full of choices. Taxes, however, are not one of them. You must file a federal income tax return if you are a citizen of the United States or a resident of Puerto Rico and you meet the filing requirements as stated in the federal income tax booklet.

Your filing status is established on December 31 of each year and depends on whether you are single or married and on your family situation. For example, you cannot claim yourself as a dependent if your parents or legal guardian already do so. Ask your parents or guardian about whom is entitled to claim you as a deduction. Only one party is allowed to claim you as a deduction. Failing to get this settled or just assuming can cause delays in processing your return and could cause penalties to be assessed against you or the party trying to claim you.

When to File

The due date for filing your federal tax return is April 15 for the preceding year. If you do not file your return by that date, you are likely going to have *failure-to-file* penalties and interest assessed against you. However, if you need more time, you may be able to get an extension of time by filing Form 4868, *Application for Automatic Extension of Time To File U.S. Individual Income Tax Return*. Avoid this if at all possible; there should be no reason why you cannot file by April 15. When you are older and faced with, for example, a home mortgage, complicated investments, home-office deductions, or self-employment taxes, you just might need a little extra time to file. But for now, while things are much simpler, get your W-2 and file. There's no need to procrastinate.

6-Step Process

If you are an employee, you will be receiving a Form W-2. This form should be sent to you by the end of January. If you have not received a W-2 by then, contact your employer. If they have not responded by February 15, contact the IRS and they will assist you in getting it. The W-2 has several copies, one to be sent with your federal tax return, one for your state tax return, and one for your records.

You may not receive a W-2, but instead receive a Form 1099, sometimes referred to as a miscellaneous income form. As with the W-2, you should have it by the end of January. Once you have either the W-2 or 1099 and have selected the proper form, sit down and follow these steps:

1. Get your employer W-2 forms together and any other records you might have.

2. Select the proper form to use, such as the 1040EZ.

3. Fill out your tax return, making sure to check it at least once for accuracy.

4. Be sure you sign and date your return.

5. Attach all required documents like copies of your 1099 or W-2.

6. Make a copy of the return for your records.

Refunds and Payments

Once your return has been completed, you will know whether you are due a refund or if you have to pay. If you have overpaid and are due a refund, expect four to six weeks before getting a check. When the check comes and the amount is correct, cash it and be thankful you didn't have to pay. However, if it is more or less than the amount you calculated on your return, you should have a letter of explanation attached to it. If you did not receive an explanation letter, wait about two weeks and then call the IRS office nearest you.

If you owe the IRS money, pay it when you send in your return. If you don't, expect to have interest and penalties tacked on. If you can't send in the total amount, send in something. It will reduce your interest and penalties. When you make out the check, make it payable to the Internal Revenue Service and in the memo section on your check, write in your Social Security number and year to which the taxes apply.

Two Kinds of Mistakes

There are two kinds of mistakes, *honest* and *fraudulent*. If you have made an honest mistake on your return, expect a letter from the IRS requesting additional information or clarification. Depending on how much time has gone by and what further information is needed, penalties may or may not be assessed. In some cases, a letter from you is sufficient; in other cases, the IRS could request an amended return be filed. If that's the case, reread the letter informing you of the need for an amended return and look for the proper form number. If you can't find it, call the IRS.

If your return is being held up due to suspected fraudulent information intentionally made by you, expect a possible personal visit by the men in black. You should also expect additional penalties, additional interest charges, and, in some cases, even criminal penalties. Your best defense against this type of mistake is thoroughly reading the applicable sections of the tax booklet and being honest.

Tax Services

If you do not want the hassle of filing a tax return and you can afford it, have a professional service like *H&R Block* file for you. Tax service companies like H&R Block base their fee on the type of forms to be used and the complexity of the return. Although every company is different, expect to pay in the neighborhood of $75 for the privilege. However, at a young age, tax returns are fairly simple, so you should at least try to file on your own. Get use to the annual tax return filing ritual, because you will have to face it every year for the rest of your life. Isn't that a happy thought?

State Tax Returns

Whether you're a full-time or part-time resident, or you just made money traveling through a given state; expect to pay taxes to every state in which you earned money. You should be filing a state tax return to every applicable state including the state in which you are registered. If you were a part-year resident of a state and earned income while living there, you will need to contact that state for tax return filing instructions.

Many states have only two forms to choose from, a long form and a short, or EZ, form. The state EZ form is usually used for those tax-payers who have earned money only in that state and made less than a predetermined amount of money. These requirements differ from state to state, so you will need to read that state's tax booklet.

Before you start filling out your state tax return, finish your federal return. The first line on many state tax returns asks for the federal adjusted gross income from either the Form 1040, 1040A, or 1040EZ. If you decide to fill out your state return first, you will have to stop on the first line and calculate that amount, so you might as well complete the federal return first.

For the most part, filing a state return is the same as filing a federal return. State tax returns, like federal returns, are due on or before April 15 for the preceding year. State returns can also be filed late if you apply for and complete the applicable extension forms. Like federal returns, if you owe or are due a refund, expect to follow a similar process. Be sure you read the booklet sent by your resident state and, if applicable, other state tax booklets. (Note: When you get ready to fill out your return, find a quiet place and follow the six steps listed for completing a federal return. Good luck!)

15

Credit Problems & Solutions

Sometimes when you are faced with a financial crisis, the choices may seem unclear, especially if this is your first time in this situation. When creditors are calling at night and hounding you with threatening letters, sometimes making the right decision can be difficult. Don't act out of haste and make a wrong financial decision that could haunt you for years to come. Instead, get help. If you have fallen behind on your payments or you simply have too much debt and can't control it yourself, call a state-operated *consumer credit counselor*.

It is a natural feeling to be confused and frustrated when faced with financial problems, especially when you don't know whom to turn to. The fact is, there are non-profit organizations in every state that counsel consumers on debt-related issues. Counselors try to arrange repayment plans that are acceptable to both parties. They can also help you calculate a realistic spending plan or budget. These state-operated services are offered at little or no cost to consumers and can usually be found in a local phone book. Most of these services handle both kinds of debt, *unsecured* and *secured*. Unsecured debts are credit cards, medical bills, utility bills, department stores, unsecured loans, gas credit cards, and taxes. Secured debts are essentially any kind of debt that has a title or lien, like a car or boat.

Debt Problems

Millions of people are having financial problems and approximately one million of those are filing for bankruptcy each year. To avoid bankruptcy, many are dealing directly with their creditors, with mixed results. However, if you are truly sincere with your creditors, you can get more time to pay, have late fees removed, and even settle for less than the original amount. For those people who honor special agreements with their creditors, even some of the derogatory information can be pulled from their credit reports.

Nobody's credit is too far gone to repair, even those who have filed for bankruptcy. Every case is different, but usually, after a few years of consistently paying on time, some creditors will start to trust you again.

Credit Bureaus

Credit bureaus gather and sell consumers credit histories and reports to credit-granters such as retail merchants, banks, and credit-card companies. While the credit bureaus themselves do not approve or deny an application, the information they provide plays an important role.

At the time of this printing, the following were the main three credit bureaus:

1. Equifax (800) 685-1111 or (770) 612-3200
   http://www.equifax.com
2. Experian (formerly TRW) (888) 397-3742
   http://www.experian.com
3. Trans Union Corporation (800) 916-8800
   http://www.tuc.com

Once a year you can get a free copy of your credit report by calling and requesting it. Most credit bureaus, before they can send you a copy, will ask for some basic information like Social Security number, current and former addresses, and the full spelling of your name.

When you get a copy, it will have a notation key which helps you understand all the terms and definitions found on the report. If you have never seen a credit report, don't expect to pick it up and read it like a book.

If you have been denied credit, get a copy of your credit report from the bureau that reported the information leading to the denial. That bureau should be listed somewhere on your denial letter. Look for the sentence that reads something like this: "*Our decision to deny credit was based on, or in part on, information received from Trans Union.*" The report has several columns of information which list account numbers, account-opening dates, dates of last activity, high credit limits, terms, balances, and past due status. Carefully read your report checking for accuracy. If you discover incorrect information of any sort, read the section on the report that explains how to file a correction change. This process is sometimes referred to as a *request for investigation*. If you file one of these forms, expect it to take between thirty and forty-five days before receiving an answer. In many cases, you can call the creditor directly and ask them about the information in question. If there is a mistake, request that the corrected information be reported to the credit bureaus as soon as possible. If the derogatory information is correct, you will at least know why you were denied credit.

Credit Scoring

Every company has a credit scoring procedure or model to rate applications and subsequently approve or disapprove them. The factors used in the scoring process are as follows and, for the most part, depending on the company, are listed in order of importance:

> ➤ Derogatory information such as bankruptcy, collections, and slow pays.
> ➤ Time at present job (the longer the employment the greater the points).
> ➤ Occupation (professionals like doctors and lawyers are given really good scores).
> ➤ Time at present address (the longer the better).
> ➤ Ratio of balance to available credit (the lower the better). For example, having a credit card with a $2,000 limit and a $200 balance.
> ➤ Being a homeowner scores big points.
> ➤ The number of recent inquires on your report (the less the better).
> ➤ Years you have had a credit file.

Credit Repair

Just because you have a less-than-stellar credit report, don't assume you'll never be able to get credit again. Each creditor sets its own credit-granting standards and conditions. Some look at your entire credit history to base a decision, while others look at the past year or so. If you have been in financial trouble in the past and have been paying on time, say for the last eighteen months, some creditors will take a chance on you. Of course, don't expect to get a platinum card with a $100,000 limit. At first, settle for applying for a gas card or look into a secured card to get your credit history back on track.

If you have seen ads for companies that claim to be able to "clean up" your credit report, consider first that you can do the same thing they can without paying them a fee. I'm referring to those private credit services that claim they can remove negative information from your report. Even if they could do that, most likely the negative information, if legitimate, will return in thirty days, or the next time your report is updated. Don't be fooled by these ads.

If you call each of your creditors and explain to them your circumstances, and make financial arrangements, you can accomplish the same thing. Think about it: It simply doesn't work the way the private credit counseling services tell you. Let's look at this example. A person charges $50,000 with six different credit cards; buys a new car and a house, and then decides not to pay. After a few months, the creditors will start calling, and very soon that person's credit report will have lawsuits, liens, an automobile repossession, a home foreclosure, and numerous negative collection agency reports splattered all over it. But wait—according to those ads, all that person has to do is call a credit counseling company or debt consolidation service and they will "clean up" all that negative information. Once that's done, this individual can go out and get more credit cards, buy a new house and car, and start over with a fresh, new credit report, God bless America. If you really think that's how it works, then you are just the kind of person these companies are looking for. The fact is, many people seek the services of these companies because they just want the creditors to stop calling. If that's the case, contact a state-operated non-profit credit counseling service to help you. Not only are they legitimate, they will usually not charge you a fee and they will be realistic about what you can expect.

Negotiating With Creditors

Creditors like to hear from you as soon as you realize you are in trouble. If they don't and you start skipping payments, they can only assume the worst. From that point on, it only gets more difficult to deal with them. You should contact them as soon as you realize you cannot make a payment. However, don't write on your Visa bill in orange crayon, "I can't pay this month." For one thing, the person opening your payment letter on the other end is probably not the customer service representative who would normally be able to help you. You should also never put a letter in with your payment, because it simply isn't the best way to inform your creditor about a problem.

Call your creditor and talk to a person, don't just leave a long, detailed message. Instead, wait for an available customer service representative. Don't be afraid of calling them when you anticipate a problem, because if you wait, they'll be calling you and the situation gets worse from there.

Once you have decided to call, explain the problem clearly. Creditors can easily understand situations like layoffs and emergency medical bills. Send in a small payment if you can; this will show that you are really sincere and the small payment will act as a good faith payment. Depending on the tone of the conversation, request that they not report your bill being late to the credit bureau right away, but give you some more time instead.

A good upfront working relationship with your creditors is your best defense against negative credit data appearing on your credit report. It might not totally prevent them from reporting negative information to the credit bureau, but if you don't call them, your chances on delaying any derogatory information is virtually non-existent.

Budget or Spending Plan

If your money is really tight and you just can't budget it in your head, sit down and put together a budget or spending plan. Call it whatever you want, just do it. Some people don't like the way a budget plan sounds, so they call them spending plans, which implies spending not budgeting. First, list all current expenses, including the following:

- Home or rent payment
- Gas, water, electric, cable, phone and trash collection
- Furniture payments and department store payments
- Groceries
- Insurance: auto, renter's, and health
- Car payment and gas
- Tuition expenses
- Taxes

Many people consider the above listed items as a spending plan, and when they stick to it and still find themselves in trouble, they can't understand what's wrong. So they give up. Their problem is simple: They are not allowing for all the other things that take money from their checking account. Individually, none of the following is big; however, cumulatively, they can destroy a spending plan if not accounted for. Consider these costs:

- Occasionally eating out
- Parking fees and tolls
- The occasional purchase for clothing and shoes
- Haircuts, cosmetics, and toiletries
- Dry cleaning and laundry
- Prescriptions, vitamins, eye care, dental, and doctor visits
- Automobile repairs, tune-ups, brake jobs, tires, and so on
- Buying compact discs, going to the movies, concerts, and hobby expenses like green fees for golf
- Film development, books, magazines, and computer hardware/software
- Pet grooming, vet bills, and pet food
- Holidays and birthdays
- Postage and office supplies such as tape, rubber bands, and glue

Individually, any one of these expenses is small; however, if you don't plan for them, never expect to stay within any kind of spending plan or budget. You should take the above list of miscellaneous items, select the ones that apply, and come up with a monthly allowance to include in your spending plan. Be assured that if you are realistic about the amount you select, you will have a much better chance of staying out of financial trouble. This is not to suggest that your spending plan be cast in stone, it just needs to be flexible enough to allow for those inevitable, and often forgotten, expenses.

Collection Agencies

If you have not stayed in touch with your creditors and you choose not to return their phone calls, don't be shocked when your account has been turned over to a collection agency. If you avoid talking to your creditors because you think it will be tough, just wait until the collection agencies get hold of you. For the most part, collection agencies could care less about your credit rating or your problems, no matter how severe they are. By the time your account has been turned over to these guys, all hope for a peaceful solution between you and your creditors is gone. If your credit situation reaches this point, don't be surprised if you can no longer talk to your creditors directly. Many of them will not talk to you once the account has been forwarded to a collection agency. These guys mean business and will inundate you with phone calls and certified mail.

A collection agency takes its orders from the creditor and therefore cannot sue you unless the creditor agrees—although most creditors usually do. If your creditor tells the agency to sue for nothing less than 100 percent of the balance, the agency cannot accept anything less. On the other hand, the creditor may give direction to collect as much as possible. With that order, the agency is in a position to bargain with you. However, don't forget that the collection agency makes a percentage off what they collect, so expect them to try to squeeze as much as they can from you. The older the account, the harder it is to collect; therefore, a collection agency gets to work as soon as it gets the case.

Unless you have some documented evidence that contradicts the validity of the account balance, expect to pay. However, if you have such evidence, make copies and forward them to the collection agency. If the matter is resolved, then the *sent for collections* note will be removed from your credit file. That is definitely a good thing.

If the collection agent becomes obnoxious, you have the legal right to tell them to stop harassing you. Write the collection agency and tell them to cease all communications with you. By law, the agency must stop, with the exception of telling you about an impending lawsuit or that the case has been dropped. If you think having your account *dropped* is a good thing, then think again. What "dropped" really means is that your creditor will tell the credit bureau to make a note that your account was written off as a bad debt. That is really damaging information, especially when a new creditor sees it. What that tells any new potential creditor is that, after all this time, you still wouldn't pay your debt, under any circumstance—not exactly flattering news to a potential creditor. It's one thing to have your account handled by a collection agency and have it paid, it's quite another to have it dropped for non-payment. Creditors sometimes order the account dropped because litigation is just too expensive. Believe me, you are the real loser in this case. Trying to explain negative statements on your credit report is next to impossible.

Avoid as much contact with collection agencies as possible. If you get into financial trouble—and millions of people do—call your creditors and try to work it out.

Derogatory Information
Time Limits on Credit Reports

The Fair Credit Reporting Act (FCRA) details the following time limitation:

Type	Limitation
Bankruptcy	10 years from the date of entry for relief
Suits & Judgments	Seven years from date of entry
Tax Liens (paid)	Seven years from the date of entry
Tax Liens (unpaid)	No limitation
Collections	Seven years
Charge off	Seven years
Criminal Record	No limitation
Other derogatory info	Seven years

16

Checking Accounts

If you have a hard time dealing with long-term relationships, you will dread the inevitable acquisition of a checking account. Friend, you will most likely have a checking account for the rest of your life. If the thought of that is less than desirable, then get over it. Unless you're wealthy enough to have someone manage your money for you, be prepared to spend one hour each month trying to balance your checking account statement. What this really means is that you will spend one hour a month trying to find a $1.78 mistake that makes you want to pull your hair out. Welcome to the world of high finance.

A check is a particular type of draft. By definition, a draft is drawn on a bank and is payable on demand. As a practical matter, checks are written on the assumption that the drawer (that's you) has funds in his or her account at the drawee bank (that's your bank) sufficient to pay the check when it is presented for payment.

Types of Checking Accounts

Most banks offer several different types of accounts. They usually range from charging for each check you write, to writing unlimited checks with no fees charged. Cost and restrictions associated with checking accounts differ significantly between accounts, so spend a little time evaluating them.

The first type of account is for those who frequently write checks and prefer keeping a moderate balance. This account almost never pays interest on your balance and has a maintenance fee around $15 per month, which is simply a charge for having the account. Another type of account has no fees, provided you maintain a daily balance of $1,000, for example, or a monthly average balance of, say, $2,000. However, if you have this type of account and do not maintain the minimum balance, the bank will charge you a maintenance fee in lieu of not meeting the balance minimums. Ask what that fee is and keep at least that amount in your account just in case your minimum balance drops. Another version of this type of minimum account balance might require a $300-per-day and/or $500-per-month minimum balance. Unlike the higher minimum balance accounts, a lower minimum balance account will sometimes have a mandatory maintenance fee.

ATM Cards

Regardless of which account you select, practically all will offer automatic teller cards, most often referred to as ATM cards. ATM cards are very convenient and allow you to do your banking whenever you want, providing you know where the ATMs are. Most ATM locations accept cards from different banks. For example, if you have a checking account at the First National Bank of Oz, you can use your card at the First National Bank of Kansas. There is one small difference in using your ATM card at another bank location, though: The other bank is likely to charge you a fee for letting you use its machine, usually around $1.25 per usage. This can add up if you make a habit of it, and it can cause you a big headache if you forget to enter the withdrawal amount fee in your checkbook. How do you know how much the other bank charges? When you first put your card into its ATM, the visual monitor readout will tell you exactly what the charge is. If you accept that charge, the fee plus the amount requested will be deducted from your account.

General Information

Before you open your first account, talk with your parents or friends and ask where they bank and if they are happy with the service they receive. Remember, you can always cancel your account and go somewhere else if their recommendation doesn't work out. However, if you're the adventurous type and want to find a bank on your own, at least take the time to go to a couple of banks and talk to their customer service representatives, all of whom will be glad to explain how the different accounts work.

Prior to entering the bank, write down some questions that will help you in making a decision. For example, ask about the different accounts and what their fees are. Find out how the minimum balance is calculated and what new checks cost. Inquire about their fees for *overdrafts*, which is just a nice term for, "Hey, you don't have enough money in your account, so we're going to charge you for it." Finally, you should ask about how long the bank holds checks before it cashes them. Many banks will hold some types of checks for several days before you can receive any funds from them. This could be particularly bad news, especially if you need some cash *now*.

Don't be intimidated when you enter the bank. Just walk over to the customer service desk, which is located away from the teller windows, and tell them what you want. Believe me, no matter how much money you have to deposit, the bank wants your business.

Be Practical and Take Your Time

Having and using a checking account is very much a part of day-to-day life. However, the simple process of writing checks and recording them should not be taken lightly. If you are a poor record keeper, you could create big problems for yourself. Making accurate entries in your check register for ATM withdraws, deposits, and checks is essential. Take the extra 30 seconds to record those transactions right after you make them, and be sure they are right. If you're like most people, your time is important and sometimes performing these menial tasks becomes bothersome. However, don't just tell yourself you'll make the entry later. Do it now, because chances are you'll forget it later. You only have to forget making an entry one time to really screw up your balance.

Common Mistakes and Check Writing Tips

Be sure that when you write a rent check for, say, $500, you don't enter $50 in your check ledger. The importance of being careful cannot be overemphasized. Another part of check writing that you should be very careful with is how you write your check. Make sure that when you write $500.00 numerically, you write out the words "Five hundred dollars" and not "Fifty." In the case of a discrepancy, the bank will use the hand written and not the numerical information. This could be bad news if your $500.00 rent check was actually worth only $50 because you wrote in Fifty and not Five hundred. If you did, you can bet your landlord will let you know real soon!

When you write a check, use all the available space either with large print or by drawing a line from the words or figures to the edge of the provided spaces. This will keep someone from altering what you wrote. For example, numerically $___50.00 can easily be altered to $150.00 and a handwritten _____ Fifty dollars can be altered to One hundred Fifty dollars . OUCH! Write as far to the left as possible and draw a line through the remaining space.

Debit Cards

These days many checking accounts are offering debit cards. Debit cards are different from credit cards in that credit cards are used to "pay later," and debit cards are used to "pay now." Debit cards are usually provided by Visa and MasterCard and can be used anywhere Visa and MasterCard are accepted. However, despite their general similarity in appearance, there is a distinct difference between a credit card and a debit card.

Unlike a credit card, debit cards have no credit line. Your available credit is directly proportionate to your current checking account balance. When you use your debit card, the money is subtracted, or debited, as the name implies, much the same as if you withdrew money from an ATM. When you use the debit card, remember to enter the amount in your check register as soon as possible. Using a debit card instead of writing checks saves you from showing identification or giving out personal information at the time of transaction. It also frees you from carrying cash or a checkbook.

If your card is lost or stolen, react to the situation the same as if you are missing a credit card. Report the loss immediately to your financial institution. If you suspect your card is being fraudulently used, also report it to your financial institution. Keep your debit card receipts and check them against your bank statement for accuracy. If you are not the kind of person who keeps receipts, at least destroy the carbon copy. This will help keep your card number safe. Finally, always know how much money you have available in your account, because the debit card is tied directly into that balance.

How to Reconcile Your Bank Statement

The following format will show you how to reconcile or confirm your balance. This format, in some form or another, should also be printed on the back of your checking account statement for your convenience.

1. Start with the balance that the bank statement has printed. $_____

2. Enter any deposits that are not included on the statement. $_____

3. Total lines 1 and 2. $_____

4. Total any withdrawals that have not been included and enter. $_____

5. Subtract line 4 from line 3. $_____

Line 5 is your balance. If it does not agree with your check register, then redo the math and try again. If still puzzled, go to the bank and have a chat.

Post-Dated Checks

Some people will do almost anything to keep creditors off their back, up to and including writing a post-dated check. If a creditor convinces you to send them a post-dated check, stop and think before you act. Doesn't it stand to reason that if you are having financial trouble now that obligating yourself to pay a debt in the future could be a shaky proposition? By writing a post-dated check, you are committing yourself to depositing the money to cover that check before it is due.

If you do send out a post-dated check, most creditors will hold it until the post-dated date arrives. They hold it because most banks refuse to accept a check if the date written on it has not arrived. However, on occasion, due to human error, post-dated checks are accepted and processed. When checks are accidentally processed before their due date, your account will be considered delinquent and insufficient balance charges will be assessed against your account.

Writing a Bad Check

Desperate times sometimes call for desperate measures. Having the heat turned off in January will, on occasion, cause even the most honest person to do whatever it takes to survive. Freezing to death vs. writing a bad check sounds like a pretty good trade-off. You know the check is bad when you write it, yet the consequences, in your mind, seem to somehow justify the crime. Using the term "committing a crime" might be a little harsh, but writing a check when you know there's not enough money to cover it is just that, a crime.

Most people who write bad checks are not concerned with the consequences; they react to a given situation and think about it later. However, if they did stop to consider the consequences, they just might reconsider. Most banks charge a fee for bad checks, referred to as returned checks, which is around $25 per check. In addition to the bank charges, the individual creditors or merchants can impose fines and, if they desire, pursue criminal charges. One final note: If the check was bad or returned because you put a stop payment on it for a legitimate reason, you will not be charged a fee by the bank.

Certified Checks and Cashier's Checks

Certified checks are sometimes called for when there is payment due on a legal contract such as the purchase of an automobile. If you need to pay with a certified check, talk to a bank teller. The teller will verify the funds in your account and then mark or stamp your check accordingly. At the time your check is marked certified, you no longer have access to those funds because the bank is guaranteeing to the name on the check that the funds are available for them.

Cashier's checks are a less expensive alternative to certified checks and provide basically the same assurance. The difference is, a cashier's check is printed on the bank's own personal account and is preferred to a personal check because it is drawn by a bank against itself. If you have an account with the bank that you want to get a cashier's check from, all you have to do is write a check against your personal account. After the bank teller verifies the funds, the bank will give you a check drawn on its account. If you do not have an account with the bank, you will probably have to give them cash.

Important Things to Remember about Checking Accounts

As painful as it is to get an overdraft charge, make no mistake about it, repeatedly having checks returned for non-sufficient funds could be damaging to your credit report. If it happens often, creditors will report your payment as late. In addition, many companies and banks will charge you for returned checks, which makes writing a check with insufficient funds a very expensive endeavor.

When you get a check made payable to you, never sign it until you are inside the bank, and always use a pen, preferably black. If you sign before that time and lose it, anyone can write "for deposit only" on the back and deposit it in their account. Take no chances; sign your checks in the bank. Also, unless you are in the bank, never write a check payable to cash. If found, it can be easily deposited into another account or cashed.

Never become lackadaisical about writing checks, using ATM and debit cards, or recording information in your check register.

References

➢ *All About Credit: Questions (And Answers) About the Most Common Credit Problems*, by Deborah McNaughton

➢ *Checkbook Management: A Guide to Saving Money*, by Eric Gelb

➢ *The Complete Idiot's Guide To Doing Your Income Taxes*, by Gail A. Perry

➢ *Complete Idiot's Guide to Online Investing*, by Douglas Gerlash

➢ *Credit Problems You Can Fix, Those You Can't, Those You Take to Small Claims Court*, by Samual E. Hunt

➢ *The First Book of Investing*, 2nd Edition, by Samual Case

➢ *The First Book of Small Stock Investing*, by Samual Case

➢ *The First Time Investor*, 2nd Edition, by Larry Chambers

➢ *Pay By Check*, by Chan

➢ *The Small Investor: A Beginner's Guide to Stocks, Bonds, & Mutual Funds*, by Jim Gard

➢ *Solving Your Financial Problems: Getting Out of Debt, Repairing Your Credit and Dealing With Bankruptcy*, by Richard L. Strohm

➢ *Taxe$ For Dummie$*, by Eric Tyson and Daniel J. Silverman

➢ *What Every Credit Card User Needs to Know*, by Howard Strong

Part 5
When "It" Happens

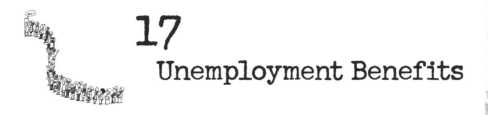

17
Unemployment Benefits

The purpose of unemployment benefits is to provide short-term, limited financial support for those who qualify while they search for another job. This state-operated program was not designed to allow people to build up benefits and then sit back and use them up, only to start working again just before the last benefit check is paid. Unemployment benefits are paid to those individuals who meet the prerequisites that will be discussed later in this chapter. Each state has an unemployment claims office that can usually be found in the phone book. Unless an employer is somehow excluded by statute from paying unemployment tax, which is very rare, employees are entitled to, and are covered by, regular unemployment insurance benefits.

Possible Exclusion

If you have been paid "under the table"—that is, without having any taxes taken out—you may still file a claim for unemployment benefits. However, before you decide to do this, you should understand a few things. First, your former employer may get into trouble for not taking out from your pay the required federal and Social Security taxes. Secondly, you may be asked to pay all of the back taxes that should have been taken out of your pay before you can collect any benefits.

There is something else to consider before you decide to file a claim that could result in benefits being questioned. The state could rule that you were, in fact, an independent contractor and therefore did not have an employer-employee relationship, which excluded you from being eligible to receive unemployment benefits. Finally, if you leave your employer to become a student or you are currently a student and not working, you may be excluded from receiving benefits.

If you are a full-time or part-time student and not looking for work, you will probably not meet the prerequisites for benefits. One of the criteria for receiving benefits requires that you actively look for work, which is hard to do as a full-time student. There are probably exceptions to this rule; however, if you are working and going to school, check with your state unemployment office for details.

Understand the Rules

Don't let other people try to explain to you how the unemployment system operates, because relying on advice from others could result in the loss of financial benefits for you. Unemployment benefits can be complicated, especially if you live in one state and work in another. Under many conditions, you are entitled to benefits regardless of where you have worked. For example, you can file in your home state against the state you worked in. You owe it to yourself to find out the rules from the unemployment benefits office, not from your friends.

Eligibility

If you have been laid off, make an appointment with your local benefits office and then be on time. When you see the unemployment insurance representative, he or she will ask you for the name and address of your former employer. If you were with that employer for less than six months, chances are you will need to provide additional employment history. Sometimes the previous employer is phoned on the spot to verify the reason(s) you were dismissed. You can never be sure what they'll say, so be prepared. Some employers issue a lay-off slip that is used as verification that you have, in fact, been laid off, and not fired. Your chances of receiving benefits with this type of documentation are very good. On the other hand, if you have been fired, your chances are slim.

Filing a Claim

While at the office, you will be required to fill out a ton of paperwork, so take your time and do it right the first time. Being called back to the office to clarify something or to provide more detail will only prolong your claim. When asked on the *application for benefits form* about what minimum wage you are willing to accept, write "the prevailing wage," even if you don't know what it is. The representative will inform you of the hourly wage that qualifies as the prevailing wage. However, if you have been working as a professional in some capacity and have been receiving a really good salary, then request an appropriate wage and not the prevailing wage.

If your claim is turned down, you will have the opportunity to appeal. If you win, you will be paid from the original date that your claim would have been approved from the beginning. If you lose the appeal, you had better start looking for work, and fast. This unfortunate situation is all too common, and unless you were able to save a little cash while you were working, times are probably going to get hard. Good luck!

Benefit Amount

If your claim is approved, your first logical question will be, "How much money will I get and for how long?" Your unemployment benefit amount is calculated based on your earnings in a past period of time, usually referred to as the "base period," which is about 52 weeks. If you have not worked the full 52 weeks, you may still be eligible to receive benefits. The total wages you earned in your base period determine your weekly benefit amount.

Benefits are based on the laws and regulations of the state in which you earned wages, and not the state you live in, if they are different. Benefit checks usually start about three weeks after you receive a confirmation letter. The good news is that, for the most part, your checks will come on a regular basis from that point on. The continuation of checks, however, is directly proportionate to how well you fulfill your obligation relative to actively seeking work and filing your paperwork out on time.

Your Obligation

Remember, you are supposed to be looking for work while receiving benefit checks. Some states send out benefit cards twice per month, asking you to list the places you've been to in pursuit of work. Be honest—if you're not, and you are confronted about a company that you listed but did not visit, you could lose your rights to this vital benefit and possibly face criminal prosecution.

Don't Procrastinate

Don't be foolish and wait until the last week before benefits run out to get serious about finding another job. Your benefits will probably be less than a regular paycheck, and even if they aren't, they will definitely run out. When they're gone, they're gone!

Unemployment insurance benefit checks are supposed to provide you with some short-term financial relief between jobs. Don't abuse it. If you do, you will be hurting yourself in the long run. For example, new creditors frown on people who have extended periods between employment. Being unemployed for a long time tells them that you are not very motivated and would probably be a risk. The same thought process is true for potential employers. Being out of work for three weeks is easier to explain than being out for three months. Also, your next prospective employer will ask what you were doing while you were receiving unemployment checks. Employers want dependable, hard-working, motivated people, so be smart and actively look for work while you receive benefits.

Throughout your working career, strive to maintain continuous employment. If you don't like your current job, find another one before you give up that steady paycheck. Finally, whenever possible, avoid the unemployment office, using it only as a last resort.

Federal Income Tax and Unemployment Benefits

Unemployment compensation could be subject to federal income tax. You must include any compensation in your total income to determine if you are required to file a return. When you receive a regular paycheck from an employer, they deduct taxes. However, when you receive compensation checks, nothing is deducted. This means you may have to pay estimated tax to meet your tax obligation. This is accomplished by sending a voucher each quarter to the Internal Revenue Service, along with a payment for the amount you estimate you owe. The formula used to calculate how much you owe is explained on the *Estimated Tax for Individuals* Form. Contact the local IRS office or the local library for the proper forms.

You should start paying estimated tax when you start receiving benefits checks. If you don't, you may owe a large amount when you file your regular return. It's possible that you could also be responsible for paying a penalty for underpayment of estimated tax.

18

Understanding Pawnshops

So, you need a little cash. If you don't have a house or car to use as collateral, or you have questionable credit and can't get a loan, you may consider a pawnshop as a source of last resort. Simply put, pawnshops can provide funds to people who are unable to secure a loan through a more traditional manner, such as a bank. Pawnshops lend money to people who are at least 18 years of age. The loans are made for different reasons and needs; however, unlike a conventional lender such as a bank, pawnshops ask no questions about what you are going to use the money for.

How They Operate

Pawnshops are operated by *pawnbrokers*, who lend money to be repaid within a specified period of time on the pledge, or *pawn*, of your personal property. Your personal property acts as a form of collateral, unlike conventional collateral such as a house or automobile. Loans are usually restricted to items such as stereo equipment, cameras, jewelry, musical instruments, computer equipment, and silverware. Most pawnshops throughout the United States require the same types of collateral; however, just to make sure, call and ask before you attempt to secure a loan. Loans are made only on articles that can be left as collateral with the pawnbroker. In other words, you must be able to deliver and leave your possessions with the pawnshop.

Buying From a Pawnshop

If you are thinking about buying from a pawnshop, consider that a majority of the items, if not all, were previously owned by someone else. You can never be sure what you're buying, although most good pawnbrokers inspect, clean, and repair the items prior to displaying them for sale. Ask if the items are sold *as is*. If they are, be very careful and, if practical, plug them in and check them out before buying. On occasion, you can really pick up a good value, with jewelry being your best value.

Before you Decide to Pawn

Before you decide to *pawn* something, it is important to note that you will probably receive only retail value for your property. Even if your item is new in the box, you will not receive what you paid for it. For example, a brand-new CD player still in the box might have cost you $400, but don't expect any more than $200. Pawnbrokers will not take a chance on losing money in the event you don't repay the debt. Therefore, the amount the pawnbroker offers is based on retail value, age, condition, plus an expected profit in case you default on the loan.

State Regulated

Pawnbrokers are subject to state regulations and municipal ordinances that control the rates of interest to be charged and the methods of disposition of the property that is unredeemed. Pawnbrokers have the legal right to retain items used as collateral until the loan is repaid. However, brokers are usually required to notify customers, better know as pawners, that the loan period has or is about to expire. This gives the pawner one last opportunity to pay the loan and collect their property. If, for some reason, the loan is not repaid within the specified time, the broker may sell the item to pay for the loan. However, the borrower/pawner has the right to redeem property at any time before a sale takes place.

The Loan

Pawnshops usually write loans for 30, 60, or 90 days, and accrue interest on a monthly basis. Many people start with a 30-day loan, which can usually be renewed at the end of the contract, if necessary. As a rule, on or before the due date, an interest payment is due for the last month or months. At this time, you may also reduce the principal amount in order to make the final payoff a little easier to handle. Make sure you ask if you can mail the payment, because some pawnshops may require the payment to be made in person and in cash.

In general, a loan may be repaid any time after it is made. When paying off the loan, the borrower may be required to have identification, especially if the loan reclaim ticket is missing. (Note: Prior to making the loan, find out what form of repayment is acceptable. Some brokers may not accept credit cards or personal checks.) As a rule, pawnshops like CASH.

Loan Default

If you do not redeem or renew a loan according to the terms of the loan, the item used for collateral becomes the property of the pawnshop. If the shop offers a period of leniency, it will most likely be stated on the loan agreement. Pawnshops want you to reclaim your items, because that was the premise from the onset of your transaction with them. Be honest with the pawnbroker, and expect the same treatment from him or her.

If you default on your loan, the merchandise to be sold is usually done so at auctions or directly to the public. In some cases, local codes require that, if merchandise has to be sold to satisfy a loan, any extra funds received above the amount necessary to satisfy the loan must be returned to the owner. Situations in which you would receive any money back are extremely rare, definitely the exception and not the rule.

Pawnshops in General

 Like any other lending institution, pawnshops want to make money and be fair in the process. Pawnbrokers are people just like you, and they are simply supplying the community with an alternative source for quick loans with no hassles and no questions. Getting a loan through a pawnshop may just be the easiest financial transaction you will ever make. For example, if you needed to get a short-term loan of $250 for say, thirty days, you might consider a pawnshop. Most banks do not want to process a loan for such a small amount and for such a short period of time. If you think that you need the services of a pawnbroker, take the time to ask about the payback period, interest rate, and general terms and conditions.

19
Personal Bankruptcy

Overview

Bankruptcy is the settlement of the liabilities of debtors who are entirely or partially unable to meet their financial obligations. The purpose of bankruptcy is to distribute, through a court-appointed receiver, the bankrupt's assets equitably among their creditors and, in most instances, to discharge them from further liability. Bankruptcy proceedings may be voluntary, initiated by a debtor (that's you), or involuntary, initiated by creditors.

A debtor has specific duties relative to filing a petition. These duties include providing a complete list of creditors, all assets and liabilities, an account of all current income and expenses, and a statement of their financial affairs.

After the petition has been filed, the clerk of the bankruptcy court sends a notice to the creditors listed on the petition. This notice informs the creditors of the bankruptcy and the date of the creditor's meeting and the time within which the creditors must act in order to participate in the bankruptcy. Once notified, a creditor must file a proof of claim within a specified time.

In many cases, the debtor is unable to pay all his or her debts, even if full value of his or her assets were to be sold off. This, as you can imagine, is an extremely painful and emotional situation for anyone to endure and should be avoided unless it is absolutely the only alternative—and even then with careful consideration.

Federal law prohibits creditors from threatening you, lying about what they can or will do to you, and invading your privacy. Federal law also allows you to stop creditors from phoning or writing you by simply demanding that they stop, regardless of how much you owe them.

Your local library most likely has a variety of books that can guide you through the bankruptcy process. However, if you can afford it, seek legal advice and read available information relative to bankruptcy prior to any legal action. The time spent will be well worth it.

Debts Usually Not Discharged in Bankruptcy

> Most federal, state, and local taxes

> Child support payments, current and late, and debts in the nature of support

> Restitution or fines imposed from a criminal proceeding

> Fees associated with filing for bankruptcy

> Recent student loans

Chapter 7 Bankruptcy

ROAD
TO
BAD CREDIT

The main reason a person files a Chapter 7 bankruptcy is to obtain a discharge that essentially gives the debtor a fresh start financially. However, the discharge applies only to the debtor's unsecured debts.

In Chapter 7 bankruptcy, a trustee gathers all the debtor's assets that are not exempt by state or federal law and distributes them in order to satisfy debts existing on the date the bankruptcy commences. The first order of business is to satisfy all the secured creditors whenever possible, giving them dollar for dollar for their claims. After the secured creditors have been satisfied, the administrative cost associated with the bankruptcy and certain other special claims, such as taxes and unsecured claims for wages, are paid. Last but not least, the unsecured creditors share equally in what is left over.

You have two classifications of property: exempt and nonexempt. Individual pieces of property may vary from state to state; for the most part, however, the following partial list represents what is considered to be exempt, or property that you can keep:

> Automobiles, unless they are extremely expensive or antique

> Necessary clothing, not to include furs

> Household appliances

➤ Your pension plan

➤ Most household furnishings

➤ Jewelry to a certain value

The following partial list is considered nonexempt, and you will most likely lose these items unless you can qualify for Chapter-13 bankruptcy:

➤ A second automobile

➤ Stamp, coin, and other collections of value

➤ Family heirlooms

Chapter 13 Bankruptcy

Regardless of your filing status, whether it is Chapter 7 or Chapter 13, the basic forms and associated paperwork are somewhat similar. Under Chapter 13, your debts could be discharged by paying all or a portion of them over time, say three to five years. Chapter 13 is a good option if you have a steady source of income to allocate for this repayment period. Unlike Chapter 7, you keep all of your property, both exempt and nonexempt, and use your income to pay all or a portion of what you owe. The courts, usually through contact with your attorney, will establish what your monthly payment will be. Deciding on that dollar amount is not up to you, so be prepared to live with the decision. Once the amount is settled, you will make payments directly to the bankruptcy trustee, who in turn distributes the money to your creditors.

If, for some reason, you cannot complete your Chapter 13 repayment plan, the trustee has the ability to modify your plan. For example, if two months after filing, you are paralyzed due to an accident and can no longer work, that type of permanent hardship might persuade the court to discharge your debts. However, if you are injured in an accident and miss a few weeks of work, you might be able to request that the trustee modify your repayment plan to allow you to get back on your feet. If the bankruptcy trustee does not discharge your debts, regardless of your physical condition, you have two basic options. Your first would be to convert, with specific requirements, to a Chapter 7 plan or you can have the bankruptcy court dismiss your Chapter 13 status and leave you in the same financial situation as you were prior to filing.

It might make you feel better to know that filing for any form of bankruptcy immediately stops your creditors from taking further legal action against you. This is definitely going to make answering the phone less stressful.

Post Bankruptcy Consideration

There are laws that protect individuals from some types of discrimination by government and private employers. Federal, local, and state government offices are prohibited from denying, suspending, revoking, or refusing to renew a license, permit, charter, franchise, or any other similar grant solely because an individual has filed for bankruptcy. Likewise, employers cannot terminate employees or otherwise discriminate against them solely because they have filed for bankruptcy. Laws are not as clear on the subject of a private employer not hiring someone because of bankruptcy. The laws only address cases in which employees are terminated because they filed for bankruptcy.

Some employers simply don't like having an employee who can't handle their finances. Although firing someone for this is unlikely, longevity with that employer could be shaky if they know an employee filed for bankruptcy. Why do some employers dislike employees that have filed bankruptcy? One reason is due in part to the increased potential for theft. An employee who has filed for bankruptcy needs money and therefore is presumed to be a greater risk with respect to stealing. Right or wrong, the perception of someone who is bankrupt is viewed as risky to some employers.

Apartment, condominium, and home owners will sometimes discriminate against you for filing. This is another post-bankruptcy consideration that is very much a reality and should be carefully considered, especially if you plan to move after filing for bankruptcy. Sad but true, this situation is played out every day throughout the country and could prove to be devastating if you are trying to move. Finally, obtaining any kind of credit could be difficult with a bankruptcy on your application.

A Glimmer of Hope

Despite the fact that bankruptcy will remain on your credit report for TEN LONG YEARS, after about three years of consistent payments combined with steady employment, your chances of obtaining new credit becomes much better. Many creditors realize that, occasionally, bad things happen to good people and some of those people are worth taking a chance on. There is much to consider about bankruptcy. However, if you have learned nothing else, remember that bankruptcy is serious business.

Other Means of Being Forced to Settle Debts

Writ of Execution on a Judgment: Once a debt becomes overdue, a creditor can file suit for payment in a court of law and, if successful, be awarded a *judgment*. If the judgment is not satisfied by the debtor, the creditor has the right to go back to court and obtain a *writ of execution*. A writ of execution, as used in this chapter, is when the plaintiff has won a court order directing an enforcement agent to sell the defendant's *nonexempt property* in order to pay the judgment against them. The writ, issued by the clerk of court, directs the sheriff or other officer to seize and sell any of the debtor's nonexempt property within the court's jurisdiction. The judgment is paid from the proceeds of the sale, and any balance is returned to the debtor.

Garnishment: The law permits the creditor, using the proper court procedure, to require persons owing creditors to turn over to the court or sheriff money owed or property belonging to the debtor. This method of satisfying a judgment for a creditor is called *garnishment*. The third party, called the *garnishee*, is legally bound by the court order. The most common type of garnishment is wages and bank accounts. The Federal Consumer Credit Protection Act limits garnishment of a debtor's wages to a specified percentage of their take-home pay and prohibits the debtor's employer from terminating him or her because of the garnishment action. Of course, not terminating an employee for garnishment is subject to debate. If an employer really wants to get rid of you, they can come up with dozens of seemingly legitimate reasons of doing so. Just as with bankruptcy, garnishment means you have less money and are therefore perceived to be a greater risk for theft.

Attachment: The statutory remedy for seizing a debtor's property under a court order is known as *attachment*. Some statutes allow attachment even before a judgment has been rendered. Statutory grounds for attachment prior to judgment are limited, usually due to the fact that the debtor is unavailable to be served with a summons or if there is a reasonable belief that the debtor may conceal or remove property from the jurisdiction of the court before the creditor can obtain a judgment.

In order to use attachment, the creditor must file with the court an affidavit attesting to the debtor's default and the legal reasons why attachment is being sought. The creditor must then post a bond sufficient to cover at least the value of the debtor's property, the value of the loss of the goods suffered by the debtor, if any, and court costs, just in case the creditor loses the suit. With the bond in place, the court then issues *a writ of attachment* directing the sheriff or other officer to seize nonexempt property sufficient to satisfy the creditor's claim. If the creditor's suit against the debtor is successful, the property seized can and usually will be sold to satisfy the judgment.

Real Estate Mortgage Foreclosure: When a mortgagor/debtor defaults under the terms of a mortgage agreement, the mortgagee/creditor has the right to declare the entire mortgage debt to be paid. This creditor's remedy for such action is called *foreclosure*. In many states, the creditor is required to sell the mortgaged real estate even if it's the person's homestead. This process is performed under the direction of the court, using the proceeds to pay the foreclosure cost and the balance of the debt. In the event there are any proceeds left over, they are given to the mortgagor. However, if the proceeds are insufficient to cover the costs of foreclosure and the remaining indebtedness, the mortgagor is liable to the mortgagee for the unpaid balance of the debt. This is a really bad situation to be in. You have just lost your home and you still owe on the debt. Under certain conditions and time limitations, the mortgagor can redeem the property by making full payment of cost, indebtedness, and interest.

Like bankruptcy, the other alternatives just mentioned will scar your credit report for a long time. Make absolutely every attempt to resolve your financial difficulties before they get out of hand.

20

Understanding the Rules of Small Claims Court

When you have a gripe with a person or business that is too small to justify the expense of a lawyer, yet too big to just say the heck with it, you could consider using the small claims court system.

Every state has a branch of its court system devoted to small claims court. This branch is also called "justice of the peace court," "magistrate's court," "county court," or "municipal court." There are probably other names; however, these are the most common. Procedures within these court systems are designed to be fair, fast, and functional.

Terms Used in the Small Claims Court System

To aid your understanding of the rest of the text in this chapter, take a few minutes and read the following terms:

- ➤ **Appeal**: A new hearing of the claims by the superior court.
- ➤ **Continuance:** A request to postpone a court date.
- ➤ **Costs:** Certain fees and charges a party pays to file and present a case or to enforce a judgment.
- ➤ **Damages:** Money claimed or awarded in court equal to the dollar value of the claimant's losses.
- ➤ **Default:** When a party to the lawsuit fails to attend the small claims court hearing.
- ➤ **Default Judgment:** A judgment entered when one party does not attend the small claims court hearing.
- ➤ **Defendant:** The person or business being sued.
- ➤ **Defense:** The defendant's facts or arguments that demonstrate why the plaintiff is not entitled to the relief requested.
- ➤ **Judgment:** The court's decision.

> **Judgment Creditor:** The party in whose favor a judgment has been awarded.

> **Judgment Debtor:** The party whom the judgment has been entered against.

> **Plaintiff:** The party who files the lawsuit.

> **Subpoena:** A writ commanding a person designated in it to appear in court.

> **Statute of Limitation:** The period of time following an occurrence in which a lawsuit must be filed.

> **Summons**: A written notification to be served on a person warning him or her to appear in court at a day specified to answer to the plaintiff.

Understanding the Rules

Small claims court primarily resolves small monetary claims or disputes ranging from around $2,500 to $7,500, depending on the state. The types of cases resolved in small claims court also differ from state to state. In general, claims involving landlords, loan default cases, and faulty repair work account for many of the cases. But no matter where you live, you cannot use the small claims court system to file bankruptcy, divorce, to file for a name change, guardianship, or to ask for an injunction to stop someone from doing an illegal act.

Each state has different rules for its small claims court system. To understand the rules of the system in your area, contact the clerk of court. The clerk knows all the current rules and procedures and is a virtual clearinghouse of information. To find the clerk, look in the telephone book under local government. There should be a listing.

Consider the Facts

Before you consider small claims court, give the facts of the case careful consideration. You don't want to waste the court's time as well as your own in trying to settle some insignificant matter with little to no facts or proof of wrongdoing. Remember, what seems to be right or wrong is not relevant; the court will be ruling on the legal aspects of the case only. You must be prepared to provide proof of all elements of your case, backing up each part with documents and/or witnesses. The first time the judge asks to see the receipt, invoice, bill, or statement of damages and you say "Um, I don't have it," your credibility as well as your case starts the long journey down the toilet of the judicial system.

Four Basic Elements of a Case

Once you have considered the facts in your case, the next step is to make sure the basic elements are present and can be proven with reasonable assurance. The following four elements are critical to any small claims case:

1. You must show that you have a legally binding contract with the other party. If you have a written agreement such as a lease, this element of your case is easy to prove. In the absence of a written contract, you will have to show that you had an enforceable verbal (spoken) contract, or that an enforceable contract can be implied for the specific circumstances of your case.

2. Be prepared to prove that you kept your end of the agreement by showing that you did what was required under the terms of the contract.

3. You must show that the other party failed to meet their obligation as outlined in the contract. This is usually the main part of the case.

4. Be prepared to show that you suffered an economic loss as a result of the other party's breach of the contract. Receipts and other forms of documentation are crucial.

Countersue

If you are being sued and you feel that the other party is really at fault, you can countersue or counterclaim. Depending on the state, if your claim arises out of the same event or transaction, you must countersue or forever give up the claim. For the most part, if the amount for which you countersue is under the limit of the state's small claims court, it makes sense to file it in the lawsuit initiated by the plaintiff. Before filing a counterclaim, check with the small claims clerk for specific rules.

Five Situations When Hiring an Attorney Should Be Considered

ATTORNEY AT LAW

The small claims court system is designed to be a *user-friendly*, no-experience-necessary type of process. However, certain situations justify the hiring of an attorney. Regardless of what your personal, preconceived notion of attorneys might be, and despite what jokes you might indulge in at their expense, you will have no greater appreciation and respect for what they can do for you than when you really need one. So, consider the following five scenarios that could justify hiring an attorney.

1. When proving your case requires the expert testimony of professionals and or subject matter experts in specific fields such as medicine.

2. When your case has been transferred/removed to a court of "superior" jurisdiction. In this case, having an attorney familiar with the rules of procedure and evidence is highly recommended.

3. When proving your case where fraud is the basis.

4. When there is much at stake and taking a chance is risky. Not spending a little money on legal fees can sometimes prove to be an unwise decision.

5. When, after considering your options, you just don't want to attempt it on your own. If you are the type that gets nervous talking to people or you think that you will become angry and violent while explaining your case to a judge, then consider hiring an attorney.

What Happens After You File Your Claim?

After you have completed your *statement of claim* or *complaint*, the clerk will send a copy to the constable, marshal, or sheriff to be served on the defendant(s). A summons will be attached to the claim, which simply states that the party is being sued. The person/defendant being served with the summons has, depending on the state and local rules, between ten and thirty days to respond. If they fail to respond in time, a judgment will be taken against them. In essence, by not responding, the defendant has lost. If, on the other hand, the person cannot be located for whatever reason, you, as the originator of the claim, will be notified by the court. At this point, it will be up to you to find another address or location where the summons can be served. The decision to pursue the matter any further is entirely up to you at that point.

Subpoenas

Depending on your case, you might consider getting a subpoena(s) for your witnesses. Discuss the need to have subpoenas with the clerk and find out about the necessary paperwork to request them and processing fees, if any. It doesn't matter if your witnesses are friends, family, or strangers—if you want to make sure they show up, consider using the court-supported subpoena approach to help you. Besides, even if someone wants to be there for you, sometimes getting off work can be made much easier if the person has a subpoena to back up his or her request for time off.

If you want specific documents as well as witnesses, you should consider the type of subpoena that requires the person to bring with them any documents or *things* that would help you support your case. If there is a charge for this type of subpoena, consider how important the document or thing is before shelling out the cash.

Can You Believe It? I've Been Sued

After the sheriff walks away leaving you with a piece of paper in your hand and a blank look on your face, it's time to pull yourself together and make some decisions. For some people, being sued comes as a total surprise; for others, they knew it was only a matter of time. Regardless of the circumstances, what you do and how quickly you do it can make all the difference in the world.

After you have collected your thoughts, sit down and thoroughly read the claim against you. Somewhere on the document the time required for your response will be noted and should be taken seriously. Even if you think the allegations are totally without merit, you still need to respond. Failure to respond in the allotted time will most likely cause you to lose your rights to contest the plaintiff's claim. If you are not required to appear, and only a written response is necessary, make sure you mail it out on time. Your formal written response, or *answer*, as it is referred to, should be mailed out as soon as possible, but not before you make a copy for yourself.

Remember, the allegation(s) listed on the statement of claim is just that, allegation(s) until proven otherwise in court. At this point, the only thing that is true is that you have been sued. If you need a few hours to calm down, take them before you do something foolish. Whatever you do, don't contact your accuser while you're mad. This will only enrage you further and, most likely, make you feel worse. Instead, collect yourself and read the document again, focusing on the specific allegation(s).

If the allegations are true and the plaintiff is right, take my advice and pay the claim. If you do not contest the claim and pay the plaintiff, no judgment will be entered against you. This makes a difference relative to your credit report, because your credit report will not show a judgment. With this in mind, if you are going to pay the plaintiff, make sure they enter a consent agreement or consent order to make it official. Once you have decided to pay, don't just drive by to see your accuser and hand over a wad of cash. If you do, don't be surprised if you have to appear in court and pay it again. If you hand over the cash to the plaintiff and have no receipt in the eyes of the court, the transaction never happened. If you decide to pay, use a personal check or cashier's check to act as a record of the transaction and require the plaintiff to give you a receipt. Just short of an official receipt from an accounting book, a sheet of paper with the amount, name(s), and date on it is better than nothing at all.

If the complaint against you is partially right, respond accordingly in your answer to the court. For example, if the plaintiff says you owe $1,200 for a service performed and the fee is $900 and you can prove it, detail why it is a lesser amount in your response. However, if you do so, be prepared to produce documentation to back up your statement. If, in reality, the plaintiff owes you more money than they say you owe them, state that in your response in the form of a counterclaim. If this is the case, you will first have the task to act as a defendant and then go on the offensive to prove why they owe you money. This is not as easy as being a defensive lineman who stops a running back at the line of scrimmage, takes the ball away, and runs for a touchdown. You will need to have adequate documentation to handle this daunting task.

If the claim is absolutely without merit and you know it without a shadow of doubt, state that in your response to the court. However, be prepared for a fight come court day. Regardless of the claim or your decision to file a counterclaim, you still need to answer the claim against you. So, write out your thoughts and respond accordingly. Even if your answer is, "I deny all of the allegations as stated on this claim against me," this response is better than nothing at all.

There are certainly other circumstances and situations involved in claims against defendants; however, the best approach is to be reasonable, honest, and responsible for your actions. Remember, depending on the claim, your chances of winning and the dollar amount or the damage to your credit report, if you lose, should not be underestimated. The long-term ramifications of a black mark on your report should be considered throughout your overall decision-making process.

Dealing With Fraud

When something sounds too good to be true, it probably is; and when a deal is just too good to be true, let the buyer beware. Seldom are things as they appear, especially when they seem like once-in-a-lifetime deals. However, despite countless warnings, many people fall prey to frivolous deals and scams every day.

Basically, fraud occurs when someone plans to deceive you and then succeeds at doing so. When this occurs, and it occurs much too often, people find themselves hurt, embarrassed, ashamed, angry, and sometimes in court screaming for justice.

The difference between cases of fraud and other small claims cases is that fraud cases sometimes award the victor *punitive* damages, also called *exemplary* damages. These types of damages are above and beyond the base claim and are meant to punish the perpetrator of the fraud. The judge awards punitive damages on a case-by-case basis and the amount is limited to the court's jurisdiction. To help the judge make a good decision, state your case in such a manner that the judge can ascertain how the fraud has affected you. Although courts are not in the business of protecting people from making bad decisions, they do aid in the prosecution and recovery of fraudulent acts.

To be successful at winning a case of fraud, you will need to do the following:

➤ Prove that the offender made a false representation to you.

➤ Prove that at the time of the false statement, the offender knew it was false and intentional.

➤ Prove that the offender intended you to rely on the misrepresentation.

➤ Prove, somehow, that you did in fact rely on the misrepresentation

➤ Prove that you were damaged as a result of relying on the misrepresentation

15 Common Sense Rules

In general, the law is applied uniformly throughout the United States, with many decisions being based on thousands of cases that have been ruled on in past similar situations. Thousands of people file small claims cases every year with the hopes that the court system will somehow see things their way. The following common sense rules are provided to help you evaluate your desire to file a small claim. Try to remove your emotions from the facts at hand and consider just for a moment what is fair and what is right.

1. When it comes to other people's property, treat it and deal with it at your own risk.

2. Don't complain about acts and situations that you have previously consented to.

3. Repair vendors and institutions are not required to give warranties. However, they can still be held accountable for being negligent or intentionally doing something wrong.

4. An accident is something that happened that was not intended to happen.

5. Unless someone prevents you from reading before you sign on the dotted line, you are bound by what you sign.

6. Businesses have an obligation to keep their premises safe for their workers and customers.

7. Know what the term "as is" means. There is no warranty on used goods unless the seller gives you one.

8. If you get something of value, plan to pay for it.

9. If you cause injury to person(s) or property, be prepared to pay for the damage.

10. If the document states that it is due by the first of the month, then paying on the second is paying late.

11. In general, a person can be held liable for their actions if those actions were foreseeable.

12. What someone will pay for something they want when they don't really need to is considered the fair market value.

13. When the seller passes a title to a buyer, a sale has been made.

14. A contract that no reasonably sane and honest person would make is rarely enforceable.

15. A corporation is a legal entity separate from the owners of the corporation.

Be Prepared

Be prepared for the other side's comments by trying to understand their side of the story, because the judge will be hearing their side as well. For example, if you are taking a former landlord to court for failure to return your $500 security deposit, have at a minimum the following documents:

➤ A copy of your lease highlighting the part that addresses the conditions under which the security deposit is to be returned.

➤ A copy, front and back, of your security deposit check.

➤ The initial walk-through of the apartment. (Note: It is customary for the landlord and the tenant—that's you—to have made a room-by-room assessment of the apartment, noting stains on the carpet, holes in the walls, cracked tile, and so on).

➤ A copy of the final walk-through of the apartment. (Note: As with the initial walk-through, both parties should have signed and agreed to this document as well.)

➤ Other relevant documents, such as correspondence between you and the landlord about damages.

What If The Other Guy Has an Attorney?

If you find out the other party has hired an attorney, don't run and hide. If your claim is relatively straightforward and you have good documentation, there is no reason to worry. The small claims court system was designed to be accessible to nonlawyers. Cases that involve lawyers are the exception, not the rule.

Sample Case

Just prior to moving out of your apartment, the maintenance man came by to fix a leaky showerhead. While he was there, his greasy boots stained the carpet, and during his repair, he cracked three pieces of tile. When you moved out, the landlord kept your deposit to cover replacement of the cracked tile and the cost of steam cleaning the carpet. If you have no documentation or proof that you did not cause the damage, your case will be difficult at best. However, if after the maintenance man left you immediately called the landlord and then sent out a letter detailing what happened, your case stands a much better chance. (Note: Make sure you send such a letter by certified mail or return receipt for your records.)

Be realistic: If you really don't have a good case with adequate back-up documentation and supporting facts, then you shouldn't consider small claims court. Don't gamble on the judge being able to see things your way. However, if you've done your homework and you feel that your case is strong, then start getting prepared right away.

Be Sure You Know Who to Sue

There is usually no question when you are suing a person, but what about a business? Is the business a partnership, sole proprietorship, or a corporation? I cannot overemphasize how important it is to know the answer.

If an individual owns the business, you have to be sure to sue the owner as well as the name of their business. For example, if you were suing a musical instrument shop called Guitars-Are-Us for damages to your guitar, you would have to know what kind of business ownership is involved. If Guitars-Are-Us is a sole proprietorship owned and operated by Eric Clapton, then your claim will be against Eric Clapton doing business as Guitars-Are-Us. If the musical shop is a corporation, you cannot sue the person(s) by name; instead, you have

to sue the corporation itself under the correct legal name. To find out this kind of information, you will need to put on your detective hat and start your search.

The county clerk's office will have on file the business name and who owns it. Prior to opening a business, individuals are required to obtain certain licenses and permits. These documents leave a paper trail, which makes it easier to find needed information.

Where To Sue

Contact the clerk of court's office for specific instructions on where to sue. The question of where to sue varies from state to state. Small claims courts serve different geographical areas. You must know where to sue prior to filing. A given court may encompass an entire county or just a small municipality. When you talk to the clerk, explain where the person or business is located and the basic facts of the case. From this information, the clerk should be able to tell you where to file your claim. Once you've found out where to file, you will need to visit the clerk's office for additional instructions. Oh, by the way, if you're the one suing, you have been labeled the plaintiff and the person or business that you are suing is referred to as the defendant. When you have filled out the paperwork, there will be a small fee to pay, usually somewhere around $50. From the time you file your claim and pay your fee, it could be from two months to six months, or even longer, before your case sees the courtroom, depending on where you live. Use this time to prepare.

How To Get Ready

While you are waiting on your court date, gather and organize all documents. Be sure you have considered what the defendant could counter with and plan a response. Planning for the other person's response is an excellent way to figure out what the judge will be hearing.

Don't be surprised if, after you have filed your case, the defendant contacts you and wants to either convince you that you don't have a case or possibly to offer a settlement out of court. Do not be intimidated, but be prepared to respond to either situation.

The Day of Court

In the event you were not able to settle out of court, get ready to fight. Arrive early on court day and become familiar with where you have to be and when. Do not be surprised if you see a lot of people outside the different courtrooms. This is not exactly a leisurely atmosphere. On any given day, several cases are being heard around the same time.

Dress casually but respectfully to the judge and court. If you're not sure what to wear, remember the dreaded "picture day" at school and go from there. When you speak, be respectful, always addressing the judge as "your honor" or "judge." Be civil, and don't interrupt, no matter what the defendant says to aggravate you. The judge will let you know when to present your case. When you do speak, take a deep breath and try to relax. Provide the facts in a chronological order. This will make your case appear organized, and the judge will appreciate that. Get to the point and be prepared to give the court any document it requests.

After the case has been heard, the judge will either deliver his ruling or announce that he reserves decision in the case, which really means he hasn't made a decision yet. If this happens, you will be notified of the court's decision, usually within a few days. Regardless of the ruling, instructions on the outcome and what is to take place will be detailed in the response letter from the court. Win or lose, you will have made your case in a court of law. If the decision is not satisfactory to you, it is recommended that you do not contest the outcome. If you had a well-prepared case with good documentation and you still lost, try to live with the court's decision.

Collecting a Small Claims Judgment

If you win your case, be prepared to collect the money yourself. The small claims court system does not collect money for you. Collecting from a reputable business or a respectable individual is relatively easy, because court-entered judgments against them are taken very seriously. However, if you win a judgment against some deadbeat, you might feel better about the victory, but actually collecting the judgment is another thing.

21
Medical Insurance

When you are young and healthy, it's hard to justify paying for medical insurance. You may feel that there are better things to spend one's hard-earned money on than medical insurance. Consider this, however: If you have to be admitted to the hospital for some reason, whom do you think is going to get stuck with the bill? That's right, the same person that has no insurance—you. Oh, by the way, don't think you can outsmart the insurance industry by purchasing insurance just before you're admitted. The insurance has this little thing called *preexisting condition* that will keep that from happening.

Why You Need Medical Insurance

Medical insurance is necessary because it provides financial protection for you. Not having insurance could mean going without medical attention or having to seek lower quality care. It also means you will have to pay the full cost of any medical services without being able to file a claim and be partially or fully reimbursed. This can be devastating, especially if there's a long hospital stay involved. Imagine you've had surgery and then follow-up physical therapy. You could have a combined bill for $5,000, $10,000, $20,000, or more. That's devastating. You could probably work out some sort of payment arrangement; however, you'd still be looking at paying back $200 to $500 per month. Insurance doesn't sound so bad after all, does it?

Medical insurance is essentially a gamble between you and the insurance company. The insurance carrier is betting that, over the long run, it will collect more money in premium payments than it will have to pay out. You, on the other hand, are counting on those benefits being available if you should ever need them.

Basic Types

There are two basic types of coverage, *group* and *individual*. The terms, premium costs, conditions, and limitations of these policies vary from provider to provider and from policy to policy.

Group insurance provides benefits to a group of individuals who are eligible due to their relationship to a particular organization or company. Group insurance is sold mainly to employers, many of whom pay all or a portion of the premium. Some policies even extend to family members such as spouses and children. If you are working for a company that offers a group medical insurance plan, take full advantage of it, because the cost will probably be less than finding a policy on your own. Another advantage of a group policy is that the cost will most likely be deducted from your check. This authorized deduction will keep you from sitting down once a month and writing a check.

Group insurance through employers usually ends when you leave the company, although in some cases there are *continuation* and *conversion* options. These options provide a couple of things. First, they are designed to help you by providing coverage while you are between jobs. Secondly, depending on the policy, they also allow you to continue your coverage with the same insurance company even after you leave. However, your monthly premium is most likely going to increase, because your employer will no longer be paying any of the cost.

Individual health insurance, sometimes called personal insurance, is sold to individuals and families. Coverage, limitations, terms and conditions, and premiums vary significantly, so shop around and compare. Unlike having a policy through your employer, purchasing a policy on your own requires you to deal exclusively with the insurance carrier or its authorized agency. With many companies, a human resource representative could assist you with problems or questions—not so when you're on your own.

Base Plan and Major Medical

Base plan insurance includes benefits for hospitalization, hospital services, supplies, X-rays, laboratory tests, and medication. Generally, this plan pays a certain amount per day while you're in the hospital, up to a maximum amount as defined by your policy. Most surgical procedures are covered in a base plan, with the exception of cosmetic surgery. In addition, base plans usually provide coverage for physicians' fees in the hospital and at their offices.

As with any type of insurance, there are limitations relative to the amount of coverage. Most, however, will pay what is referred to as *reasonable and customary* costs. Expenses above those reasonable and customary are not covered and, therefore, will have to be paid by you, the policyholder. "Reasonable and customary" refers to a range of services for which the insurance company would limit or exclude for payment. A simple example would be a physician charging $100 for an office visit when reasonable and customary fees for that service are only $85. In this case, the insurance company would notify you of the cost discrepancy and pay according to the standard $85 fee. You would have to pay the extra $15 out-of-pocket plus any portion that the insurance company did not pay. Understanding how policies pay is another reason why you really need to understand medical policies before you decide on the one that's right for you.

Major medical insurance is just what is sounds like: protection for serious illness or injury where costs can range from $250,000 to $1 million. Deductibles and coinsurance are associated with major medical because, without them, the premium cost would be significant and unaffordable to most people.

The deductible amount is the amount that you, the beneficiary, would have to pay before the insurance company would start paying. These deductible costs are usually paid on an annual basis, with somewhere around $200 per year being a standard amount. Depending on the policy, deductibles work like this: If your medical bill is $1,000, you must pay the first $200 of that cost and the insurance company, depending on the illness or injury, would pay either all or a portion of the $800 balance. However, once the deductible is paid for the year, again depending on the policy, subsequent bills are paid with no deductible being required from you, the policyholder. In other words, after you pay that first $200 deductible, the next $1,000 bill would be paid without any deductible payment from you. Many standard policies have a $200 per-person, per-year deductible.

Coinsurance is the fixed percentage that the insurance company will pay after the deductible has been satisfied. Some plans pay 50 percent, while others pay 80 percent of the cost. Using the previous example, the balance after deductible was $800, so if the plan pays 80 percent, $640 (80 percent of $800) will be paid by your insurance company and the remaining $160 is your responsibility.

Most policies have a *stop-loss* clause or provision that limits the amount of money that an insurance company will pay either in a given year or over the life of the policy. Some policies have a $1 million lifetime limit, and every time a bill is submitted for payment, the remaining amount payable is listed on the statement. For example, the statement might read, "You have used $8,543 against your lifetime limit of $1 million."

How to Decide on the Right Policy

Before you can determine what policy best suits your needs, you will first have to consider all the information covered in this chapter. You will also need to understand what your medical history is. Your medical history is more than just your past and current medical conditions. It also includes the medical history of your parents and, in some cases, your grandparents. For example, if your parents have cancer and your grandparents also have cancer, the likelihood exists at a higher than normal rate that you, too, might develop cancer sometime in your life. With that in mind, the policy you select should have a relatively large amount of coverage. It could also be more expensive, depending on the insurance underwriter who reviews your application for insurance.

When trying to make a decision, consider the variations of policies offered by the different carriers. Policies and their content can be complicated, so before you make any decision, decide on what you really need. The following partial list of questions should be considered throughout your selection and decision process:

➤ What outpatient services, if any, are available and what are the coverage limitations?

➤ If you are denied coverage on initial application, when can you reapply?

➤ How comprehensive is the coverage, and what does it include and disallow?

➤ What special services are included, like rehabilitation, mental illness, and so on?

➤ Is the policy renewable and, if so, will the premium change?

➤ How much are the monthly premiums?

➤ What percentage of the charges is paid, for example, 50 percent or 80 percent?

➤ What is the deductible amount, and how is it applied to a charge from a provider?

Medical Terms and Definitions

The following is a partial list of standard medical terms and definitions that will help you when researching a medical policy:

➤ **Allocated Benefits**: The maximum amount payable for a specific service as itemized in the policy contract.

➤ **Beneficiary:** The person designated or provided for by the policy terms to receive the proceeds upon the death of the insured.

➤ **Benefits:** The amount payable by the insurance company to a claimant (that's you) or to the party to whom the payment is assigned.

➤ **Certificate of Insurance:** A statement of coverage detailing the provisions of the policy issued to an individual insured under a group.

➤ **Claim:** An application or form used to request payment from the insurance company as provided for by the policy.

➤ **Contributory:** A group insurance plan issued to an employee under whom both the employer and employee help pay the cost of the plan.

➤ **Co-payment:** The amount you must pay for a service or benefit as provided for by the plan.

➤ **Covered Charges**: The amount of expenses covered by the plan.

➤ **Deductible:** The amount you must pay before the plan pays benefits.

➤ **Disability:** A limitation of physical or mental functional capacity resulting from injury or sickness.

➤ **Effective Date**: The date the insurance policy begins.

➤ **Eligibility Date:** The date on which an individual member becomes eligible to apply for insurance under the insurance plan.

➤ **Eligible Employee:** Those who meet the eligibility requirements under a group health insurance plan.

- **Eligibility Period:** The specified time following the eligibility date during which an individual member of a particular group will remain eligible to apply for insurance under a health insurance policy without evidence of insurability.

- **Grace Period:** Time period after a payment is due during which the policyholder may make payment without penalty or loss of benefits.

- **Health Maintenance Organization (HMO):** An organization that provides a wide range of health-care services from a specified group of providers at a fixed payment.

- **Lapse:** The termination of a policy for failure to pay the premium within the specified time required.

- **Limitations**: Statement in the policy that indicates what supplies or services are not fully paid for.

- **Long-Term Disability Income Insurance:** Insurance payable to provide a reasonable replacement of a portion of an employee's earned income lost through serious, prolonged illness or injury during his or her normal work career.

- **Maternity Care**: Prenatal and postnatal care and delivery by a covered hospital, physician, or other covered practitioner, including a nurse or midwife.

- **Outpatient Services:** Care provided to a person in an outpatient department of a hospital, in a clinic, another medical facility, or in a doctor's office.

- **Policy Term:** The period for which an insurance policy provides coverage.

- **Pre-admission Certification**: The process whereby you or your doctor is required to contact the policy provider before admission to a hospital. Your plan determines the appropriateness of the admission and the length of stay by using established medical criteria.

- **Preexisting Condition:** The physical or mental condition of an insured person that first manifested itself prior to the issuance of their policy.

- **Reasonable and Customary Charge:** One of two benefit maximums that plans use as the amount of your medical expenses they will cover for a particular service.

➤ **Reinstatement:** The reestablishment of coverage after coverage has lapsed.

➤ **Waiting Period:** The time between the date of the enrollment or application and the actual date the policy is effective.

Health Maintenance Organization (HMO)

HMOs are usually the cheapest form of health care. As a member of an HMO, you pay the least per visit, sometimes referred to as co-pay, and in monthly premium costs. The downside of the HMO is their reputation for providing only the minimum services when you are being seen by an HMO doctor. Another limitation is the list of physicians from which you can choose. Most HMOs provide you with a list of physicians that you must see, depending on the need. The HMO pays the physicians on that list, so don't expect to get the best of everything. The doctor decides what tests or procedures are necessary and whether referrals should be made for other services. If you are lucky enough to convince an HMO doctor to send you to a specialist, they will be using the *list* in choosing the referral physician. If you know of a better doctor who is not on the list and you are determined to see him or her, expect to pay a larger percentage of the bill. However, HMOs are usually better than conventional insurance carriers by paying for and providing good preventative services. The thought there is that by paying to keep you healthy, you will cost the HMO provider less money over time.

Still More to Remember

It's possible that your parents' medical insurance policy will cover you for a short time after you leave home. Of course, there are a variety of prerequisites and exceptions that could apply to that type of coverage. However, if the coverage is available, stay on that policy for as long as you can or as long as your parents will allow, whichever comes first. If your parents' policy doesn't cover you, start calling around for rates and policy information. No matter what policy you end up with, just accept the fact that, like auto insurance, you will probably have medical insurance for the rest of your life. This probably doesn't make you feel any better right now, but it will someday give you much peace of mind.

22

Traffic Court

"I Hope That's an Ambulance Behind Me"

How many times in your short driving career have you been riding along and noticed flashing lights behind you, only to find out that it was just an ambulance wanting to pass? Well, if it hasn't happened yet, it probably will. Either way, seeing those lovely lights in the rearview mirror can conjure up that sick feeling that only the thought of getting a traffic ticket can give you. Even if you consider yourself a good driver, chances are that one day the local police department is going to pull you over for a little chat about your driving habits. Knowing how to deal with this encounter is what this chapter is all about.

Pull Over

The name of the agency that enforces traffic laws for each state may differ. One state might have a Department of Motor Vehicles, while another will regulate through a Department of Public Safety. Regardless of what these departments are called, they perform basically the same function.

When you see the lights flashing behind you, prepare to pull over. If the policeman just wants to get around you, let him pass. However, if it's you he's after, he'll stay behind you until you pull over. To increase your chances for a pleasant encounter, pull over as soon as possible. As a rule, you are supposed to pull off on the right shoulder in a clear area. If you are in the far-left lane and the policeman is behind you, turn on your right turn signal and start working your way over. This will show the officer that you are trying to comply, thus easing any concern he might have about you wanting to evade his authority. Never give the local police or state trooper any reason to question your intentions. Once you have safely made it to the right side of the road, come to a complete stop and turn the engine off.

If you are pulled over in the daytime, stay in your car and let the officer approach you. If it's nighttime, he may direct you to get out and move to the rear of your car, all the while shining a light on you. If you are riding with someone who is pulled over, remember that the officer wants only the driver to get out, so stay in the car unless told otherwise. Many policemen are killed each year as a result of routine traffic stops. No matter how non-threatening you think you are to the officer, according to him, you could be an armed robber or drug dealer willing to shoot if provoked. Once you are pulled over, be careful how you react. Keep your hands on the steering wheel and remain still unless directed to do something else. If the officer wants you to get out, do so slowly and keep your hands where they can be easily seen.

Some people become highly agitated when they get pulled over, while others pull out their pocket version of the United States Constitution and start rattling off their rights. Use a slightly different approach—one which could work in your favor, depending on the reason you were pulled over. Be polite and cooperative by letting the officer speak first and then by complying with his request. Remember, this individual is just doing his job, nothing more, nothing less. So don't have an attitude and give the officer a reason to tighten the legal system around your neck.

Listen First, Talk Later

Now that you have pulled over and stopped, be prepared to answer some questions. Most of the time, the officer will start off by requesting to see your driver's license, registration, and proof of insurance. If the officer walks back to his patrol car, he is probably going to be calling in your license and registration information for confirmation. If he stays next to your car, he is probably going to do one of two things: write you a ticket right off the bat or give you a warning. Of course, he could be writing your ticket in the patrol car after he calls in your license. It's hard to tell what's going to happen; however, if he is considering a warning, your attitude and willingness to cooperate could weigh heavily in his decision. Follow his instructions and let him finish the initial line of questioning. It's best to let him do his job without interruption at first.

The first thing out of your mouth should be polite and respectful. Each situation will be different, so respond accordingly to what has just taken place. There are no magical words that can erase the officer's actions to this point, so don't waste your time and his by trying to do so. At the same time, be careful about what you say in respect to the traffic violation, if there was one, remembering that what you say can be used against you in traffic court. If you were stopped for traveling 65 in a 25 zone, expect to get a ticket unless you are bleeding to death or taking your wife to the hospital. Even under those circumstances, it's not a given that you won't be ticketed once you arrive at the hospital.

A friend of mine gave the worst excuse I have ever heard for speeding back when I was about 20 years old. I was riding to work one day with a friend who would do anything to keep from being late for work. One day, about five miles from the job, his tire blew out, but he refused to stop. Instead, he started speeding up faster and faster. As I was about to question his mental stability, 5-O turned on his lights and tried to pull him over. My friend didn't stop until we were in the parking lot at work. Here's the good part. His excuse was, "Officer, with a flat tire, the only way you can keep it from going completely flat is by speeding up and allowing the centrifugal force to keep air in the tire." After shaking his head, the officer wrote him a ticket. The good news is, we were not late for work.

Oh Boy, I'm Getting a Ticket

If the kind officer decides to give you a ticket, just accept it. You have the option to fight the ticket in court, but for the time being, just sign it and drive on. Avoid a verbal confrontation with the officer, don't plead like a whimpering little kid, don't argue, and don't challenge the officer's decision to give you the ticket. And forget about trying to bribe the officer into letting you go. Remember, the patrol car probably has a dash camera and will likely record the entire ordeal. Don't make matters worse for yourself. After the 6'4" twenty-five-year veteran of the police force explains the nature and violation for which you are being ticketed, respond with humility and then sign on the dotted line. On the other hand, if the officer has not yet written the ticket and is just telling you why you were pulled over, then your initial response could be the difference between getting a ticket or walking away with a warning.

Signing the ticket is not an admission of guilt; it is merely a written confirmation from the officer relating to your violation. Depending on the violation, you may be asked to turn over your driver's license. If this happens, the ticket you get for the violation acts as a substitute license until you appear in court. The court date, as well as the time and location, will be on the ticket. Make sure you know where it is and how to get there. Don't even think about refusing to give the officer your license, because if you do, you will likely end up in jail wondering who to call to bail you out.

Search and Seizure

Just in case you didn't know it, the United States Constitution provides some protection against invasion of privacy and improper search and seizure. However, despite what the Constitution says, your rights may be voided under certain circumstances. For example, if there is evidence of a crime or an illegal substance in "plain view," an officer has the right to search your vehicle and take possession of the contraband. So, if you are going to be traveling with a grenade launcher and fifty pounds of crack cocaine, make sure you put them in the trunk.

If the local policeman has reasonable grounds to suspect that you have committed a crime or are about to, then you may be frisked for a weapon or searched more thoroughly. For example, if you are sitting in your car behind the First National Bank of Oz at 4:30 in the morning, don't be shocked if you look suspicious to a drive-by patrol car.

Driving Under the Influence/
Driving While Intoxicated: DUI/DWI

Under certain circumstances and in certain states, you could have your car searched if you are being arrested for driving under the influence (DUI). There are other conditions in which your car can be searched after being arrested; however, at that point there is little you can do once the handcuffs are slapped on. Whether or not the search was legal will be a subject for your defense attorney to figure out.

If your car is being impounded, it could be searched from top to bottom. Laws vary, so before you get too excited, realize that the officer probably has a better working knowledge of what he can do than you do.

Driving under the influence, or driving while intoxicated, includes alcohol, drugs, and even prescription drugs. If you are driving unsafely or erratically, you could be pulled over for *probable cause*. If this happens, the officer may require you to get out and perform several activities to determine your mental capabilities relative to driving a car safely. These dexterity tests are designed to see if a driver is fit to drive a car. If the officer smells alcohol or drugs, your chances of being there for a while are high.

If it is determined that you are under the influence or intoxicated, you could be arrested and taken to jail. The situation after that gets worse, with large fines, jail time over the weekend or longer, skyrocketing insurance premiums, and the suspension of your driver's license for six months or so. Right about now, you're thinking that a designated driver policy sounds pretty good.

Take my advice, if you get a ticket for DUI, get an attorney. A DUI is a misdemeanor that will be recorded, giving you a permanent police record. Depending on whether or not you have prior tickets of a similar nature, or any tickets for that matter, the outcome could be determined by how good your attorney is. This misdemeanor will come back to haunt you for years to come, so be careful. Most job and loan applications ask if you have ever been convicted of a crime. Up until now, the answer was probably no.

Out-of-State Tickets

What happens if you are given a ticket out of state? For the most part, expect the same basic treatment. The out-of-state police department will notify your home state's Department of Motor Vehicles or Department of Public Safety. They do that as a courtesy to you. After all, they want you to get full credit for your driving habits while driving through their lovely state; isn't that considerate of them? But how about your insurance company? Won't you need to call them so they can raise your premium? Relax, the out-of-state notification process is very efficient. You're in good hands!

Drug and Alcohol Test

I'll bet you thought there would be no more tests after you graduated from school. Guess again! On occasion, after being pulled over, an officer may want you to take a quick dexterity test to examine you for possible drug or alcohol usage. If the officer smells alcohol or drugs on you, or in your car, or if you are acting peculiarly, you could be asked to take more dexterity tests. If the officer sees that you are having difficulty in performing relatively simple activities, like walking a straight line or reciting the alphabet, then you will most likely be given either an alcohol or a drug test.

A quick preliminary test for alcohol is the Breathalyzer test. If more testing is required, they will not be asking you, they will be telling you. If you refuse to take a drug or alcohol test, you will likely be considered guilty in the eyes of the court. Also, if you refuse, you could be arrested and taken to jail. If you are alone, or the passenger(s) with you are also questionable drivers, the police officer will probably tow your car away. Once the car is towed away, it will be searched and any illegal items found will be inventoried and potentially used against you, come court day.

Suspension of a Driver's License

Each state has its own list of offenses that meet the criteria for suspension. However, no matter where you are, at least some of the following criteria apply nationwide:

➤ Being ticketed for DUI

➤ Driving a vehicle involved in a hit-and-run accident

➤ Leaving the scene of an accident

➤ Fraudulent usage of a driver's license

➤ Failing to report an accident that caused damage

➤ Driving without proof of insurance

Going to Traffic Court

When you get a ticket, you have the right to go to court. Consider your options carefully, because the outcome could result in jail time, huge fines, or a loss of driving privileges. The court you go to depends on the charge. Your case could be heard in municipal court or circuit court.

When you arrive at the courthouse *early*, proceed to the clerk's office or window for directions to the right floor and room, and to also verify the approximate time your case will be heard. Just as a reminder, dress appropriately for the occasion. If you are not sure what to wear, just remember the dreaded "picture day" when you were in school. When you find the right floor and room, go in and sit down. If you have an attorney, wait outside for him and take his advice. If you don't have an attorney, just sit quietly until your name is called. Hopefully, you have rehearsed what you are going to say. After the charges are read to you, you will have two options: to plead guilty or not guilty.

I Plead Guilty

If you don't have an attorney, ask the judge if you face jail time if convicted. Depending on the circumstances, you could be allowed to seek an attorney before you plead guilty. Be very careful if you do not have an attorney. At least research what kinds of penalties are handed down for the charges you face. This is no laughing matter; be very sure you know what you are doing before you decide to represent yourself in traffic court.

Going to traffic court is not a casual event in your life, so take it very seriously. When you plead guilty, you are admitting to the court that you committed the violation. If you plead guilty, the judge will tell you what your sentence is, or what the fine is, or both. Aside from the potential fines and imprisonment, you could be sentenced to attend traffic school. Don't even think about not going if sentenced.

The reason you should do a little research before going to court is because, if you are fined, the court usually wants its money right then and there. Be prepared to pay, or have a good excuse why you can't. Saving your money for a WWF pay-per-view event doesn't cut it. If your license was seized, you will probably get it back after you pay the fine. This is, of course, dependent on the charge, violation, and number of traffic offenses you have committed. If the judge wasn't planning on reinstating your license, at least ask for your license back with a *drive back and forth to work only* restriction.

Not Guilty

If you are truly innocent of the charge, or you did not do what the ticket is accusing you of, plead not guilty. However, when you plead not guilty, be prepared to go to trial. Most likely, after you plead not guilty, the judge will schedule your case for another date. If there are circumstances that will not allow you to be there on that day, request another date, with "request" being the key word. The extra time will allow you to think about getting an attorney or to start preparing your own defense. If you have witnesses and they are unwilling to come to court, the clerk of court can issue subpoenas.

In the event you cannot afford an attorney, and jail time could result from a conviction, the court may appoint an attorney for you. Remember, while you are preparing for your defense, the prosecutor is preparing his case. Expect to see the arresting or ticketing officer and witnesses on their behalf when you get to court.

Depending on the circumstances, you may be allowed to have a jury trial. If you refuse a jury trail, you cannot change your mind later. In the absence of a jury, only the judge will hear your case. On the day of the trial, the prosecutor will ask you questions if you decide to testify on your behalf. You have the right not to testify, so consider the option and make your decision carefully. Once both sides have given their respective arguments and closing statements, the judge or jury will decide the case. If you are found innocent, go home and be happy. However, if you are found guilty, the judge will inform you of your sentence and what you have to do next.

Avoid this time-consuming process by driving carefully and choosing not to drink and drive.

23

What to Do After an Automobile Accident

When an accident or loss occurs, regardless of whose fault it is, you must promptly notify the insurance company. Be prepared to give the insurance company the who, what, when, where, and how of what happened and if there was any damage or loss. In addition, you need to give a brief description of what happened and report the names of those involved, including any witnesses. If you were involved in a hit-and-run accident, or had your automobile stolen, you must also provide your insurance company with that information. This information is required by most policies, and failure to promptly notify them could jeopardize your claim. Reporting this information to the person who sold you the policy, probably the agent, is the same as reporting it to the company.

After the Smoke Clears

Your ability to remember the following steps are directly proportionate to how serious the accident is and whether or not you are badly injured. If you don't already have a pen and small notepad in your glove compartment, put one in there, it will come in handy on occasions other than writing down pertinent accident information. Depending on your physical condition and emotional state, try to remember the following steps immediately following an accident:

➤ If you or anyone else involved in the accident has a cell or car phone, make sure someone calls 911 and reports the accident. Whoever make the call needs to give the operator the location and physical condition of those involved in the accident.

➤ If the accident resulted in a rear-end collision, turn off the ignition and get out of the car as soon as possible. Due to the location of the fuel tank in proximity to the point of impact, fire and explosion are potential hazards. (Note: Regardless of impact location, always turn off the ignition after an accident to reduce the potential for fire.)

➤ Stay as calm as possible and get out of harm's way. Move to the side of the road and away from traffic.

➤ Unless you have collided with a tree, building, light pole, or animal, or you have run into a ditch, other people will be involved. When you talk to them, do not discuss who is at fault and never talk about the limits of your policy.

➤ If you have the presence of mind, get out that pad and pen from the glove compartment and write down the other driver's name, driver's license number, make/model/year/color of the car, and license plate number. While you are waiting for the police, write down other important information, such as your account of what happened; who was visibly injured or claiming to be injured; the date, time, and weather conditions; and anything else that you think might be important later.

➤ If you are taken to the hospital or you drive to a doctor shortly after the accident, make sure you save and organize any and all documents and receipts.

Notify Your Insurance Company

Once you have cooperated with the police investigation and you are safely home or at work, stop and call your insurance company. Contacting your insurance company as soon as possible after the accident does two things: It helps you give a more accurate description, because the accident is still fresh in your mind, and it meets a requirement as spelled out in most auto policies relative to reporting accidents. Also, the sooner you file a claim, the sooner your repair work or expenses, if any, can be attended to. To expedite the claim you should do the following:

➤ Cooperate with the company/agent as required by your policy throughout the investigation and any defense of the claim or settlement.

➤ Promptly send in copies of any notices or legal papers received in connection with the accident or loss.

➤ Visit a doctor for exams as required by the company and send your agent all copies.

➤ Provide written authorization for the company to obtain medical reports and other pertinent documents.

➤ Take reasonable steps to protect your car from further loss. For example, if you can drive the car home and the back window was shattered, place something over the area to keep water out.

➤ If your car was towed away or is non-operational, ask your agent about coverage for a rental car. You should know the answer, but either way, if you are entitled to a rental, make sure you rent the type of car that is included in the policy. If you rent a Mercedes Benz and your policy pays for a Pinto, be prepared to pay for the difference. Also, make sure you know how long you are entitled to use the rental and, by all means, save the paperwork.

➤ Allow the insurance company to inspect and appraise the damaged property before it is repaired. The company may want to inspect even if the vehicle has been totaled. This is usually done to begin assessing the current value of your auto in preparation for a settlement.

Drinking and Driving

Drinking is a reasonably acceptable social aspect of life and, unfortunately, young drivers such as you have taken notice of that acceptance. Even without alcohol, teen-aged drivers are involved in a large number of accidents, which is partially due to inexperience and the occasional peer pressure to drive recklessly. Drinking and driving is not only illegal, it is often deadly.

Contract for Life

The *Contract For Life* is a document drafted for parents and young drivers with specific guidelines, promises, and obligations. The following is a sample contract.

CONTRACT FOR LIFE

DRIVER: I agree to call you for advice and/or transportation at any hour from any place if I am ever faced with a situation in which a driver who is responsible for driving me home has been drinking or using illicit drugs. If I am the driver and have been drinking or using illicit drugs, I also agree to call for advice and/or transportation. I have discussed with you and fully understand your attitude toward any involvement with drinking and using illegal drugs.

Signature_____   Date_____

PARENT: I agree to come and get you at any hour, any place, no questions asked, and with no argument at that time, or I will pay for a taxi to bring you home safely. I expect we would discuss this matter at a later time.

Signature_____   Date _____

Effects of Alcohol on Driving

Alcohol is a depressant, which impairs the decision-making and control processes of the brain. Drinking alcohol slows down the activity of the brain, and when it is consumed faster than the body can dispose of it, a gradual build-up will take place. This build-up is called the blood alcohol concentration, or BAC. The BAC is usually stated as a fraction of one percent. Many states consider a BAC of 0.10 (unit of weight/percentage of volume) as legal proof of intoxication. However, BACs in lower levels, such as 0.02, still affect a driver's ability to operate a vehicle, therefore increasing their potential for an accident. Remember, the higher the BAC, the more the driver is impaired.

Even if you are smart enough not to drink and drive, realize that others may not be so bright. You are not alone on the highway, so stay focused. If you notice someone driving recklessly, protect yourself by driving defensively. Be alert—if the driver is behind you, let him or her pass; if in front, slow down and let the driver pull ahead. If the driver is really weaving and you have a car phone, call 911 and report the driver. You could be saving someone's life by making the call. In any event, stay away from them. Many drivers, although intoxicated, are not impaired to the point of weaving, which makes them even harder to spot. The inability to spot these drivers is dangerous, because at any time they could start driving recklessly and cause an accident. While you are driving, stay alert and drive defensively, because you can never tell when you will encounter a drunk driver.

Many drunk driving accidents occur after a social gathering such as a party where alcohol is consumed. If you arrive at a party with friends, make sure you have a designated driver for the ride home. If not, either plan to spend the night or just avoid alcohol altogether. Remember the *Contract For Life*. If you're the host of the party, refuse to serve alcohol to a guest who is obviously intoxicated or is soon going to be driving home. Avoid pressuring anyone to drink under any circumstance, especially if they are going to be driving. If you're hosting the party or just there having fun, never let an intoxicated guest leave when you know they are driving. Instead, make them stay until they sober up, call them a cab, or be a friend and drive them home yourself.

Bottom line, don't drink and drive!

Driving Record Point System

The insurance plan for which your policy is rated uses past accidents and convictions as part of the determination of your monthly premium cost. The driving record point system has been established so those drivers who have no points receive the lowest premiums. For the most part, each time you receive a ticket and are convicted of the violation or have an accident, you have points assigned to your record. The more points assigned to you, the higher your insurance cost grows. The time limit that the points remain on your record differs from state to state, so you will need to check with your agent for that answer. The following circumstances contribute the greatest number of points and should therefore be avoided at all costs:

- ➤ DUI/DWI involving alcohol or drugs or refusal to take a sobriety test
- ➤ Failure to stop and report when involved in an accident or leaving the scene of an accident
- ➤ Manslaughter, homicide or assault arising from the operation of a motor vehicle
- ➤ Reckless driving or driving to endanger the safety of others
- ➤ Driving without a valid driver's license or during a period when your license is suspended or revoked
- ➤ Racing or engaging in a speed contest
- ➤ Fleeing or attempting to elude police
- ➤ Committing a felony with an automobile
- ➤ Making a false accident report

➤ Lending a vehicle registration or driver's license to another person

➤ Operating a motor vehicle without the owner's authority

➤ Improper passing of a school bus

Lesser violations result in fewer points, although your goal should always be no points.

Protecting Your Car from Thieves

The best policy here is common sense and being aware of where you are. To help you protect your car, remember some of the following points and know what to do in the event something does happen.

➤ Before you get out of your car, store packages or valuables in your trunk or out of sight. Don't tempt a potential thief by displaying something that can easily be taken.

➤ When you park, look for a locked garage or a patrolled parking lot. If these areas are not available, at least park in a highly visible and/or well-lit area.

➤ Always remove your keys from the ignition and lock your car, even if you're going to leave it unattended for only a few minutes.

➤ Make it difficult for a thief to tow your car by parking with the front wheels turned sharply to the right or left and apply your emergency brake.

➤ Purchase and install a steering wheel locking device.

➤ Activate all anti-theft devices you have when not using the car.

In the unfortunate event that theft does occur, call the police and your insurance company as soon as possible. The quicker you notify them with accurate information, the better chance law enforcement will have in the recovery of your car or in apprehending the thief. When you call and report the theft, make sure you give them the make/model/year/color and license number. When it comes to protecting your car, you can only do so much. However, to stack the deck in your favor, use some, if not all, of the previous tips.

Stopping after you have seen an accident

If you are unlucky enough to drive upon an accident scene, there are many things to remember. If you decide to stop and help, first of all, pass well beyond the crash before signaling to pull off the road. By pulling past the wreck, you allow others to see what has happened. If you stop before the wreck, others may not see what is going on and you could be the cause of another accident. Now that you are off the road and out of the way, turn on your emergency flashers and raise your hood—this indicates trouble.

Carefully approach the accident while looking around for hazardous situations such as downed wires, leaking fuel, and fire. If any of the vehicles is running and you can reach the ignition, turn off the engine. This will reduce the chance of fire or explosion due to sparks and leaking fuel. (Note: Unless there is immediate danger, don't move an injured driver to get to the keys.)

If you have a cell phone or there is a phone booth close by, call 911 and stay on the line to answer all questions. Check for injuries by calling out to those in the cars and seeing if they are responsive. If they are moving, tell them to remain still until help arrives. Sometimes victims can injure themselves because they are in shock and are unaware of their injuries. Unless you are trained in first-aid procedures, just stay there until help arrives and try to calm the victims.

References

- *Automobile Accident Checklist*, by Jon R. Abele
- *Bankruptcy Step-By-Step (Barron's Legal-Ease Series)*, by James John Jurinski
- *Bounce Back From Bankruptcy: Step-By-Step Guide to Getting Back on Your Financial Feet*, by Paul L. Ryan
- *The Complete Idiot's Guide to Manager Health Care*, by Sophie M. Korezyk
- *The Confused Consumer's Guide to Choosing a Health Care Plan: Everything You Need to Know*, by Martin Gottlieb
- *Consumer Bankruptcy: The Complete Guide to Chapter 7 and Chapter 13 Personal Bankruptcy*, by Henry J. Sommer
- *The Educated Guide to Speeding Tickets: How to Beat & Avoid Them*, by Richard Wallace
- *Fight Your Ticket...and Win!*, 7th Edition, by David Wayne Brown
- *How to Talk Your Way Out of a Traffic Ticket*, by David W. Kelley
- *The Insider's Guide to HMOs: How to Navigate the Managed-Care System and Get the Health Care You Deserve*, by Alan J. Steinberg
- *Nolo's Law Form Kit: Personal Bankruptcy*, 2nd Edition, by Stephen Elias
- *Out of Debt: How to Clean Up Your Credit and Balance Your Budget While Avoiding Bankruptcy*, by Robert Steinback
- *Surviving an Auto Accident: A Guide to Your Physical, Emotional and Economic Recovery*, by Robert Saperstein
- *Traffic Ticket Defense*, by Mark D. Sutherland, Esq. and Chris Sutherland

Part 6
Life Skills
and Social
Necessities

24

A Few Good
Things to Know

Adversity

Have you every heard of the old saying, "There's only two certainties in life—death and taxes?" If you have, you could probably add another one to the list, placing adversity right after taxes. Adversity comes in many forms and degrees of difficulty, ranging from not having enough money to cover a check to experiencing the loss of a close friend or family member. In dealing with the two main certainties, death and taxes, you know that around April 15 of every year, taxes are due. The other certainty is death, and, well, there's nothing you can do about that, which leaves adversity as another unpredictable and therefore difficult situation to deal with.

Adversity can bring stress, uncertainty, and a sense of hopelessness. It also creates tremendous anxiety, frustration, fear, panic, grief, and sadness. Adversity makes you question life, the God you believe in, and, just as important, your self worth. When you experience adversity time and time again, you start to question your ability to bounce back and move on. If you can't seem to quickly overcome what has happened, then slowly, over time, you will become less confident and, therefore, less likely to deal with subsequent problems.

Although difficult to accept at times, you could look at adversity as one of life's great teaching tools. You see, life teaches us whether we want to learn or not; and some of life's lessons are hard to accept. With that in mind, you have some control over adversity by how you live your life. By working towards being selective and mindful about your relationships, jobs, your finances, and health, you can reduce the incidence of adversity. For example, the loss of a job often causes great adversity. So, by being a good employee, working hard, and being punctual, you can reduce the chance of being fired or laid off. The same goes with your finances: By keeping a close eye on your credit cards and personal spending habits, you might eliminate the adversity that comes from financial troubles like collections agencies, and bankruptcy.

When adversity strikes, don't say to yourself, "Why do all of these things seem to happen to me?" Instead, take responsibility for what has happened and stop thinking of yourself as a victim. For the most part, much of the adversity that you will experience can be traced back to something you have failed to do or not do. If you don't take responsibility for your actions, you will become complacent about what happens to you and, therefore, less likely to see what has to be done to make your life better.

When confronted with adversity, most people have a tendency to fear the worst. Think back to the last time you were faced with a difficult situation. How did you react? Was your life suddenly shifted into a state of temporary insanity, or were you calm and collected? In either case, remember that the first few hours of a difficult situation are the worst. That's the time when you are the most afraid and least likely to think things out. You might have thought, "How will I survive this or am I destined to struggle for the rest of my life?" In reality, when adversity strikes, most people usually start trying to resolve the issue right away. By the end of the day, most people will have started to consider their options and are well on their way to selecting the right one. Things always look the worst at first, but over time, a reasonable person can usually work things out.

The next time you are faced with difficulty, consider the following thoughts before you start to reason your way through:

> ➤ In the overall scheme of things, how does this situation affect the rest of my life?
> ➤ Will I remember this five or ten years from now?
> ➤ Consider what resources you have available, not the ones you don't.
> ➤ Realize that, in a few hours, the situation will probably not appear to be as bad.
> ➤ Remember that you can't always control what happens to you.
> ➤ Regardless of what has happened, you can't change it, so move on to how to make it better.

- ➢ Try to put the situation in perspective.
- ➢ If the adversity is about a loved one, try to remember the good things at first. There will be plenty of time to think about the bad.

So, how much of what you have just read will you remember and try to change about your ability to deal with adversity? Take my advice and stop reading for a while and just think about what you have just read. If you can conquer the frustration and fear that usually accompany adversity, you will live a much happier and more productive life. The only difference between those who fall apart when bad things happen and those who seem to put things together is their belief in themselves. If you confront adversity believing that you will be able to work it out, then you probably will.

Self-Esteem

Here are two pretty good definitions of self-esteem: the first is the way you see yourself, and the second is your own feelings of self-worth. These two simple definitions describe a very complex part of life. The complexity lies within the many factors that determine whether or not a person has a healthy dose of self-esteem. For example, some people are greatly affected by the opinions of those they respect, while others could care less. Also, some people cannot seem to concentrate and focus if they feel their efforts will not be appreciated; others try their best and move on.

To know whether or not you have a healthy portion of self-esteem, consider how many of the following statements you can agree with:

- ➢ I really don't have any need to put others down.
- ➢ For the most part, I can laugh at myself from time to time.
- ➢ When I'm criticized, I do not completely fall apart.
- ➢ I am relatively comfortable with who I am.
- ➢ I am relatively confidant in my own abilities.
- ➢ I do not become defensive when my work or opinions are questioned.
- ➢ When confronted with problems and setbacks, I can usually work them out.

➤ I am relatively confident about how I look.

➤ I do not have to constantly try to prove myself to anyone.

➤ I know how to be confident without becoming too overbearing.

If you can't honestly agree with the previous statements, then try to implement positive change in your life. Few things in life can negatively affect your ability to live a happy life and give freely and lovingly to those you cherish than having low self-esteem. If you don't think much of yourself and your abilities, don't expect others to either. If the self-esteem statements listed above are not prevalent in your life, start practicing the following steps as soon as possible:

➤ Rely on your opinion of yourself, instead of what others may think of you.

➤ Rely on your ability to make decisions.

➤ On occasion, take chances and stop being afraid of failure.

➤ Realize that you will make mistakes, and you will learn from them.

➤ Stop putting yourself down and start focusing on your good qualities.

➤ Recognize what your needs are and work to fulfill them.

➤ Set realistic goals and reward yourself when you achieve them.

➤ Learn to forgive yourself.

Low self-esteem can lead to depression and can keep you from reaching your true potential in life. Read these self-esteem building steps over and work on them on a daily basis. Soon, with a little effort, you will start feeling better about who you are and what you can achieve.

Conflict Resolution

Have you ever noticed the way some people deal with conflict? It's as if they have received special training on the subject. The way they seem to present themselves during the whole ordeal is as impressive as their ability to bring the situation to order and final resolution. If I'm talking about you, then stop reading and move on, because you have mastered a vital skill. If you don't think resolving conflict is a skill, then think again. Having the ability to resolve conflict successfully is a skill that requires the patience of a saint and the fortitude of an Army general. To help you hone your conflict resolution skills, consider working on the following steps:

➤ Always remember there will be at least two sides to every story. If you cannot accept that, you will never be effective at resolving conflicts.

➤ When a conflict is presented to you, stop what you are doing and listen. The first few sentences from the person presenting you with the conflict will usually be the most critical to grasp. You must take the time to listen.

➤ If you are the one bringing conflict to someone, make sure you can control your emotions. People have a tendency to talk back in the same manner in which they are talked to. So, if you're firm and controlled, they will most likely respond to you in the same manner. However, if you jump in with both feet and start yelling, expect the same response from them. Of course, there will always be those personality types who will yell back regardless of how you confront them. Still, the advantage will be yours if you can remain somewhat calm, because you will be able to think and react more rationally.

➤ Try to examine the conflict piece by piece and identify the root cause of the problem. The faster you can do this, the better off you'll be.

➤ When you initially get involved with someone to resolve a conflict, make sure you have the time to somewhat work through the issues. Do not just lay out your side of the story and walk away. Hear the other person out and start the resolution process as soon as possible.

➤ While keeping your emotions in check, discuss possible alternatives to resolve the situation. If either of you starts to get angry, stop. If you fail to stop, you will most likely make the situation worse. If it takes days to calmly resolve the conflict, so be it.

Learn from each conflict you're involved in and focus on what worked. You will surely need the skills next time around. Although each situation will be different, the basic analytical skills previously mentioned and maintaining self-control will serve you well.

Stress

If you want to live longer and keep your hair from turning prematurely gray, you will need to be able to effectively cope with stress. Few things in this world will wear you down and ruin your life faster than the inability to deal with stress. For some, stress is a part of everyday existence. For those unfortunate souls, they will have to learn to cope or be doomed to a miserable existence. Stress causes tension and denies its victims the ability to properly function and reason. I'm a firm believer that everyone can benefit from a little help in this area. So, here are a few helpful tips:

➤ First, accept the fact that life can be stressful.

➤ Try to put life's little problems in proper prospective.

➤ Learn to effectively identify stressful situations.

➤ To help combat the inevitable effects of stress, try to do something fun every day.

➤ Learn to be flexible and have the desire to compromise when needed.

➤ Eat right, get plenty of sleep, and exercise regularly.

➤ If driving to work is stressful, try leaving for work a little earlier each day to allow for stressful traffic problems and delays.

➤ If you keep your feelings inside, learn to let them out in a controlled manner.

➤ Be confident of your ability to deal with stress by thinking positively.

➤ Avoid simple everyday stressful situations; manage your time and money.

➤ Try to organize yourself and your belongings.

Anger Management

Experiencing anger is part of our day-to-day lives and should, therefore, be managed and understood when at all possible. As with any behavioral skill, anger is best controlled when you know how to deal with it. Anger can serve as a great motivator, inspiring all of us to deal with problems and develop innovative solutions. The best way to control anger is by learning to talk about what is bothering you and to not keep your emotions bottled up inside. Sometimes just talking and listening to others about a particular problem or feeling you're having will make things better. The first thing to remember about anger is that it's okay to have certain feelings about something or someone, but it is unacceptable to act out those feelings in a harmful manner. So, when you start to feel angry, stop, take a few long breaths, and think about somewhere that makes you happy or relaxed. This little exercise is sometimes referred to as going to one's "happy place."

I don't claim to have all the answers, but I do know that yelling is not going to solve anything except the debate over who can yell the loudest. When you feel anger coming on, notice how your body reacts and learn to recognize those feeling. Anger causes you to be disrespectful, spiteful, and insensitive to others. In addition, feelings that accompany anger can play a role in your desire to become violent towards other people as well as yourself. It can interfere with your ability to perform adequately at work and can put tremendous stress on personal relationships with friends and family. Ultimately, anger and the emotions that usually come with it can cause serious mental and physical problems. Understanding that you have a problem dealing with anger is a big step in doing something about it. If you need help, talk with your doctor and get their advice. To do nothing could prove to be detrimental to your health as well as your relationships.

Getting Organized

When was the last time you said, "Where are my keys or has anybody seen my wallet?" If your answer to that question was today or yesterday, then maybe you need to really concentrate on this section. Developing good organizational habits is tough, especially if you were not raised that way. You see, for the most part, people have the tendency to model or adapt their habits after their surroundings as a child. I don't know of anyone who is a neat freak that was not raised in a home that was well kept, clean, and well organized. If you fall in that category, then becoming organized should be easy—that is, if you're not already that way. However, if you could never seem to find things as a child, then you probably live in somewhat of a start of disorganization today.

Whether you just want to get better at being organized or you need to start from scratch, follow these seven basic steps:

1. Keep things that you frequently use in an easy-to-get-to place. For example, put the scissors, tape, pencils, rubber bands, envelopes, and stamps together in a desk or kitchen drawer.

2. File important papers like insurance documents, real-estate papers, and birth certificates in a safe container. If you can afford to, buy a fireproof box.

3. Put all of your monthly bills together and create a system like a simple spreadsheet that shows when they are due, when you paid them, and how much you paid.

4. File all warranties and manuals separately.

5. Keep an up-to-date address book and put a calendar together with important dates on it such as birthdays for family and friends.

6. If you decorate your home for every holiday, label boxes for your decorations and store them away.

7. Put things back after you use them, and finish a short-duration project instead of putting it down and starting another.

I realize that not everyone wants to be organized, and if you're one of them, you have just wasted ten minutes reading this section. However, if you took the time to read it anyway, maybe you really want to get your life in order. If that's the case, get busy!

Body Language and Listening

When you talk to someone, you can usually tell whether or not they are interested by their body language. A person's body language changes as they become more or less enthusiastic about what is being said. If interested, they will stand up straight and look at you; if not so interested, they will probably be looking away and appear uncomfortable. Think back to the last time you felt that a person was really listening to what you had to say. Now think back to a conversation you wanted to have with someone who appeared to care less about what you had to say. There was most likely a big difference in the two.

If you realize through observation that people are not interested in what you are saying, try to change your approach. There are several things you can do to make whatever you say more interesting. First, you can alter your speech pattern by changing the volume and tone to emphasize important words or thoughts. You can also help your delivery come across better by making sure you respect a person's personal space. Another good practice is to maintain eye contact.

There's just something insincere about talking or listening to someone who will not make eye contact with you.

When it comes to being a good listener, practice the following steps:

> ➤ Never interrupt the person speaking. Not only is it rude, you can't truly listen to someone if you are thinking about what you are going to say before they have finished talking.

> ➤ If you are not sure about what is being said, ask for clarification.

> ➤ Face the person talking and be careful not to turn away.

> ➤ If you are sitting, don't slump, instead, sit up straight. Sitting up straight will not only be more polite in appearance, it will help you breathe better when you talk.

> ➤ Maintain relatively consistent eye contact.

> ➤ When someone is talking to you, stop what you're doing and listen. It's hard to be a good listener if you're watching television or reading a magazine.

Decision Making and Problem Solving

Have you ever tried to solve a problem only to find out that every time you turn around, new pieces to the puzzle were constantly being uncovered? Trying to make an informed decision is impossible without knowing what the real problem is right from the beginning. It is not only suggested that you identify what the problem is before trying to solve it, it's essential. Even the simplest problems require all the information prior to solving. However, regardless of the level of difficulty, use the following steps to solve problems and make decisions:

> ➤ Clearly define the problem before moving on.

> ➤ Develop some possible alternatives.

> ➤ Review the possible alternatives.

> ➤ Make a selection based on the best available information.

> ➤ Implement your decision to solve the problem by applying all of your resources.

> ➤ If the problem was not solved, regroup and select one of the other alternatives.

Making the right decision to solve a problem is challenging; trying to do so under pressure or in a crisis situation is difficult at best. If at all possible, never put yourself in that situation. Remember, you have control over some potential problem situations, so work on them as need be. A good example of preventing a problem would be contacting a bill collector and explaining why you can't make this month's payment. Postponing the phone call will only make the situation worse. Doing nothing is not going to make the problem go away. In many cases, it will likely turn a small problem into a very big one. The longer you wait to address a problem, the less time you will have to mitigate the damage. Do yourself a favor and get in the habit of taking responsibility for yourself. The sooner you do this, the sooner you will develop a good thought process for making decisions and solving problems.

Dealing With Depression

Many dictionaries define depression as the condition of feeling sad or melancholy. It can also be defined as a psychotic or neurotic condition characterized by a person's inability to concentrate or by having feelings of dejection and guilt. This disproportionately intense reaction to life's trying events called depression is sometimes accompanied by strong feelings of sadness, loss, and rejection.

Few people go through life without periodically dealing with some level of depression and the lonely, unhappy state that goes along with it. There are three basic levels of depression: normal, mild, and severe.

Normal depression can be caused by the natural reaction to life's situations, such as the loss of a loved one, losing a job, not getting that promotion, or the failure of a relationship. These events usually happen to everyone at some time in their lives. Some of the emotions and conditions that usually go along with normal depression are despair, changes in appetite, guilt, and even insomnia. The term "normal" is used because most people normally recovery from it. Now the normal recovery period of depression associated with not getting a promotion might take a few days, loss of a loved one could take several years. The key here is still eventually coming out of the depression at some point, which is normal for most people.

Mild depression can come from anywhere at any time with no defined reason. For some who experience mild depression, the holidays themselves seem to bring on a sense of sadness. Have you ever known anyone who seemed to get depressed around Thanksgiving or Christmas? In some cases, this form of depression comes from bad experiences on or around those holidays. For some people, they remember sad occasions on a particular day and the event causes them to subconsciously go into a state of mild depression. For example, if someone ends a significant relationship on February 3 of a given year, then every February 3, they relive the sadness associated with it. This type of mild depression, although slightly more unpredictable than normal, can still be recovered from in a reasonable amount of time.

People with mild depression can still function, but when they go into these states of depression, their friends and family members have a hard time understanding what's going on. The misunderstanding comes from not knowing about the specific dates that trigger depression; therefore they are left with wondering why the person seems so sad. When depression is obvious, in these cases communication between those involved is critical and, in some cases, can serve to be the best medicine for all parties.

Severe depression often causes despair and hopelessness so intense that the person loses interest in life, becomes incapable of experiencing pleasure, and prefers to just stay in bed. Severe depression is by far the worse form of depression, leaving the sufferer with such sadness, irritability, anger, frustration, and anxiety that they become unable to adjust to normal life. Thoughts of suicide can often accompany severe depression, which is why having the ability to recognize it is essential for those suffering from it and for those who know someone experiencing it.

If you or someone you know is suffering from depression, remember that sometimes it helps just to talk. Depression is a medical condition that responds well to treatment. If you're not sure whom to talk to or whom to advise a friend to talk to, consider a health care professional. If there is a family doctor available, use them, because they will be familiar with the patient and their specific needs and condition. Together, the two can discuss treatment options such as counseling and or antidepressant medicines.

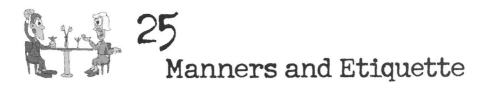

25
Manners and Etiquette

Having good manners and exercising proper etiquette are signs of refinement and class. Conversely, the lack of good manners and etiquette usually signifies either an insufficient lack of proper upbringing or an unwillingness to conform to established codes of conduct and behavior. In any event, the perception of one who does not practice good manners is not very flattering.

Dining Manners and Etiquette

For the most part, people are reasonably conscious about how they behave at home and in public, especially when it comes to table manners. Of all the behavioral attitudes and practices performed by humans, table manners, or the lack thereof, are probably the most noticeable. This is probably because most people, whether they practice them or not, can spot bad table manners a mile away. So, do yourself and your dining guest a favor and be more conscious of your table manners.

For those of you who need reminding, here are fifteen tips to practice at the table:

1. When you first sit down to the table, do not take your napkin and flop it open like a bull whip and then stuff one corner under your neck. Instead, unfold the napkin and place it on your lap. When you need to use it, lightly dab the area, don't wipe your face with it as if you were using a washcloth.

2. Be conscious of how you sit at the table. Do not slump down in the seat, rock the front legs of the chair off the floor, or sit on the very edge of the seat. Sit up relatively straight and keep your elbows off the table.

3. If you have packages with you or a cell phone, place them somewhere other than on the table. If you have a cell phone or pager, turn it to a silent alarm while you are dining.

4. This tip has two parts. If you are dining with a small group, remember to wait until everyone has been served before you start eating. However, if you are dining at a large event, such as a wedding reception or banquet, wait until those at your table have been served. It is not necessary for everyone in the room to be served before you start indulging.

5. When you pick up a utensil and start eating, remember that the utensil does not go back on the table. For example, once you have finished using your knife, place it back on your plate, making sure that even the handle does not rest on the table. Oh, by the way, don't use you're eating utensils as pointers when you are talking. Waving around a knife as you explain how you caught "the big one" on Cumberland Lake last weekend is rude.

6. When you chew, keep your mouth closed and do not talk with your mouth full. There is nothing that you have to say that is so important that you can't wait until you swallow.

7. Dining is supposed to be enjoyed, so relax and slow down. This is probably not going to be your last meal, so practice good manners and pace yourself. You do not want to be eating pie and gulping down coffee while the rest of the table guests are enjoying their salads. At the same time, don't be waiting for your appetizer to cool to exactly 74.3 degrees while your guests are waiting for the check to come.

8. When eating bread, break off a small piece and butter it. Do not butter a large slice and set it on your plate.

9. If you are sitting in a smoking section with table guests, don't light up until everyone at the table has finished eating. Even after dining, if someone at the table does not smoke, ask if it would be all right to burn one. I have dined with guests who smoke as soon as they have finished cramming their double-bacon-cheeseburgers down their necks, and I have also dined with those who need a cigarette between courses. If at all possible, wait to have a cigarette until you're away from the table.

10. When confronted with the dreaded place-setting dilemma, remember that if you use the outermost utensil first and work your way in, you can't go wrong. However, if you are going somewhere that you expect to encounter a very formal setting, read up on the latest rules and etiquette first; you'll be glad you did.

11. I should not have to say this, but I am still amazed at those who blow their nose at the table. Do not blow your nose at the table and refrain from putting on lipstick, combing your hair, and cleaning your fingernails with your handy-dandy Swiss Army knife. One last thing—if you have something stuck in your teeth, excuse yourself and remove it in the bathroom.

12. Cut just enough food for a single bite. Don't sit there and section off everything on your plate as if your waiter was going to remove your knife the first time you set it down.

13. If you really enjoy dunking your jelly doughnuts in your coffee, dipping your cookies in your milk, or mixing all the food on your plate together to look like a Picasso painting, do that in the privacy of your home.

14. If you accidentally belch, loudly smack your lips, or slurp your soup, simple say "Excuse me." If you know that a particular beverage makes you belch, avoid it, or at least drink it slowly. If you eat slowly and use proper manners, you will not be smacking your lips together or slurping your soup.

15. Have you ever seen anyone push their plate away from them or scoot their chair back and cross their legs after eating? If you haven't, it's probably just a matter of time. The act of pushing away your plate looks as if you are glad to finally be finished with that meal. Pushing your chair back looks as if you are telling the rest of the table guests that you are ready to leave now! It's rude to do either.

Greeting People

Make a good first impression when you first meet someone in person. You may not remember their name, what they do, or where they live, but you will remember whether or not you liked them. There's just something about a pleasant first encounter. When first introduced, say hello, how are your doing, good morning or evening, but say something. Don't try to be cool and just nod in the general direction of someone talking to you. People may appear to be standoffish, but they will usually come alive when greeted or spoken to.

If you are seated and someone is introduced to you, stand up and greet them, unless you are in a tight spot behind a table or bar. If someone offers their hand to you, shake it while looking them in the eyes. Apply moderate pressure and shake the hand for only a few seconds. Everybody has a pet peeve—getting a poor handshake from a man is mine. I can't stand extending my hand to another guy and feeling like I am holding a dead fish. If you are going to shake someone's hand, shake it! I'm not talking about squeezing the life out of them, on the other hand, don't make me want to check your pulse to see if you're alive.

Using the Phone

Unless you're from some Third World country, you have probably used a telephone a few thousand times to date. Yet many people can't seem to get the basic courtesies down. Before I give you some helpful tips on proper phone etiquette, I want you to ask yourself these two questions: Do you have a paper and pen close by the phone? Do you have a comfortable place to talk on the phone when you make and receive calls? If you did not answer yes to these questions, do something about it. Now, in order to help those of you who just can't seem to grasp the proper usage of the telephone, here are some useful tips:

> ➤ When you call someone, identify who you are first; don't make him or her ask who's calling.

> ➤ If someone calls you, say hello, don't just wait for them to begin speaking.

> ➤ Do not try to eat a double-decker sandwich and drink a milkshake while talking on the phone. Just because the other person can't see you, don't think they can't tell if your mouth is full.

> ➤ Take your time when you talk and try to be as clear as possible while maintaining proper volume.

> ➤ If you are in a crowded nightclub setting, do not use a phone unless you have to. The person on the other end will probably not be able to understand you unless you yell, and who wants to hear that over some loud music?

➤ Just as in person, don't interrupt while the other person is talking.

➤ When leaving a message on an answering machine, keep it short, clear, and to the point. Remember—clarity, brevity, and impact.

➤ If you are calling from a pay phone, consider the amount of time you are using the line. Of course, if no one is waiting, talk all you want.

➤ Unless something critical is happening or going to happen, do not put your phone guest on hold. Once in a while it's okay, if you know them, but even then, don't put them on hold for more than a few seconds. Remember, their time is as important as yours, so be courteous.

➤ While talking, allow the other person time to respond. Have you ever had a one-sided conversation on the phone, one in which you could not seem to get a word in? Well, remember that feeling and never do that to anyone else.

➤ Don't call someone late at night or during the dinner hour unless you really know him or her well. How do you feel when the phone rings while you are asking for more mashed potatoes or when you have just lain down for a long winter's nap?

➤ If you are one of those extremely important people who have to call someone on their cell phone as soon as they get in an automobile, be cautious and very careful as you drive. If the call was so important, why not make it before you leave home or wait five minutes until you get home? What's the rush? I just don't get it!

➤ Be polite. If someone calls you, have the decency to call him or her back as soon as you can.

➤ If the line becomes disconnected, the proper callback responsibility is that of the original caller. If both of you try to reconnect, it will only delay the reconnection time, because both phones will give busy signals until one stops trying to call back.

➤ If you have to cut a phone call off short, do so politely.

How Much Do I Tip ?

This section will really make a tightwad uncomfortable. Why, I know people who are so tight they could take a penny and squeeze a booger out of Abraham Lincoln's nose. Unless the person providing you a service is doing such a bad job that you can't seem to think straight, leave a tip, even if it's a small one. The reason for this gesture is simple. You don't know why the person is having such a hard time providing for you. As far as you know, they could have just received some really bad news or there are other factors that you are just not aware of. In any event, you should leave something; after all, most people who receive tips count on them to pay their bills. You might be thinking, "Well, if they were concerned about their tip, they would try harder." Remember what I just wrote—there just could be some underlying circumstances that you are not aware of. I don't know who coined this phrase, but it is appropriate in this case: "Forgive them—it will teach them a lesson." How fitting a thought. There are many different situations where tipping is appropriate, but for the sake of brevity, only the most commonly used services are mentioned.

Everyone is different, but use these suggested tips when in doubt:

> ➤ When dining out, tip around $2 or $3 dollars for the valet who brings your car around. If you need to check a coat, $1 will do nicely. While inside the restaurant's bathroom, tip the attendant $1 for splashing on some cologne or putting some breath mints in your pocket. After the meal, tip 20 percent, and even more if your dining in a five-star establishment. If you arrived by taxi, tip the doorman about $2 for calling you a cab. If you think these costs are high, then consider that, for most people, going out to a really nice restaurant is rare; therefore, tipping should be figured in the total cost of the evening.

> ➤ For relatively short taxi rides, say a $4 fair, tip $1, for longer rides, say a $15 fare, tip between $2 and $3.

> ➤ When visiting the hairdresser, figure on giving the shampoo assistant $2 and the hairdresser around 20 percent of the cut or style price. If you're a regular customer, you will probably hear your hairdresser talk about someone else who gave a small tip,

and you can gauge your tipping habits accordingly. If the hairdresser also does the shampoo, give them a little extra. Although tipping with cash is great, consider giving your hairdresser something else, like tickets to a show or a box of gourmet chocolates.

➤ When you order food delivery, consider how far they have to drive and how much easier it is for you to have it delivered. You should tip at least $2 for this service. If you are ordering a large amount of food for a party or gathering, bump it up to $5. Remember, this will probably not be the last time you have food delivered by this person. Put yourself in their shoes— would you like to drive your personal car across town during dinner rush hour and deliver Chinese food to some guy on the fourth floor for $1?

General Rules

Let's keep it brief and review some of the following helpful tips. Although not all of the tips relate directly to manners and etiquette, some are simply bits of helpful advice.

The following tips can help shape your character:

➤ Take pride in how you present yourself and your personal appearance.

➤ Refrain from being obnoxious, boastful, arrogant, crude, and loud.

➤ Be considerate, sympathetic, and compassionate when needed.

➤ Avoid road rage by practicing patience.

➤ Learn to be firm, direct, and unambiguous when times call for it.

➤ When in doubt, give the benefit of the doubt.

➤ Get in the habit of saying "please" and "thank you."

➤ Don't be stingy with handing out compliments and congratulations.

➤ Whenever possible, be optimistic.

➤ Avoid pessimistic people.

➤ Instead of criticizing and complaining, learn to understand and adapt.

➤ If you have roommates, treat them and their possessions with respect.

➢ Respect your elders.

➢ Pass along useful and helpful information to those who can benefit from it.

➢ Accept who you are and only change what needs to be changed.

➢ Remember who you call when things are good and who you call when things are bad. Wouldn't it be nice if they were the same? That would be a true friend.

➢ Develop hobbies and interests early in life; they will really come in handy when you get old.

➢ Buy what you need first, and then buy what you want.

➢ Stay in contact with your family.

➢ Guys, learn to raise and lower the toilet seat!

References

➢ *Letitia Baldrige's Complete Guide to The New Manners For The "90S*, by Letitia Baldrige's

➢ *Say Please, Say Thank You*, by Donald McCullough

➢ *Etiquette: Guide to Modern Manners*, by Charlotte Ford

➢ *Miss Manners Guide For The Turn-Of-The Millennium*, by Judith Martin

➢ *Undoing Depression: What Therapy Doesn't Teach You and Medication Can't Give You*, by Richard O'Connor

➢ *The Eight Essential Steps to Conflict Resolution: Preserving Relationships at Work, at Home, and in the Community*, by Dudley Weeks

➢ *Manage Your Time The Lazy Way*, by Toni Ahlgren

➢ *Stress Management For Dummies*, by Allen Elkin

➢ *How to Raise Your Self-Esteem*, by Nathaniel Branden

➢ *The Anger Workbook*, by Lorrainne Bilodeau

Index